HITLER, JESUS, AND OUR COMMON HUMANITY

To Cookie —

Love,

Blessings

&

Shalom —

Rolf Menachem

Gompertz

12/29/2019

HITLER, JESUS, *and our* COMMON HUMANITY

A Jewish Survivor Interprets Life, History, and the Gospels

Bruce W. Longenecker

CASCADE *Books* · Eugene, Oregon

HITLER, JESUS, AND OUR COMMON HUMANITY:
A Jewish Survivor Interprets Life, History, and the Gospels

Copyright © 2014 Bruce W. Longenecker. All rights reserved. Except for brief quotations in critical publications or reviews, no part of this book may be reproduced in any manner without prior written permission from the publisher. Write: Permissions, Wipf and Stock Publishers, 199 W. 8th Ave., Suite 3, Eugene, OR 97401.

Cascade Books
A Division of Wipf and Stock Publishers
199 W. 8th Ave., Suite 3
Eugene, OR 97401

www.wipfandstock.com

Citations of the Bible are primarily taken from the New Revised Standard Version, except in instances where translations have been provided by the author.

The photo of Rolf Gompertz © Marissa Roth; used with permission.

ISBN 13: 978-1-62564-988-1

Cataloging-in-Publication data:

Longenecker, Bruce W.

Hitler, Jesus, and our common humanity : A Jewish survivor interprets life, history, and the Gospels / Bruce W. Longenecker.

xiv + 188 p. ; 23 cm. Includes bibliographical references.

ISBN 13: 978-1-62564-988-1

1. Gompertz, Rolf. 2. Holocaust, Jewish (1939–1945)—Influence. 3. Jewish children in the Holocaust—Germany. 4. Kristallnacht, 1938. 5. Holocaust, Jewish (1939–1945)—Moral and ethical aspects. 6. Good and evil. 7. Jesus Christ. 8. Bible. Gospels—Criticism, interpretations, etc.
I. Title.

D804.3 M265 2014

Manufactured in the U.S.A.

In memory of Danny May,
my childhood friend, twice taken away.

And in honor of
Tom Göbel, Alma Herrmann, and Anna Coffee Baer,
each of whom did something
to affirm "our common humanity"
when most did nothing.

Contents

Acknowledgments | ix
Abbreviations | x
Introduction | xi

PART 1: *Kristallnacht,* **The Narrative** | 1

1. November 7, 1938 | 3
2. Early Night, November 9, 1938 | 8
3. Deep Night, November 9–10, 1938 | 12
4. Early Morning, November 10, 1938 | 16

PART 2: *Kristallnacht,* **Before and After** | 19

5. The Immediate Aftermath of *Kristallnacht* | 21
6. Before *Kristallnacht* | 34
7. Interpreting the Gompertz *Kristallnacht* | 43

PART 3: Crafting a Contribution | 49

8. Crafting a Jewish Life | 51
9. Crafting a Literary Corpus | 60

PART 4: The Gompertz Jesus-Novel | 69

10. Corollaries of Violence | 71

CONTENTS

PART 5: The Voice of Rolf Gompertz | 101

11. Speeches of the Heart | 103
12. An Appreciation | 114

PART 6: Gompertz in His Own Words | 119

13. Snapshots | 121
14. Rolf Gompertz's First Diary, Extracts | 138
15. Rolf Gompertz's Second Diary, Extracts | 157
16. Rolf Gompertz's Third Diary, Extracts | 159

APPENDICES

Appendix 1: Who am I to Write This Book? | 167
Appendix 2: A Reading of Matthew 27:25: "His blood be on us and on our children" | 170
Appendix 3: Further Reading | 181

Bibliography | 185

Acknowledgments

Financial support for this project has generously been supplied by the Department of Religion and the Institute for Oral History at Baylor University.

My thanks also go to early readers of this project, including (in alphabetical order): Tricia Aven, Dick Bond, William Henderson, and Nick Zola.

I owe significant thanks to my friend David Baker, who set out the conceptual foundations of the narrative in chapters 1 through 4 of this book, and who contributed many of its better features. The literary weaknesses of the narrative are my responsibility.

Special thanks go to Rolf Gompertz himself for reading through the penultimate version of the book and offering invaluable help in fine-tuning some historical details.

Abbreviations

Deut	Deuteronomy
Ps	Psalm
Isa	Isaiah
Ezek	Ezekiel
Zech	Zechariah
Matt	Matthew

Introduction

THIS BOOK TELLS THE redemptive story of a Jew who narrowly escaped the Holocaust against the Jews in 1939–45, and of how his experiences of Nazi Germany transformed him.

It is a story of his lifelong struggle against forces that nearly swallowed up his life—not unlike the time when he fought for his life in a swimming pool, while a German lifeguard sat in his seat and watched the Jewish boy drowning.

It is the story of a quest for justice and peace amidst prejudice and conflict—not unlike the time when he watched his father bravely stand up to a Nazi soldier pointing a gun at his face.

It is the story of a man who found that words could be used as ammunition in a war against concentration camps, hatred, and evil—not unlike the time when Nazi soldiers came to take his father away and these words of solidarity escaped his young lips: "Father, if they take you, I'm going with you."

It is the story of Rolf Gompertz—a simple, kind-hearted, astute interpreter of his times, who has bequeathed to us a life worthy of appreciation and emulation. As a young Jew in Nazi Germany, he was part of a marginalized minority on the receiving end of systemic and systematic hatred. But as his life unfolded beyond Germany, he found his voice and spoke of the need to embrace our common humanity. He found he could do little other than to speak, to speak as a Jew, and to speak in response to Adolf Hitler, offering an ideology that ran directly counter to the ideology that had inevitably shaped world-shifting events during the early years of his life.[1]

1. Hitler, of course, bought into the ideology that propounded the Darwinian supremacy of certain white Europeans while demonizing other groups of people—including

According to Rolf, we are all here for one reason: to improve the world, and in that sense, to redeem the world, wherever we are—or as Rolf likes to put, "to bloom where you stand." This is the story of where and how Rolf has bloomed.

The story of Rolf Gompertz was markedly shaped by the lives of two other Jews, one from his own time and one from a much earlier day.

1. Around the year 30, Jesus of Nazareth, a Jew who was perceived to be a trouble-maker by the elite, is crucified by Pontius Pilate, the Roman governor of Judea.

2. In November 1938, Herschel Grynszpan, a Jew from Poland, killed Ernst vom Rath, a little known German functionary working in Paris.

The first of these two moments became a powerful resource in Rolf's evolving understanding of the use and abuse of power, as he (a Conservative Jew throughout his life) increasingly found an unexpected camaraderie with a persecuted Jew from long ago. And the second of these two moments unleashed a groundswell of anti-Semitic activity on the night of November 9–10, 1938, which would come to be called "The Night of Broken Glass," or *Kristallnacht*. Rolf would later describe that night as "the most powerful memory I have."[2]

Hitler would have viewed the events of that night as driving his country closer to realizing his vision for the German Fatherland—a vision that included what was later named among the Nazi leadership as "the final solution" to "the Jewish question." It was a vision that a young Rolf Gompertz characterized in his diary as "a glaring example of all the forces of Evil, and the utterly hateful, despicable, corrupt effect upon the self, mankind, and the universe of a Perverted Ego."[3]

The "hateful, despicable" and "corrupt" events of *Kristallnacht*, and the immediate run-up to it, are recounted in narrative form in the following section of this book—a narrative that focuses on one small family: Oskar, Selma, and Rolf Gompertz—the Gompertz family of Krefeld Germany.

---

homosexuals, gypsies, the disabled, Jehovah's Witnesses, and, of course, the Jewish people.

2. This derives from an email correspondence between Rolf and myself, dated November 24, 2009. In Appendix 1, I outline the history of my relationship to Rolf.

3. See Rolf's diary entry for November 24, 1949, cited in chapter 14 below.

PART 1

Kristallnacht: The Narrative

1

November 7, 1938

Bismarckstrasse 118, Krefeld, Lower Rhineland, Germany;

10:15 PM

"Why did he have to be a Jew?"

"Who?" asked Selma Gompertz. She stopped dusting the stairway banisters and joined her husband in the parlor of their apartment, located on the second and third floors of *Bismarckstrasse* 118. "Do you mean Jesus of Nazareth?" she proposed with a smile.

"No, no. I'm being serious. Listen to the radio. A Jewish boy shot a German diplomat in Paris . . . a man named vom Rath."

Selma's face darkened abruptly as she seated herself on the floor by her husband's side. "Is he dead?"

"No. At least, not yet."

Oskar turned up the volume on the parlor radio, slightly. The two listened carefully until martial music began to play. He turned the radio off.

"Who was the shooter?" asked Selma.

"Grynszpan. Herschel Grynszpan. He's only seventeen. His parents are Polish Jews who were being deported from Germany with about 15,000 others. Apparently they're caught up in that mess at the border, and Grynszpan became angry about it. The Poles don't want any Jews back, you know, and now that group of Jews is in limbo between Germany and Poland. Neither country is accepting them."

Selma nodded. "Nobody wants them."

"Nobody wants *us*, you mean."

"Don't take this too far, Oskar," said Selma, softly.

"Too far? You heard how angry that radio announcer was."

"Well, that boy Grynszpan had no business shooting a helpless man."

"I never said that he did," said Oskar. "I just wished he wasn't a Jew. If vom Rath dies, things will get worse for us than they already are."

Suddenly nervous, Selma cast a look at the stairway leading up to her son's third-floor bedroom. "At least it was in Paris and not Berlin," she said. "And the shooter's only seventeen and the son of immigrants. It's not like a *German* Jew did this."

"Selle, think about it for a minute. He's a Jew and he shot a *German* diplomat. It doesn't matter that it happened in Paris. You know what the Nazis will do with this. Have you forgotten the Jewish boy from America they executed last June?"

"They didn't do that simply because he was Jewish. He was a radical, conspiring to assassinate Hitler."

Oskar left his upholstered chair and began to pace. "And now a Jewish boy shoots vom Rath in cold blood in his office. If that man dies, Selle, it will be a *Jewish* crime. And in case you've forgotten, we are Jews."

Selma smiled. "I've not forgotten, Oskar." Selma led her husband to a wooden chair where she removed a bandage from his right eye to examine the incisions he received from a minor surgery in the previous week.

"You see what is happening, don't you?" Oskar said, tilting his head backward as she performed her short inspection.

Selma stiffened, and said nothing. She was not blind, but neither was she one to abandon hope easily.

Released from his wife's examination, Oskar walked to his parlor window to watch from the second floor as a stream of taillights passed along the rain-slicked street below. His town had blossomed under Hitler, as had the whole of Germany. For that he was glad, but while prosperity blossomed for some, it was often different for most Jews.

"You've seen the placards against Jews that are plastered all throughout the city," said Oskar. "Hideous, insulting cartoons."

"Of course. I try to make sure that Rolf doesn't see them."

"They're getting worse," said Oskar. "Every week there are new ones, and every week they become increasingly blatant in condemning us." He shook his head. "I saw enough hatred in the trenches of the Great War to last ten lifetimes. It scares me, Selle, how hatred can grab hold of people and erode any sense of their common humanity."

Selma went to her husband. "There is always hope, Oskar, and we Jews never abandon hope."

Her hand slipped into his. Oskar was silent, and continued looking out the window. She tugged at his arm, trying to pull him back into the room. He turned to her, gave a gentle smile, but he didn't budge. When she put her full weight into it, the pair lurched awkwardly into the room, stumbling over each other until they both landed on the familiar comfort of the old davenport sofa. Selma tossed her head back in laughter, while Oskar pulled the right side of his suit coat out from under his hip.

Selma reached over and adjusted Oskar's tie. "We must cling to moments of hopefulness, Oskar. Some of those placards have been ripped down. *Frau* Probst baked us a *Strudel* last week. And your eye doctor . . . he's not a Jew, but he keeps you as a patient."

"Selle, you are burying your head in the sand. You hear the radio; you read the newspaper!"

"Maybe the soup is not always served as hot as it's cooked."

Oskar closed his eyes and drew a deep breath. "Selle, think about it. Even your good friend Trude won't allow Doris to play with Rolf anymore. The boundaries of society are being redrawn, Selle, and we Jews are on the outside."

"But Trude probably didn't *want* to keep Doris away from Rolf."

Oskar turned toward his wife. "You are a good woman, Selle. But don't let hope cloud your judgment. Remember that awful parade when Jews were mocked? What did our neighbors do?"

"Yes," replied Selma quietly, "they laughed."

"They enjoyed watching Jews being mocked. Our *neighbors* did that! And last week you told me that *Frau* Merkel won't buy her family's food from *Baum's Deli* anymore. Then there's Pfarrer Schmidt from the Lutheran church; he's been one of the 'Brown Shirts' doing Hitler's dirty work against Jews for the past five years. And, of course, you remember the incident in the swimming pool when Rolf nearly died!"

"Yes, yes, I remember," clipped Selma. "I will never forget the look in Rolf's eyes when he told me about it. He was so confused."

Oskar shifted uneasily in his place, then self-consciously touched his bandage. "I just want us to be realistic about all this."

Selma nodded. "I understand, Oskar. But I still believe they will only let it go so far and no further."

"You believe, or you hope? And haven't they already gone too far already?" Oskar sighed, heavily. "I really do wish I could see things your way, Selle, and I will try to hope for the best. But I'll never forget my Papa reading that Viennese archbishop's speech in the newspaper: 'The Catholic bishops promise their cooperation with National Socialism.' Their *cooperation*, Selle. If Christian leaders are supporting all this, why should we expect our neighbors to be any different?"

Selma reluctantly released some information of her own. "One of Rolf's school mates called him an 'alien' the other day—a 'non-Aryan *guest*' of Germany," she said, her hand anxiously stroking the brocade upholstery of the davenport.

"You see! That's exactly what I'm talking about. That stuff comes directly from the Nazis, and it is infiltrating everything. Even that American carmaker, Ford—he thinks just like them. An 'international race,' he calls us. They don't want us to be Germans, or French, or Dutch, or American— they want us to be seen as foreigners no matter where we go, no matter what land we've lived in, or the number of generations we lived there. Our neighbors are believing this stuff. That's why when a 'Jew' shoots a German, it doesn't matter where he or his parents were born, he's just a Jew . . . like us."

Despite her devotion to hope, Selma Gompertz was not ignorant of the clouds that had gathered over her beloved city of Krefeld, or over the whole region of the Lower Rhine where Gompertz families had lived for centuries—or over the whole of the new German Reich. "I am not suggesting that times are good, or that we are not in danger—or that this shooting is meaningless," she replied. "Believe me, dear Oskar, I worry when your barber has to sneak over here at night to cut your hair, and Rolf's. I do understand the dangers."

Oskar took a breath. "I know you do. Forgive me, Selle, I'm agitated tonight. This announcement has me worried. And people so easily forget that 100,000 Jews like me fought for the Fatherland in that terrible war, with 12,000 of us spilling our blood in the field." His voice began to rise. "They actually believe that hotheaded Jews like Grynszpan represent us in their rebellious and unlawful acts!"

Selma stroked her husband's hair, tenderly. "Shhh, Oskar. I know. But let's not wake Rolf."

Herr Gompertz fell silent. He never involved his ten-year old son in talks like these. Both he and his wife had shielded him the best they could, hoping the boy could simply be a boy learning to love God, others, and life itself. The flushed veteran took a breath. "I just want my family to be brave and to stand strong."

Selma kissed his cheek. "And to never lose hope, and to always find beauty, and to never stop loving."

Outside some horns began to blow. A fire whistle sounded several blocks away and some voices could be heard shouting something from *Bismarckstrasse*. Oskar Gompertz took three long strides to the window, then returned to his wife's side. His face was strained with worry. He took her hand and she leaned into his embrace.

2

Early Night, November 9, 1938

Bismarckstrasse 118, Krefeld;

7:25 PM

Selma let the knife slide into the sink, dried her hands on the dishcloth, and turned off the kitchen radio. She paused for a moment. The world had changed in the last forty-eight hours.

She left the kitchen and went into the parlor where Rolf was reading aloud to Oskar, whose doctor had advised him not to read until his eyes improved. She went and stood in front of Rolf, extending her hand as if she were inviting him to dance. Rolf put down the book and stretched out his hand toward her. His mother leaned in to take hold of it, then leaned back, pulling him up off the davenport.

"What is it, *Mutti*?"

Selma said nothing, but began to sway her son from side to side, while standing in one place. Rolf chuckled at the affectionate attention. Then Selma took the lead and stepped her son over toward the door of the parlor, in what equated to Rolf's first lesson in dancing the Fox Trot. Just past the door, a twirl ended the lesson. Mother and son smiled together before Selma took her young son by the shoulders and aimed him toward the steps leading up to his bedroom. A gentle pat of his bottom was the motherly signal to go up and get ready for bed.

Rolf resisted. "Why, *Mutti*? It's only 7:30 and you said I have no school tomorrow."

"Well, I think it would be better . . . "

Suddenly suspicious, Rolf asked, "What's happening *Mutti?*" He looked into the parlor at his father. "*Vati?*"

Since the vom Rath shooting two days earlier, trouble had been brewing in the streets of Krefeld. Rolf knew something troubling was in the air. Despite the problems of the past, never before had he seen his father and mother looking so worried. It was their silence that was the worst of it—a silence that covered deep unspoken concerns. He knew that much. And he knew that being Jewish was part of the problem. But he did not understand why. He only knew that he was proud of being Jewish, and proud of his mother and father.

"Please tell me," Rolf persisted. "Are we in danger?"

Selma turned her face away from Rolf and pressed a handkerchief to her eyes. With a sob that was barely audible, she shared a glance with Oskar, and then vanished into the kitchen.

Oskar got out of his leather chair and went over to his son at the foot of the stairs outside the parlor. Squatting in front of him, he said, "Your mother is tired, Rolf, and there's been some trouble outside. It will all pass. We'll be fine, my son. But for now, maybe we all need a good night's sleep. Okay?"

Oskar tussled Rolf's hair and smiled reassuringly. Rolf smiled back, though with a hint of doubt. He nodded obediently, turned, and started heading up the stairs.

His father called after him. "And I've got an appointment with the doctor early in the morning, so I won't be far behind you, son."

Oskar waited to hear Rolf's door close before joining his wife in the kitchen. "What's the matter, Selle?" he asked. "Why are you crying?"

Selma seemed pale. "Vom Rath has died." She went to Oskar's side and tucked her head into his chest, releasing a flood of fear and tears. "After Grynszpan pulled the trigger, he said he hoped the whole world would hear his protest," she said. Looking up into Oskar's troubled eyes, she wiped tears from her cheeks. "Now the world will surely hear it. You were right, Oskar. We're in terrible danger."

🏃

For the next hour, the house was relatively quiet. Oskar and Selma Gompertz sat together in the parlor. Rolf was asleep in his bed. The clock on the parlor mantelpiece ticked away the seconds.

Suddenly shouts came from the street below and glass began to shatter. Oskar and Selma raced to the parlor window. Shadowy figures were running down the street and hurling rocks into the glass of storefront windows.

Oskar quickly threw the curtains closed. He ran out of the parlor and tripped his way down the staircase to the ground floor, where he made sure the heavy lock on the front door was engaged. Then he made his way back up the stairs, finding Selma in the parlor frantically putting a few small family heirlooms into a bag.

"What are you doing, Selle?"

"I don't know, I don't know." She grabbed more trinkets for her bag. "They want us out of here, Oskar. They'll stop at nothing to get us out of here. And nobody will stop them now. Nobody will *want* to stop them, now that a Jew has murdered a German." She looked at her husband wide-eyed. All color had drained from her face. The bag suddenly slipped from her hand and fell to the floor. Something inside of it broke.

Oskar went to her, took her into his arms, and she began to sob.

"I didn't want to tell you, Oskar, but a boy threw a broken brick at Adele and me this morning. The brick just missed my head, and the boy was shouting, 'Sarah, unwanted Jew.' His mother did nothing to stop him. She looked at me for a moment, and then she just looked down and carried on with her sweeping. She wasn't going to do anything to stop him. I should never have left the house but . . ."

Oskar held his wife more tightly.

"They banished all Jewish newspapers yesterday," Selma continued. Her voice was almost a whisper. "We won't know anything about what's going on. And they boarded up the center today. That's where I was going with Adele. Now it will be hard for Jews to talk to one another."

A siren screamed by the house. Oskar stepped over to the window and peeked between the curtains. Dull flames lit the sky here and there. He instinctively cast a look in the direction of his family's magnificent synagogue that stood a fifteen-minute walk away at *Petersstrasse* 99. Something on that block was ablaze. A moment of reflection and he knew what it was. Saying nothing to Selma, he stepped away from the window closed his eyes for a long moment.

"We must pray, Oskar," said Selma, softly. "We must pray together." She picked up her bag of heirlooms and hid them in a cabinet, before sitting down at one end of the sofa. Reaching over to the table next to her, she picked up the Hebrew Bible that lay there. Then she padded the seat next to her, gently bidding her husband to join her. Oskar went over and sat next to his wife, kissing her on the cheek.

"Perhaps, Psalm 116 tonight," Selma said, leafing through the pages of the Bible. She found the passage and began to read. "I love the Lord." She paused, her chin quivering slightly. She drew a fresh breath. "I love the Lord because He hears my voice and my cries for mercy. Because He has inclined His ear to me, I will call upon Him as long as I live. The cords of death encompassed me and the terrors of the grave came upon me; I was overwhelmed with distress and sorrow." Selma paused to look at her husband.

Oskar took her hand, squeezed it lightly. "The next verse too, darling."

With her eyes fastened to her husband's face, she finished the passage in a confident voice. "Then I called upon the name of the Lord: 'O Lord I pray, save my life.'"

11

3

Deep Night, November 9–10, 1938

Bismarckstrasse 118, Krefeld;

2:00 AM

The sounds of loud, constant banging on the front door awakened young Rolf Gompertz who had been fast asleep three floors above. At first confused, he sat up and listened. Bang, bang, bang. He ran to the top of the stairs and could hear husky voices far below: "Open up or we break the door down!" A chill down rode his spine.

Rolf looked down from the banister outside his third-floor bedroom and saw his parents, standing bolt upright by the banister on the second floor below him. They looked up at him. He could see fear in their faces.

"Open this door, Jews!"

Rolf watched his father make a move to descend the staircase, but his mother stopped him. "No, Oskar," she said. "You can't see well with one good eye. You almost fell the last time." She shouted down the stairway: "I'm coming, I'm coming!"

Frightened, Rolf ran back into his room to grab a small suitcase. He frantically threw a bundle of clothes and his little teddy bear inside of it, then raced down the steps. "*Vati!*" He cried. "If they take you, I'm going with you!"

Selma could feel her heart pounding as she approached the front door. She laid one hand on the knob and gripped the key with the other. She hesitated. She thought of her son; a cold rush of fear washed over her.

"Open this door, Jew! Open it now, or we'll bash it down!"

Upstairs in the parlor, Oskar embraced his son. "I'm proud of you, Rolf," he whispered.

Trembling, Selma twisted the key in the lock. But before she could turn the knob, the door was hurled into her, knocking her against the wall. She tumbled to her side and watched a half-dozen Nazis, armed with rifles, storm past her and up the wide staircase. Stunned momentarily, she gathered herself together, and then shouldered the front door back into position.

Oskar stood wide-legged and ready for the "Brown Shirts" who were thumping loudly up the steps.

The Nazis burst into the parlor. "The kitchen, Jewish pigs!" barked their leader. "Now!"

Oskar stood still as stone, staring into the eyes of the Nazi in charge.

His resilience drew the ire of the commander, who walked slowly over to Oskar. Standing two feet away, the Nazi said in a low voice. "The kitchen, Jew. Get into it, now. You don't want to test me, I assure you."

Oskar took hold of Rolf's hand. The two of them stood together. Only their chests moved as their lungs sought to draw air.

"Get into the kitchen," shouted the Nazi, "or we'll drag your dead circumcised bodies into it."

"No, no," shouted Selma, now rushing into the room. "We will not be locked up!"

"Selle! Silence."

"No, Oskar, don't let them lock us up!"

Was there any other way?

Then Oskar said as calmly as he could, "Selle. Rolf." His eyes still trained on the Nazi leader, he continued with the confidence of a military soldier speaking to his troops. "We'll be alright. Come. Follow me."

The little family left the parlor, each step yielding more of their home to the Nazis. But Oskar had no intention of being imprisoned in the kitchen, leaving the home exposed to Nazi plunder. Entering the hallway with the Nazis behind in the parlor, Oskar whispered "Quickly!" to Rolf and Selma as he darted to the back room that he used as his office.

Rolf and Selma dashed to join him.

With sounds of Nazi boots and curses filling his ears, Oskar yanked open the top drawer of his desk and pulled something out of it. "Better an end with terror than terror without end," he said quietly, under his breath.

Enraged Nazis stormed into his office moments later. Five of them pointed their guns directly at Oskar. The Nazi leader, surrounded by his men, folded his arms. "I think you may have made a mistake."

Oskar extended his closed right hand toward the man. He then cautiously opened it to reveal what he had taken from his drawer. None of the Nazis said a word.

The only thing between the Jewish family and the Nazi guns was a small medal that Oskar held. It was his Iron Cross—the coveted medal for battlefield bravery awarded by the German government for outstanding service to the country during The Great War.

Mustering his composure, Oskar hollered at the Nazi leader. "Is this the thanks I get for serving the Fatherland with courage?" There was a moment of silence before he repeated his question, this time with controlled composure. "How you're treating us now—is that the thanks I get? Is this how you treat a hero of the Fatherland?"

Rolf waited, breathlessly, his mother's arms around him protectively as they stood watching at the side of the room. He felt her squeeze him tightly, anxiously. What would the intruders do? Maybe just a few curses? Insults? Maybe "Damned dirty Jew?" Or maybe a rifle butt crushing into his father's face? Maybe a bullet in the head?

Rolf's heart was racing and his mouth felt suddenly dry. He waited. His mother waited. His father waited.

Everyone waited.

The clock on the office mantelpiece struck two. Rolf wanted to shout something, but what? He wanted to run, but where?

The two men stared at one another—the diligent Nazi commander and the soldier decorated twenty years earlier for bravery in the battlefield.

After what seemed an eternity, the wait was over. The Nazi turned away. Saying nothing, he signaled to his men to follow. Obediently, they joined him as he left the office, walked through the passageway and descended the stairs. The only noises were the scuffling of Nazi boots on the steps of the Gompertz family apartment.

Rolf remained frozen; his mother too was fixed in her place. It was Oskar who moved first. Dropping the Iron Cross back into his desk drawer, he went to his wife and son and embraced them.

Out in the darkness of the night, Rolf could hear women crying, shouts of anger, and glass breaking. "I would have gone with you, *Vati*, if they had taken you," he said.

4

Early Morning, November 10, 1938

Bismarckstrasse 118, Krefeld;

8:30 AM

The sun had not been up for long when Oskar unlocked the front door, opening it just wide enough to peer out onto *Bismarckstrasse*.

Furniture and other furnishings were strewn all over the street—the possessions of Jews that had been left for non-Jewish scavengers to collect. But not much of it was of any use to anyone, most of it having been broken apart or set alight in the dark hours. Things of any value had already been smuggled away.

Oskar opened the door wider, then walked out of his home. Glass crunched beneath his shoes as he stepped out onto the sidewalk. He closed the door behind him and locked it carefully. He thought of the words he had said to Selma before leaving the apartment. "We can't let them enslave us in our own home."

He had to leave early enough to make his 9:00 AM appointment with his eye doctor. Oskar lifted his coat collar around his neck, then hurried along, keeping his head down while he walked.

Oskar's appointment had only just commenced when it happened again. Selma and Rolf were in the kitchen, cleaning up after breakfast. Then fists pounded once more on the downstairs door.

"Open up." More banging. "Open up in there."

"Oh no," whispered Rolf. "Not again."

"Go up to your room, son," said Selma, her face turning white as she realized their vulnerability.

Rolf did not budge.

Selma fixed her eyes on him for a moment. Then she removed her apron, and quickly descended the stairs in a nervous clip.

"Open up, I said! Open the door, now!"

"One moment," Selma said, trying to adopt her most polite tone. "I am coming. Just a minute please."

Selma stood to one side as she twisted the key. This time the door was hurled open but it bounced harmlessly against the wall. "How can I help you?" Selma's voice exhibited no fear.

Two Nazis pushed past her, one answering, "We've come for your husband."

Selma thought she recognized one of the men. "My husband is not here," she shouted.

Something caught her attention outside. There, not five yards from her, was a truck whose cargo was Jewish men, held at gunpoint. Her heart sank. She knew some of them. They stared out at her. Blank faces. Empty eyes. A compassionate smile instinctively appeared on Selma's face. Mindlessly she shot out an instinctive wave of her hand, only to withdraw it abruptly in mid-motion a second later.

Raised voices from within her apartment returned her attention. One of the Nazis was cursing and insulting Rolf. Selma whirled about and raced up the stairs. "Leave him," she shouted as she went. "Leave him alone. You've not come for our children. Leave him alone."

It was a calm voice that greeted her as she entered the kitchen. "Where is your husband, *Frau* Gompertz?"

Selma recognized the man. She had passed him many times on the neighborhood streets, sometimes with Oskar, and always with a polite nod.

Now her attention turned to Rolf, who managed a nervous smile to indicate that he was fine. Then she replied to the Nazi, "He is at the doctor's office. His eyes are recovering from surgery." She went over to Rolf, wrapped an arm around him, and pulled him tightly to her side. Then smiling and tilting her head to one side, she added gently, "We just want to be left alone. We haven't caused anyone any trouble."

The man paused, then leaned forward, his face close to Selma's. "We will be back for him," he scowled, staring her straight in the eye. "We will be back, *Frau* Gompertz."[1]

1. In the narrative of the first four chapters of this book, the scenes in which Rolf was not present have been entirely conjectured. In the scenes where Rolf is present, the historical bedrock of the narrative has been solidly laid in Rolf's testimonials over the years, with only minimal artistic license. I have added two things that certainly did not take place. First, Rolf does not remember standing next to his father and his father saying "I am proud of you, Rolf" as the Nazi's broke into the house; I hope the reader will excuse the point, which both (1) represents a reality of the relationship between father and son, and (2) seems appropriate in a context where Rolf has just expressed his willingness to "go with" his father. Second, Oskar was not saying the words "Better an end with terror than terror without end" as he pulled his Iron Cross from the drawer of his desk. Those words were added since (1) they link to Selma's reading of Psa 116 earlier in the narrative, where "terror" is mentioned, and (2) this saying was one that Oskar said to Rolf later in life (see Rolf's diary entry for March 9, 1952, which appears in chapter 14 below), and seemed well-suited at this point in the narrative as well.

PART 2

Kristallnacht: Before and After

5

The Immediate Aftermath of *Kristallnacht*

The events recounted above are exceptional, in both senses of the word—
"extraordinary" and "virtually unique." The experiences of the Gompertz
family during the horrific events of *Kristallnacht* must certainly be one of
the only stories, or perhaps the only story, throughout the whole of Germany in which a Jewish home was raided by Nazis but left intact without
incident.[1]

But if those experiences were extraordinary, what happened to the
little Gompertz family in the immediate aftermath of the events of *Kristallnacht*? How did those extraordinary events get resolved?

This chapter addresses those issues, tracking the initial movements of
the Gompertz family during the years of World War II. In order to put those
developments into a larger context than the one provided by the narrative
above, it will be helpful to triangulate the story recounted in the previous
four chapters with two eyewitness accounts of *Kristallnacht* published in
British newspapers. When placed alongside these newspaper testimonials,
the story of the Gompertz family recounted above is shown not to be deficient in its verisimilitude.

1. It is not surprising, then, that the Gompertz family's experiences of *Kristallnacht*,
along with the experiences of two other Jewish families, were dramatized in a BBC
television production entitled "Days that Shook the World" (October 28, 2003; Lion
Television).

What the Papers Said

In the wake of *Kristallnacht*, the British newspaper reporter Hugh Carleton Greene published eyewitness reports about what he himself had witnessed on the streets of German cities. These extracts speak for themselves.

> I have seen several anti-Jewish outbreaks in Germany during the last five years but never anything as nauseating as this. Racial hatred and hysteria seemed to have taken hold of otherwise decent people. I saw fashionably dressed women clapping their hands and screaming with glee [and] respectable middle-class mothers [holding] up their babies to see the [anti-Semitic] "fun." . . . There were remarkably few policemen on the streets. Those who were there, when their attention was drawn to the outrages which were proceeding before their eyes, shrugged their shoulders and refused to take any action. Several hundred Jewish shopkeepers were . . . put under "protective custody" for attempting to shield their property. A state of hopeless panic reigns . . . throughout Jewish circles. Hundreds of Jews have gone into hiding and many businessmen and financial experts of international repute have not dared to sleep in their own homes.

In another newspaper, Greene reported the following:

> Mob law ruled in Berlin throughout this afternoon and evening as hordes of hooligans indulged in an orgy of destruction. On the *Kurfürstendamm*, the interior of every Jewish shop was systematically demolished by youths armed with hammers, brooms and lengths of lead piping. In Dobrin, a fashionable Jewish café, the mob smashed the counter and the table and chairs and then stamped cream cakes and confectionary into the floor. Weisz Czarda, a restaurant owned by a Hungarian Jew, was invaded by another horde which cast chairs and tables out on to the street.[2]

Whereas Greene expressed nausea at the events of *Kristallnacht*, most of the German population had become systematically numbed to the increasingly outrageous injustices carried out against the Jews even prior to the Holocaust. Had non-Jews felt the sting of things and then simply cowered out of concern for themselves, their families, their businesses, their wellbeing? Or had they never really felt the sting at all? Had some of them

2. These two reports are listed as coming from *The Daily Telegraph* and *The Times* between 8–16 November 1938 in Smith, *Foley*, 304.

relished the sight of it all? Were they internally conflicted, or had they simply adopted a willful blindness?

Such unresolved issues will continue to be debated. But regardless of how they are answered, the effect was the same—the abandonment of the Jews to the worst elements of Nazi society. One Christian pastor is reported as saying that the events of *Kristallnacht* "did not move me colossally,"[3] and he was not alone in failing to speak out. The Gestapo reported that there were no protests over the events of *Kristallnacht,* and most pastors and priests did not mention the event on the Sunday that followed. With a few exceptions, the general population had invoked a collective shrug as the Nazi program forged ahead.[4]

It is against the backdrop of this much larger picture that the storming of the Gompertz home by Nazi operatives must be placed. As it was for millions of Jews throughout Germany, so too for the Gompertz family, life would never be the same after *Kristallnacht*.

The Gompertz Family in the Wake of *Kristallnacht*

The Nazis never did come back for Rolf's father, Oskar. That fact has remained cloaked in mystery ever since. Why did they not come back a third time? We will never know.

One other mystery from that night also remains—that is, why the Nazi leader who stormed the Gompertz residence on *Kristallnacht* yielded to the Iron Cross that Oskar held up between them? We will never know for sure. One hypothesis will be registered later in this book that takes its cues from Rolf's worldview as a means of explaining that mystery.[5]

3. Barnett, *For the Soul of the People,* 140.

4. This is in line with the story recounted by Hannelore Mahler who was born in Krefeld in 1921, six years before Rolf. Although her father was Catholic, her mother was Jewish, and consequently she was Jewish as well, under German law. She survived in Krefeld until September 1944, when she and the last remaining Jews in the city were deported to a German death camp. She survived the death camp and was liberated in May 1945, whereupon she returned to Krefeld and later began a family. She recalls, however, that on the Sunday morning when she was finally accosted by the Nazis, she and other captives were led through the streets of Krefeld. The timing of the march coincided with the release of congregants from local church services, as people left church buildings. "They had to have seen us," she is later reported as saying. But they said and did nothing. See Johnson and Reuband, *What We Knew,* 117.

5. In one episode of the film *Hitler on Trial: The Truth behind the Story* (1:04 into the film), an elderly Jewish man approaches Adolf Hitler (in May 1931) and shows him the

Despite these remaining mysteries, what happened in the aftermath of the incident is clear. The little Gompertz family remained intact, living tentatively for the next few months in their two-storied residence in their hometown of Krefeld. Part of that time they shared their apartment with another Jewish family, the Meyers family. The parents and their two teenage girls were in need of accommodation after the Nazi's destroyed their home in the events of *Kristallnacht*.

In early 1939, the Gompertz's rabbi in Krefeld, Rabbi Arthur Bluhm, was given the task of rationing emigration rights to members of his synagogue—the beautifully ornate "Krefelder Synagogue" at *Petersstrasse* 99 that had been gutted by fire during the events of *Kristallnacht*.[6] The emigration out of Germany by selected members of his synagogue happened in bursts. German officials provided the rabbi with quota numbers issued by the American government, allowing a limited number of individuals to come to the United States. The rabbi then had to choose who would be included, without exceeding the quota limit. In this unenviable task of virtually deciding who would live and who would die, Rabbi Bluhm usually gave preference to those families that had children. Once the quota of emigrants was filled, Rabbi Bluhm could do nothing but wait to be provided with new quota numbers—a practice that stopped completely once war was declared in September 1939.

The Oskar Gompertz family was soon chosen to be on Rabbi Bluhm's list of Jews eligible for emigration out of Germany. This was, of course, good news. But it also meant that they would be stripped of their possessions and reduced to poverty. The German authorities would allow them to leave the country only if they left virtually all of their possessions behind—in effect, forcing Jews to donate to the Nazi cause through decimating their personal resources. Because of this, countries that were willing to accept Jewish refugees from Germany often required documentation demonstrating that the refugees had a sponsor who could support them for at least five years, if necessary.

The United States of America, being still in the grip of The Great Depression (1929–39), was one of these countries requiring a sponsor

---

Iron Cross presented to him for service to the Fatherland in the war of 1914–18. Having already identified himself as a Jew, the man's short speech to Hitler ends with the words, "So you see, this is my country too. Good day to you," whereupon Hitler says nothing but walks out of the room.

6. A few days after *Kristallnacht*, Rolf walked by the site of the synagogue, shocked and saddened by the extent of the destruction.

before accepting Jewish refugees. But the Gompertz family had a relative in Los Angeles who, although only a distant cousin whom they had never met, was willing to act as their financial sponsor. This was Anna Coffee, a wealthy childless widow who looked kindly upon her relatives' dire situation. Without her, the lives of Oskar, Selma, and Rolf would probably have ended in a German concentration camp. Also instrumental in orchestrating their emigration out of Germany was Julius Baer, a cousin of Selma's who had fled Germany prior to *Kristallnacht*. He helped the Gompertz family in their efforts to gain Anna Coffee's assistance. Later (at a date prior to 1945), he and Anna married, with her name then changing to Anna Coffee Baer.

All the pieces fell into place. The Gompertz family was included on Rabbi Bluhm's list, had a sponsor in the United States of America, and their departure from Germany fell within the limited time-period during which the USA permitted Jewish immigration from Germany into America.

But there was sadness. While arrangements for their own survival were now in place, they would be leaving behind precious family members—leaving them in the clutches of Nazi ideology. This included Selma's two brothers and two sisters, their spouses and families, Nanni Herrmann (Selma's stepmother), and Oskar's father Moritz.

As things turned out, however, Rolf and his parents would not have to say sad farewells to Rolf's grandfather Moritz. About two months before Rolf's family emigrated, Moritz came to their house to visit. But he slipped and fell on the way, causing serious damage. He died a few days later, surrounded by his family. It was a much better death than the one that would have waited for him along a different trajectory of events.

In April 1939, the Gompertz family boarded a ship (half passenger, half freight) and sailed to California through the Panama Canal. On June 11, 1939, less than three months before the official beginning of World War II, they disembarked from their boat at San Pedro harbor and met Anna Coffee. Stepping onto American soil, all three of them kissed the ground. They were poor, but they were free from the horrors of Nazi Germany.

They were driven to Anna Coffee's home in Beverly Hills, riding in a black Cadillac. She had wanted to keep them nearby her own home, so she rented an apartment for them in Beverly Hills. There, on 114 North Almont Drive, they started their new lives.[7] But they soon moved to a very small apartment on 248 Alexandria Avenue in Los Angeles, where they could live more cheaply. This was crucial for a family who wanted to be financially

---

7. Rolf attended one semester of elementary school while living in Beverly Hills.

self-reliant as soon as possible. Having been allowed to take the equivalent of ten dollars per person out of Germany, they knew how important it was to live a frugal lifestyle in those threadbare days.

During the first two or three years of living in America, Oskar tried his hand at three different low-paying jobs. His first job was with a clothes cleaning firm, delivering laundry to its customers. Then he became a door-to-door salesman of home goods. Then he took a position as a shipping clerk. These proved to be tough ways of making a living, and the family did little more than live hand-to-mouth on what Oskar earned. So Selma was required to take on work as well, unlike their days in Germany. She became a masseuse, and had a number of clients, including Anna Coffee.

After three years or so of scraping by, Oskar joined up with another Jewish refugee from Germany, Max Weil, who had founded a pottery factory and who would eventually go on to produce ornate collectible pottery. Oskar helped to administer Max's company, the California Figurine Company, for the next seventeen years. Oskar began to draw a somewhat better salary, although, as Rolf would later say, it was "nothing to write home about." He continued: "We never went without. We lived in a very small apartment. We always had a roof over our head, always had food, always had clothes. Took modest vacations, you know, at a certain point."[8] Slowly the family put together a life in their new surroundings. In due course, the family was able to fulfill their goal of repaying Anna Coffee for all of her expenditures on their behalf.

Meanwhile, all correspondence between Jews in America and Jews in Germany came to an abrupt halt with the outbreak of World War II in September 1939. Not long after arriving in Los Angeles, Oskar subscribed to a German Jewish newspaper published in New York under the name *Aufbau*, or "Reconstruction." An extremely popular newspaper among Jewish refugees, it was a powerful anti-Nazi voice and one that spoke directly to the interests of Jewish refugees from Germany. It was also one of the few ways that Oskar and Selma connected with their former life in Germany and kept abreast of developments there.[9]

Rolf had no interest in connecting with his former life; he was simply an eleven-year-old boy adjusting to his new environment. The biggest hurdle in that adjustment, of course, was the language barrier. Oskar, who

8. These comments were made to me when interviewing Rolf in May 2011.

9. Moreover, for two years after the war, the *Aufbau* newspaper frequently published the names of Jewish Holocaust survivors and Holocaust victims.

knew some English from his German school days, had hired a man to tutor Rolf in English before they left Germany—even prior to *Kristallnacht*, but the tutelage increased in frequency as the family waited to immigrate to the United States.[10] Nonetheless, despite those efforts, the linguistic foundations laid during that time were not robust.

Rolf's early exposure to the English language in the United States came in two forms. The children on the block where the family lived welcomed him among them, and as he played with them on the streets he inevitably started to learn their language. But things were not easy at first. One day early on, Rolf ran from the playground to his home and cried to his mother, "It's no use, *Mutti*. I don't understand them, and they don't understand me." But not long after that, he came home and triumphantly announced to her, "*Mutti, Mutti*, I can understand them now. And I don't even have to look at their lips any more when they talk."

Rolf also was helped to learn English when Anna Coffee enrolled him in a summer school for arts and crafts. The teacher there took it upon herself to teach him English in order to prepare him for the beginning of the school year just a few months away.

By the time school started in the fall of 1939, Rolf could function pretty well with his English. But obviously there were going to be deficits in his learning for the first few years. In the second week of school at Horace Mann Elementary School, his teacher Mrs. Chase gave his sixth-grade class a fifty-word spelling test. Of those fifty words, Rolf got thirty-five words wrong.

But things were set to change as time progressed. Rolf went on to become an English major at UCLA (where he later received both a BA and an MA in English), an editor of a weekly newspaper, an employee of NBC's public relations department, and an author of half a dozen books—all of which are discussed in later chapters of this book. His grappling with the English language after emigrating from Nazi Germany gave him a love for language that has stayed with him for the rest of his life.

His first triumph in using language effectively came only a week after he failed his first English spelling test in September 1939. Mrs. Chase had set each child in his class the task of writing some poetry and then standing up and presenting it to the rest of the class. But if a person's vocabulary is limited, the options for putting together a decent rhyme are similarly limited. So, while all the other students were writing away, Rolf had to think

10. Selma started to learn English only when the family arrived in the United States.

of words (1) that he knew, (2) that rhymed, and (3) that could be put together meaningfully into a poem. "Finally, at the eleventh hour," he later recounted, "I managed to scribble something down." And when it was his turn to share what he had written, this is what he read out to the class:

A MONKEY AND AN ELEPHANT

> A monkey and an elephant,
> They played once in a zoo,
> There came a tiger and a lion,
> And both of them said, "Boo!"
> The monkey was so scared at once,
> That he jumped on a tree,
> From there he looked in the lion's face
> And laughed: "Hee, hee, hee, hee!"

His classmates broke out in spontaneous laughter, enjoying his piece of literature.

Although Rolf's poetry would greatly improve in years to come, this was an important moment in his life. Rolf had experienced humor in Germany, of course, but there the humor of non-Jewish people was frequently directed at and against the Jews—as Rolf himself had come to know even prior to the events of *Kristallnacht* (as outlined in the next chapter). So when his non-Jewish classmates laughed with him, rather than making fun of him, Rolf's face must have beamed with pleasure, satisfaction, and, in a sense, triumph. The sharing of humor puts a person within a group. So, as Rolf later expressed it, the laughter of his classmates "was a wonderful and welcome sound. In that moment, I felt accepted by my classmates—and by America!"

In 1940 Rolf turned thirteen, and celebrated his *bar mitzvah*. Once again it was Anna Coffee who paved the way for this. Rolf had not undergone the five years of training that Rabbi Jacob Cohen normally required prior to a *bar mitzvah*, but Anna Coffee persuaded him that an exception was required in exceptional circumstances. And so Rolf's *bar mitzvah* went ahead on the Sabbath of Hanukkah—a Jewish holiday that (all the more appropriately, in this instance) focuses on the remembrance of the freedom gained by the Jewish people from their foreign oppressors who sought to destroy their identity.

Not much of the ceremony stuck in Rolf's long-term memory except for the reading from the prophet Zechariah: "Not by might, nor by power, but by my Spirit, says the Lord of hosts" (Zech 4:6). It is a verse that Rabbi Cohen charged Rolf to remember and it has accompanied Rolf all his life. Rolf was frequently called upon to give speeches as his reputation increased later in life, and he often included the verse toward the end of a speech. What is the Spirit of God, according to Rolf Gompertz? It is love. And so the verse captures within itself two worldviews and contrasts them, denouncing "might" and "power" (the driving forces behind Nazi ideology) and affirming "love."

As a boy in both Germany and later the United States, Rolf was captivated by a fascination for Native Americans. Although this might look like an incidental feature of his childhood, there is a sense in which it might be indicative of deeper facets of his personality and developmental identity. This is how he orally described his interest in Native Americans—or as they were called back in the days of his youth, American "Indians." (I leave this as an extended quotation simply to allow the reader to capture some of Rolf's natural charm. He spoke these words to me in a recorded interview when he was eighty-three years old.)[11]

> Before I decided that I was Jewish, I decided I wanted to become an American Indian, and tried real hard to be one. It goes all the way back to Germany. I decided I would become an American Indian. And I thought, when we came to America, that was going to be it. . . . And we came to Beverly Hills, and I looked around—didn't find any American Indians. (So that was the only disillusioning thing I found about America.)
>
> Fortunately, as a teenager, I became an Indian guide with the Woodcraft Rangers. It's sort of like Boy Scouts, only modeled on Indian lore, Indian life. That was it for me. . . . [During summer camps with them] I played [an] American Indian. I got the job of beating the tom-tom every morning to wake kids up, and then at night to put them to bed. And [I] chanted Indian chants and so forth. I had a ball with it, and even made myself a tom-tom out of cowhide and made myself a war bonnet. I couldn't find any real eagle feathers, so I used turkey feathers. And I couldn't find any beadwork, so I made my own beadwork. And I played Indian.
>
> And one day I came to the realization, "You're never going to be an Indian. You're Jewish." [He laughs.] And I finally said, "Oh, all right. Well, that's another tribe. Let's discover, let's find out what

---

11. The only change I have made in a few places is the bringing together of words that were separated by a few others. The appearance of multiple occurrences of ". . ." would prove distracting.

that is all about. What is being Jewish?" That was one of my ways into Judaism.

Rolf dates this "conversion" of interest from Native Americans to interest in Judaism to the summer of his seventeenth year. That was 1945, the very year when Hitler committed suicide, American combat in Europe ended, and Nazi Germany was finally crushed by Allied and Soviet forces once and for all (with Germany's unconditional surrender taking place on May 7 of that year).

It might not be coincidental that Rolf felt able to begin a slow but progressive journey into his Jewish identity only once state-sponsored Nazism was finally trounced. Until then, perhaps his imagination was able to place his secret identity safely among a different ethnic people—a people who had adventurous and intriguing stories written about them, but also a people who had experienced the slow drip of persecution, apartheid, and genocide by those who controlled societal power. Those were experiences that even the young Rolf of *Bismarckstrasse* 118 could relate to and identify with. (See especially the next chapter.) Since both the Native Americans and the Jews of Germany were people-groups that were progressively written out of their larger national macro-narratives, it might not be surprising that young Rolf was fascinated by the micro-narratives of Native Americans at precisely the time when micro-narratives of Jewish Germans were being silenced and, at times, tragically extinguished. His identification with Native Americans resembles what Kafka called "interior emigration."

After the war ended in May 1945, communications with Germany opened up once again. The names of those who had been murdered and the names of those who had survived slowly began to trickle out. Like other Jews who had immigrated to other countries outside of Europe, Oskar and Selma were desperate to hear news about members of their family. They learned of some survivors among their family, and to them Oskar and Selma frequently sent care packages of food, clothes, and other supplies that would come in handy.

These survivors included Max and Alma Herrmann, and Otto and Ilse Herrmann—Rolf's uncles and aunts on his mother's side.[12] Each couple had their own incredible story to relate. Otto and Ilse had been sent to two concentration camps, *Theresienstadt* and *Auschwitz*, and survived them both.

12. Rolf's father became an only child after two sisters died in early childhood.

Max and Alma had a much different story. As a Christian married to a Jew, Alma was regularly called in for questioning by the German Gestapo. "When are you going to divorce your Jewish husband?" she was asked. And each time she indicated that she had no intention of doing so. But as things progressively worsened for Jews, she realized that simply refusing the Gestapo's pressure to divorce Max was not a long-term strategy. If she and Max failed to take an initiative of some kind, the Nazis would do so instead. Consequently, Alma devised a strategy that would ultimately save Max's life.

Colluding with her sister, Erna Kampert, Alma arranged for Max to move into the basement of Erna's house in a neighboring village. Erna's husband Ernst was a German soldier serving on the Russian front when the two sisters devised their strategy. When Max moved into the basement of the house, Erna and Ernst's daughter, a young girl by the name of Edeltraut, was coached never to say anything to anyone about Uncle Max living in the house.[13] Then Alma went to the Gestapo and reported the sad news that her husband recently cracked under the pressures placed on the family and committed suicide. The Nazi officer was pleased to hear it, and closed the case on Max. Meanwhile, Max spent several years of his life huddled away in a small, clammy basement, coming out of his confines for some fresh air only briefly at night.

Max's life was in danger because he was a Jew, of course; if the Nazis had discovered him, he would almost certainly have died in one of the Nazi concentration camps. But Alma and Erna had joined him in his danger, putting themselves in an extremely precarious position; although they were not Jewish, by helping a Jew they had placed their own lives in jeopardy. In the end, human ingenuity and the bonds of love preserved them all, and they, rather than the Nazi establishment, survived.

Rolf also had a half-aunt who survived, Selma's half-sister Helene Herrmann. She escaped from Germany as a teenager, managing to make her way onto a children's transport train that was headed to "Palestine" (as it was called then, or "Israel" as it is known now).

Other members of the Gompertz's extended family were not so fortunate. This included at least eight people:

13. This was recounted in an email (sent to Rolf in early December 2012) from Billy Hermann, son of Alma and Max Hermann, who remembers this from "stories my mother told me." He also informed Rolf in that email that Edeltraut is currently living next door to the home in which she grew up in the city of *Stokum*. Max and Alma had lived in the village of Unna.

- Rolf's grandmother (by marriage) on his mother's side, Nanni Herrmann;

- his aunt, Grete von Minden;

- his uncle and aunt, Siegfried and Irma Stern;

- his cousins Irmgard, Klaus, and Kurt Stern, and Irmgard's baby.

All of them were murdered in German concentration camps—a fate shared by six million other Jews, and a fate that Rolf, Oskar, and Selma had only narrowly escaped.

There was one other person important in Rolf's early life who did not survive the Holocaust against the Jews. That was Dr. Isidor Hirschfelder, one of the best pediatricians in Krefeld and the doctor who delivered Rolf at birth. He had moved to Krefeld in 1906, when he was twenty-eight years old, and over the years he had become well known and respected for his work with infant and maternal care. He frequently did not charge his poorer patients for his services. Like Rolf's father, Dr. Hirschfelder had also served in the German army in World War I and had received the Iron Cross medal in recognition of his outstanding services to the country.

Rolf remembers three childhood incidents pertaining to Dr. Hirschfelder. When Rolf had whooping cough, Dr. Hirschfelder came by to see him. When the doctor decided that it would be best to give Rolf an injection, he prepared the needle to be injected into Rolf's bottom, whereupon little Rolf said to him, "That's not where I have my cough."

The other two incidents involved the doctor getting wet. Once the doctor tried to wash his hands in the bathtub but the water came out of the overhead shower instead—a funny moment for a very young boy to see. Another time, the doctor tried to examine little Rolf, while Rolf was laying ill in bed; but Rolf had a full bladder and eventually could no longer control it, resulting in urine squirting all over the doctor's face.

As the Gompertz family would learn after the war was over, Dr. Hirschfelder's life ended tragically. On October 29, 1941, the night before he was to be deported to Auschwitz, Dr. Hirschfelder stood behind his desk in his home, put a gun to his head, and blew his brains out. On his desk were photos from World War I and his 1st class Iron Cross. He was sixty-three years old (born March 11, 1878). Today a street in Bockum near Krefeld is named after him. So too his name is the emblem of an educational unit in Herongen that dedicates itself to immersing children to the wonders of nature.

☥

Kristallnacht—the Night of Broken Glass. It was a night in which more than a hundred synagogues were burned, more than seven thousand Jewish businesses were vandalized or destroyed, more than 25,000 Jews were arrested and taken to concentration camps, ninety-one were killed in their homes and untold numbers were beaten. And for ten-year-old Rolf Gompertz, the trauma of that night would prove ultimately formative. Reflecting upon *Kristallnacht* years later, Rolf characterized it, "the most powerful and memorable experience" of his life, as the "dress-rehearsal for the Holocaust."

And he was right about that. *Kristallnacht* devastated Jewish communities in Germany, proving to have been directly ruinous to the lives of untold hundreds of thousands of German Jews. But beyond that, the most horrific aspect of it was not simply the devastation that it unleashed on the night of 9–10 November in 1938, but the evils that it set in play in months and years to come.

As the "dress-rehearsal for the Holocaust," the horrors of *Kristallnacht* arc forward to the evils of the Holocaust. And it was to those evils that Rolf would later apply himself in what he would call his "response to Hitler."

But in order to understand where Rolf's life was to go in the future, we need also to understand a bit more of Rolf's life prior to *Kristallnacht*. It is to those issues that we now turn.

6

Before *Kristallnacht*

THERE WERE GOMPERTZES IN Germany centuries before Hitler came to power in 1933. Records suggest their presence there at least as far back as the 1600s. The name "Gompertz" (or its alternative "Gomperz") is perhaps a combination of two Spanish words: the name Gomez and the name Perez. Alternatively, it may be a combination of Gomez and the word Iberes or Ibertes—the latter either functioning a separate name or as an identifier of the Iberian region (i.e., the Spanish region). The name would then mean "Gomez from Iberia."[1] Either way, it seems that the Gompertz family left Spain during the Spanish Inquisition of the late 1400s and early 1500s, when Spanish Jews and Moslems were required either to convert to Catholicism, to be burned at the stake, or to leave the country.[2] Evidently, the flight of Jews from Nazi Germany was not the first time that Gompertzes were forced to leave their homeland because their Jewish identity ran contrary to the overarching preferences of the ruling authorities.

By the 1930s there were roughly five thousand Gompertzes in Germany, with a number of them being based in the city of Krefeld. The Gompertz family is credited with bringing tie manufacturing into the city, an offshoot of the silk industry that still thrives in the Krefeld area.

Rolf's mother Selma had three brothers (one of whom died early, in a drowning accident) and two other sisters. Selma's parents were no longer

---

1. This hypothesis derives from Kaufmann and Freudenthal, *Die Familie Gomperz*.
2. Other wings of the Gompertz family converted to Catholicism, then Protestantism.

living by the time Rolf was born; her step-mother "Nanni Herrmann" was grandmother to Rolf in his youth, although she would later be murdered in the gas chambers of Auschwitz. Moritz Gompertz, Rolf's grandfather on his father's side, worked as a butcher in Krefeld until his death in 1939. He was a widower who at that time had only one living child, Oskar.

Although Oskar worked in the silk industry as a traveling salesman, he and Selma met through Moritz's business. As a young woman, Selma was employed in a department store in Krefeld. She frequently purchased meats in the butcher shop operated by Oskar's father, and one of Oskar's female cousins noticed her as a fine Jewish girl and pointed her out to Oskar. "You should meet her in the store sometime," she said to Oskar. And that's exactly what happened. They married on April 20 in 1926, the same day that an aspiring German politician by the name of Adolf Hitler turned thirty-seven years old, and the same year that he wrote his political ideology in *Mein Kampf*.

Although the couple were not rich, Oskar was successful in his job, and his income allowed them to enjoy a comfortable lifestyle. Selma did not need to work to add income to the family finances, and Rolf remembers being given many of the toys that he wanted as a boy. The only thing he never got while in Germany was a dog.

Oskar, Selma, and Rolf were Conservative Jews, falling between the more conservative Orthodox Jews and the more liberal Reformed Jews. They worshipped at the Krefelder Synagogue, which was later destroyed in the events of *Kristallnacht*. Rolf was the first boy to be born into the congregation after Arthur Bluhm was made the rabbi at that synagogue in the late 1920s. Rolf's Hebrew name was Menachem ben Shimshon v' Sarah—Menachem son of Shimshon and Sarah. Shimshon was Oskar's Hebrew name and Sarah was Selma's Hebrew name. Menachem means "comforter."

Rolf's birth nearly brought death. During childbirth, Dr. Hirschfelder thought that a decision would have to be made as to whether to save the mother's life or the baby's life, instead of losing both of them. In the end, both mother and baby survived the ordeal. But Rolf weighed just over two pounds at birth. Having been due on February 28, 1928, he was born two months premature on December 29, 1927. So for the first two months of his life, he was kept in an incubator. Selma was told that if she could keep him alive until he was seven years old, he would have a good chance of growing old naturally. Consequently, Selma and Oskar became very protective of little Rolf in the early years.

If Rolf was born weak and vulnerable, he was also born Jewish in the Germany that Hitler would soon control. This ensured that Rolf's early life would be vulnerable to threatening societal forces. His parents, of course, did everything they could to ensure that Rolf was protected from the rising tide of anti-Semitic sentiment that was sweeping through Germany in the 1930s—a sentiment deeply rooted in European history. But they were not able to protect him from it altogether. Rolf remembers a few such incidents.

In an interview with me in 2011, Rolf articulated things in this way:

> At the time Hitler came to power I was five years old. Five years later I'm ten years old, and so very much, very much aware of the effect, because there were signs all over the place, all over town— "Jews not wanted!" (*Juden unerwünscht!*) So we were not allowed anymore in restaurants or swimming pools or this, that, or the other. So it was very obvious to us where we stood . . . it was apparent to all of us, the whole Jewish community.

The ten-year-old Rolf who encountered the Nazis in his own home on *Kristallnacht* was well aware that being Jewish in Nazi Germany could draw tactics of intimidation from non-Jews.

Rolf had already undergone a few formative experiences by that point in his life. Attending a Jewish school until the summer of 1938 would have buffered this somewhat, but only somewhat. The ugly face of Nazism could not be avoided, despite the most strenuous of parental efforts. As he wrote to me once, "They [my parents] shielded me from what was going on as much as possible." But it was impossible to protect him completely. Consequently, as he says, "I saw and experienced enough to know!"

One of Rolf's earliest memories of anti-Semitic attack was in 1935 or so, when he was about eight years old. The Nazi newspaper *Der Stürmer* ("The Attacker") was published by Julius Streicher on a weekly basis and circulated throughout the whole of Germany between the years 1923 and 1945. It was a decidedly anti-Semitic tabloid paper that reveled in besmirching the reputation of the Jewish people. In doing that, one of its favored strategies was to caricature Jews in ludicrous ways, intending to foster anti-Semitic ridicule at a people thought to be strange, inferior, and unwanted. The newspaper was circulated within Krefeld as well, and it was inevitable that Rolf would come across it. That day came when Rolf and Selma were walking along the street and passed a newspaper stand that had displayed the caricatures prominently. As a fun-loving young boy, Rolf was obviously curious about the "funny pictures" (as he later recalled them) portrayed across the newspaper and ran to take a look at them. Before he got a good look at them, his mother yanked him away, followed by a stern warning, "No, Rolf, we don't look at those." Although he would not have been able to put a name to the phenomenon, he knew that being Jewish was a thing to be ridiculed in Hitler's Germany.

A year or so later, the same message received stark reinforcement. A parade marched past their apartment at *Westwall* 32 (where they were then living). Rolf, curious by the frivolity and noise, ran to the living room window to watch the proceedings. But it wasn't a simple civic parade; it was a Nazi parade intent on stirring up anti-Semitic sentiment in order to "cleanse" the city of Jewish presence and become *Judenrein*, "free of Jews." Rolf was not able to watch all of it, since Selma rushed to the window and closed the curtain before he had a chance to watch it all. But he had seen enough already. German Nazis had masqueraded through the streets as caricatured Jews. They wore long black coats, black hats, and prayer shawls. They held prayer books and scrolls of the Torah. They donned large hooked "Jewish" noses as part of their costume, and danced down the street looking as ridiculous as possible.

As anti-Semitic pressures increased within Krefeld, the Gompertzes found that their non-Jewish friends and associates began to distance themselves from them. So, for instance, the barber who had cut Oskar's hair for many years said to him one day, "Mr. Gompertz, please don't come to my barbershop anymore. I cannot be seen giving you or your son a haircut." His business would have suffered if he were seen to cater to a Jewish constituency. But he was not ill-intentioned, and added, "However, if you call me, I will continue to give both of you haircuts at night, in your home." And that's what happened. Good people, unintentionally caught up in the evils of Nazi society, had increasingly to distance themselves from Jews.

The same phenomenon resulted in the rupturing of close friendships. One of Selma's best friends was a Christian woman named Trude Pilling. Rolf called her his "aunt," and her daughter, whose name was Doris, was Rolf's age and one of his best playmates. One day "Aunt Trudy" had a frank conversation with Selma, informing her that being Selma's friend was becoming too dangerous; the two of them could no longer be friends, nor could Doris and Rolf. Selma gave Rolf only a brief explanation, but he understood even what she kept from him. Never again did Rolf see Doris, nor did Selma ever again see Trude.

The danger of befriending Jews in Nazi Germany was reinforced through the interminable signs that were plastered everywhere in the towns and cities (including Krefeld) saying "*Juden unerwünscht!*"—quite simply, "Jews unwanted!"[3] But what happens when a restaurant or a shop or a swimming pool or a playground or a museum or a cinema or a theater or a beach or a park or an exhibition or a hotel does not display the signs? Does that mean that Jews are wanted? Or at least that they're accepted there?

This was an issue that resulted in a near-death experience for Rolf. In the summer prior to *Kristallnacht*, a new swimming pool was opened in Krefeld. Rolf had taken some lessons in another of the city's public pools, but that had been five years earlier, and in the meantime he had not been allowed to swim, because he was Jewish. But when the new pool opened in 1938, Rolf, now ten years old, explored its environs to see if any signs prevented Jews from entering. Seeing none, he rushed home and asked his mother if he could swim there, since "it doesn't have a sign!" After pleading with his mother, Selma eventually allowed him to go swimming, not imagining for a moment how it would turn out.

Rolf returned to the pool with some money, changed into his swimming trunks, and rushed into the pool area. With a lifeguard on duty overlooking the water, Rolf jumped into the deep end of the water. In the five intervening years since his lessons, however, Rolf had forgotten how to swim. He only realized this moments after he was already immersed in the water. Struggling and thrashing about, Rolf bobbed, sinking down into the water and gasping for air whenever his head punched through the water's surface. He felt he was drowning, just as his mother's brother had died in a drowning accident.

In the end, his frantic efforts overcame his inability to swim, and he managed to make it to the side of the pool. Coughing and spluttering out water, he pulled himself up a nearby ladder. After spending a few moments to catch his breath and regain his focus, Rolf picked himself up. He then noticed the lifeguard, still sitting in his chair overseeing the water. He had seen the whole thing and not bothered to do anything to help the struggling boy. Instead, he motioned to Rolf, instructing him to approach. Rolf

---

3. Compare Flew, *There is a God*, 13: "I was greatly influenced by these early travels abroad during the years before World War II. I vividly recall the banners and signs outside small towns [in Germany] proclaiming, 'Jews not wanted here.'"

hurried over and looked up at the lifeguard. "Didn't you see the sign?" the
lifeguard's voice boomed. Rolf left the pool quickly, and ran home, certain
that the lifeguard would have let him die in the pool because he was Jewish.
To have saved a Jewish boy from drowning would have gone against the
ethos of the culture. When Selma heard what had happened, she could not
forgive herself for allowing him to go in the first place.[4]

On top of all this, seeing "the writing on the walls," 150,000 Jews had
already fled Germany prior to *Kristallnacht*. That number included Rolf's
own uncle Julius Baer. Those departures testify to the growing perception
of the approaching danger among German Jews (and within the Gompertz
family), and would have heightened the sense of insecurity for the Jews
who remained behind. Many of them clung to the belief that things had
reached their worst, and could not get any worse. Repeatedly, this belief
was proven false.

There must have been redemptive moments in Rolf's life prior to
Kristallnacht, initiated by people who swam against the tide of systemic
evil. Rolf can really only remember one, however—the tutor in Krefeld
who came by the house to teach Rolf English. His name was Tom Göbel.
The day after *Kristallnacht*, Tom came to the house (itself a brave thing to
do), expressing concern about what had happened and offering assistance
in any way possible. Oskar asked Tom if he would be willing to protect
some valuable family documents. Tom agreed. He went to the house on a
bicycle at a pre-arranged time and collected them, keeping them safe for
the family.[5] Rolf knows of other redemptive moments (as in the case of his
aunt Alma and her sister's family), but for the most part they did not touch
his little life.

What we see, then, is Rolf's world getting a little smaller and a little less
secure with each passing day. A thicket of dense, intertwining anti-Semitic
initiatives had overgrown Rolf's little world, with only the smallest sliver of
light getting past the encroaching darkness. Even his own name, given to
him by his parents, was not impenetrable against Nazi encroachment. On
August 17, 1938, a new ruling was passed that would require Jews who did
not already have an identifiably Jewish name to adopt a new middle name
by the first day of 1939, so that their full names would advertise clearly

4. In an email on December 9, 2012, Rolf wrote this to me: "I have no idea how the
lifeguard knew that I was Jewish. I must have acted very uncertain and insecure. I had
never been there before. He put 2 and 2 together."

5. The papers were returned to the family prior to their departure to the United States.

their Jewish identity. Males were to add "Israel" as a middle name, and women were to adopt "Sarah" as a middle name. Consequently, at ten years of age, Rolf Gompertz knew that his name would soon become Rolf Israel Gompertz. Even his own name could be imprinted by the Nazis for the express purpose of making him much more easily identifiable as a Jew and, consequently, all the more exposed.

In that context of a world shrinking in size, vulnerable to Nazi encroachment, and increasing in danger, Rolf's family played a huge role in keeping his outlook healthy and his demeanor happy. This is quite a testimony to the quality of their family life.[6] In fact, in Rolf's own words, life with his parents was "a good life," simply because he "had good, loving parents." He remembered his mother in this way:

> My mother was a cheerful, joyful, imaginative person, a romantic. I spent a lot of time talking with my mother. She was a good listener, a wonderful listener, and she always had time for me. She knew how to draw me out. I always felt understood.

Regarding discipline at home, Rolf noted that his mother operated by means of "affection training," in which she sought to motivate proper behavior by encouragement and approval. "She was kind, gentle, and loving," he said, "but she could also be firm. . . . My mother barely ever spanked me, but the threat was always there."

And the threat prompted him to excel in adopting workable strategies for pain avoidance from a very young age. He tells the story of the broken mirror in this way:

> When I was still quite young, my mother dressed me on the dresser. When she had to go out for a moment, I amused myself

6. Rolf said this about his parents in an interview with me in May 2011: "I want to pay brief tribute to my parents, and say I was really raised in a loving home, with a very loving mother, very understanding mother, very empathetic mother, and a very good, good father. Good values, and so I—whatever love I have incorporated in my thoughts was felt far before I had any thoughts on the subject. I experienced it."

This tribute to his parents was not a rhetorical gesture at an opportune moment. Others have testified to this repeatedly in questionnaires about Rolf that they have returned to me. For instance, Ulrike Gruenberg, whose family provided residence for Rolf in their family home for a week in 1987, wrote this (in a questionnaire returned to me) about Rolf's relationship with his parents: "Rolf has told us several times about his kind and caring parents. Their deep love had given him the strong basis for his own life." So too Bill Kiley, one of Rolf's NBC associates, wrote (in a questionnaire returned to me): "I watched his love and adoration for his aged parents when they'd come to the office to visit."

with a hand mirror that was lying next to me. Suddenly, the mirror slipped out of my hands, fell to the floor, and broke into pieces. I knew I was in trouble. What to do? Before I could think of anything, my mother walked into the room and saw the damage. I suddenly knew what to do and went into action. I cried and cried and cried, and called out, "*Mutti, Mutti*—Mommy, Mommy, you don't have to spank me . . . I'm crying already!"

Rolf's father fell in line with cultural expectations and left Selma to raise their young son. But Oskar was not aloof. Rolf remembers his father's disciplinary style being an extension of his good-natured character:

> He only spanked me once, it was more a little "potch" on the tush rather than a spanking. I don't even know what the occasion was any more. However, he felt so bad about it that he apologized for it for the rest of his life. He was really a non-violent, kind-hearted soul.[7]

If family was a mainstay of safety and security for a young Jewish boy growing up in Nazi Germany, the outside world was at times a source of confusion. Rolf remembers one incident that makes the point. Rolf's best friend in Krefeld was a Jewish boy named Otto Strauss. When they were both nine, Otto proudly announced to Rolf that he (Otto) was looking forward to turning ten years of age because ten-year old boys could join "The Hitler Jews." Rolf knew that something was wrong with this picture—"The Hitler Jews" didn't sound like an official Nazi-sponsored program, or at least one that a Jew should be actively seeking to join. Rolf then realized that behind Otto's mistake lay a confusion of two German words. Otto had heard "*Juden*" ("The Hitler *Jews*") instead of "*Jugend*" ("The Hitler *Youth*").

Otto had probably imagined that, by joining a group of "Hitler Jews," life might become better for him and his family. It looked to Otto that his participation in "The Hitler Jews" would enable his Jewish and his German identities to be reconciled. He pinned his hopes on this eventuality, imagining that the discrimination against him and his family would fall

---

7. Dee Stone, the wife of Stanley Stone, a long-time friend of Rolf's, remembers Rolf's parents in this way (in a questionnaire returned to me): "Both of Rolf's parents had that rooted European elegance. His mother's hair was silver gray and beautifully coiffed. She had a lovely face which was lightly made up. She had that old European way of carrying herself. Rolf picked up that demeanor of his parents and it has been a part of him all of his life. The way he dresses is his own, probably not unlike his father." Ron Gompertz, Rolf's son, remembers Rolf's parents in this way: "his mother was very spiritual, his father was hard-working."

away as a consequence. But, of course, this was an ill-founded pipe dream. The circle could not be squared. If Jews were not welcome within Germany, they certainly were not welcome within the enclave of Aryan purity that marked out "The Hitler Youth."

The solution to Otto's situation did not ultimately lie in establishing a place for him within German society, of course. But neither were he and his family among the millions of Jews who were murdered systematically by the Nazis in the years to come. Otto and his parents made it to New York City, even before *Kristallnacht*. He and Rolf would continue their friendship on American soil, between Los Angeles and New York, until Otto's death in 1987.

Rolf's years on American soil will be the focus of chapter 8 below. But before progressing to Rolf's emerging life as an adult, it is helpful to consider what we have seen thus far in the story of Rolf Gompertz—a task to which the next chapter is dedicated.

7

Interpreting the Gompertz *Kristallnacht*

Enough of the story has been presented to allow us now to take a step back from it, in a sense, and to consider something of the meaning of it all. The "narrative plot" has been registered, with plot points forming arcs forward and backward, and the events of *Kristallnacht* serving as the foundation for many arc-points. But we might take a moment to reflect on the narrative's significance.[1] What is it that we are really seeing once all the plot points have been put together? What is the kernel of importance that can transcend the plot details?

I want to propose that at the heart of it all is the little comment made by ten-year-old Rolf Gompertz as half a dozen Nazis were storming his family home, the only place where he felt secure from those societal forces that "he understood he did not understand"—forces that were progressively eroding the fabric of moral decency and nurturing a deadly cancer within the world in which little Rolf lived. His uncle Julius had already fled the country, and so too had a good number of other Jews. People who shared his ethnic identity were realizing that their lives were in danger, and those who did not share his ethnic identity were distancing themselves from his family. The enclave of safety did not extend much beyond his little family, comprised of his mother and his father. But Rolf must have suspected that even they could not protect him from the worst, if it were to happen.

1. This recalls Richard Hays's point (*The Faith of Jesus Christ*, 28) that "stories have an inherent configurational dimension . . . which not only permits but also demands restatement and interpretation in non-narrative language."

Against this backdrop, it is Rolf's one sentence to his father at 2:00 AM during the dark hours of November 10 that reveals the heroic heart of humanity: "Father, if they take you, I'm going with you."

There are, of course, many heroic moments and heroes in the story told thus far. Among their number I would include the following:

1. Rolf's English tutor in Germany, Tom Göbel, who risked helping the Gompertz family by keeping some important documents safe for them;

2. Anna Coffee, who by all accounts went well out of her way to spread her beneficence to a family in need. Without her, the lives of Rolf and his parents would likely have been snuffed out in concentration camps, several years before Rolf's eighteenth birthday; and

3. Alma Herrmann and her sister's family, who put their own lives in danger in order to save the life of Alma's Jewish husband, Max.

There must be stories behind and within these mini-stories that deserve to be told, but unfortunately the specific details of these people's heroism are probably lost forever.

But we do have another heroic moment to consider, from the Gompertz household on the night of *Kristallnacht*. Just a little Jewish boy, Rolf went to bed that night not knowing that, before the first light of dawn, Nazis would raid his family's house, invading his safety zone and threatening to bring death to the only place where he was most alive and most loved.

It was the night that the fatherland caved into its worst tendencies—tendencies that it had been carefully nurturing for several decades, grooming the population for this "dress rehearsal" of the horrors that were looming on the horizon.[2] As George Clare has well said:

> Race hatred was not invented by Adolf Hitler. He was only the
> executor of the vile thoughts of others before him. All the venom
> of the nineteenth century spurted into the mind of this one man.
> He was the personification of the evil of a whole century. He alone

2. When asked in 1922 what he would do if he ever rose to power in Germany, Hitler replied: "If I am ever really in power, the destruction of the Jews will be my first and most important job. As soon as I have power, I shall have gallows after gallows erected, for example, in Munich on the Marienplatz—as many of them as traffic allows. Then the Jews will be hanged one after another, and they will stay hanging until they stink. They will stay hanging as long as hygienically possible. As soon as they are untied, then the next group will follow and that will continue until the last Jew in Munich is exterminated. Exactly the same procedure will be followed in other cities until Germany is cleansed of the last Jew!" This extract is from Toland, *Adolf Hitler*, 116.

brought to a conclusion the thoughts and writings of others and thus arrived at the ultimate, the final, solution to the hatred of centuries: murder on such a huge scale that the human mind cannot grasp it.[3]

The cultivated biases of the fatherland would soon result in the slaughter of more than six million of Rolf's people, roughly 5,000 every day. Those millions would include children just like him, whose only wish was to live fruitful, happy, and rewarding lives. Rolf's wish would come true; for a million and a half other children whose light was snuffed out by the Nazis, it would not.

Little Rolf understood that he didn't understand those tendencies. He didn't understand, he couldn't understand, how people all around him could overflow with hatred. Surrounded by the love of his father and mother, Rolf's worldview had already been nurtured in ways that ran in direct opposition to the worldview nurtured by the fatherland. Even in the small world of this ten-year-old Jewish boy, hatred was known for what it is—a disease that corroded the mysterious realities embedded with life itself. The tragic evil that had increasingly surrounded Rolf in his ten years of life had not managed to destroy his love of life, nor his life of love.

And so, in a critical moment that defined him in his most tender years of youth, Rolf did what he could to affirm what he had already been taught to cherish, and to stand up against the ethos of hatred that threatened the values that his parents had imbued within him. "Father, if they take you, I'm going with you," he called out, packing his suitcase in readiness.

Perhaps Rolf opposed this ethos of hatred simply because it was directed against him, against his family, against his people. Or perhaps there's more to it than that. Perhaps he opposed it simply because it was evil. Perhaps he opposed it simply because it fell to him to play his part against evil, where he had been "planted," in a sense, at *Bismarckstrasse* 118 in Krefeld Germany.

To say that Rolf opposed the ethos of hatred that had grown up all around him may give things too sharp a point, of course, for Rolf was only ten. But the defining moment in Rolf's young life testifies to the fact that, although his was only a childish form of opposition, it was still opposition. "Father, if they take you, I'm going with you." Even in the days of his childhood, when the culture around him did everything possible to strip him

---

3. Clare, *Last Waltz in Vienna*, 29. See further his elegant reflections in his "Epilogue," 255–57.

of his humanity and nothing to help him, he did not oppose hatred simply because it was pointed, like a loaded gun, right at him and those whom he loved dearly. He opposed it simply because it was hatred.

At just ten years of age, Rolf was not to know how the events of *Kristallnacht* would go on to change his life. Nor was he to know how his changed life would then go on to influence thousands of other lives, not only in America, but even the fatherland itself, Germany. But his knee-jerk reaction to "go with" his father into dark uncertainties already testified to attributes that were taking hold in the character of the young boy—including a resilience of conviction, a dedication to love, and a pursuit of life. These characteristics are the hallmarks that would characterize Rolf's life throughout the decades that followed—putting in play yet another arc, one that takes us well into his adult years.

During those years, Rolf would spend much of his time in the continued effort to oppose hatred and the abuse of power. If at ten years of age he could only offer to "go with" his father into a horrific future, as an adult he was able make much more tangible and constructive contributions to the offsetting of hatred.

As we will soon see, Rolf's faith would empower him to redeem memories of violence, hatred, and exile through his deep reflections on reconciliation, transformation, and the community of humanity. Perhaps most laudable is the way that Rolf chose to remember his encounter with Nazism. As Miroslav Volf has argued, "We are not just shaped by memories; we ourselves shape the memories that shape us."[4] What we will see as the narrative of Rolf's life unfolds is that he chose to shape the memories that shaped him not by repressing them, denying them, boxing them up, and hiding them away; instead, he chose to bring them out, front and center, and expose them to the light of truth in a fashion that neither denied them of their evil nor gave their evil the final word about the meaning of life. It was not easy, and in the 1980s there would come a moment when Rolf was forced to come face to face with his own suppressed fears and hatred. But in the end, Rolf chose to employ what we might call "redemptive remembering"—a form of remembrance that keeps the hated moments of hatred intact while seeking nonetheless to find a redemptive alternative that does justice to the moments of evil without allowing them to determine or erode the character of one's own life. For Rolf, that redemptive alternative is encapsulated in the appreciation of what he calls "our common humanity."

4. Volf, *The End of Memory*, 11.

That phrase gets to the heart of what was to become an impressive literary corpus spanning Rolf's adult years. One of Rolf's publications from 2002, a pamphlet for family and friends entitled *Menachem's Mantras & Other Verses, Stories and Thoughts*, repeatedly teases out his lauding of "our common humanity." In the following extract, for instance, he uses the phrase itself in his essay entitled "Jews and Germans II":[5]

> If there is a central truth to be snatched from the flames of *Kristallnacht* and the Holocaust, it is this: That we must always remember our common humanity. In case of conflict, in case we are forced to choose between ideology and our common humanity, we must choose humanity.

This paragraph would later become a central tenet in the speeches that Rolf would commit himself to, during the autumn of his life (see chapter 11 below).

鬼

The theme of choosing our common humanity over and above everything else would go on to form the backbone of Gompertz's literary corpus. Included in that corpus is a collection of poetry and prose (*To Life, To Love*), a book about spirituality (*Sparks of Spirit*), a modern comedy-drama (*The Messiah of Midtown Park*) and two biblical novels—one from the Hebrew Bible (*Abraham, the Dreamer*) and one from the New Testament (*A Jewish Novel about Jesus*).

It is toward Rolf's Jesus-novel that we are now moving—a book originally conceived in the early 1950s but executed only in the early to mid 1960s. It is a book that he calls "an affirmation of faith and belief in the triumph of the spirit over persecution and oppression—whether in the form of pagan Rome or Nazi Germany."[6]

This is a slightly different view to the one expressed by Anne Frank in her diary entry of July 15, 1944. There, she spoke of the innate goodness of the human heart: "It's really a wonder I haven't dropped all my ideals,

---

5. Gompertz, *Menachem's Mantras*, no pagination. Worthy of equal note are his "Jews and Germans I" and "Jews and Germans III" from the same volume. The first speaks of being bound together for eternity in a story that must involve transformation for the sake of life, and the third speaks of building bridges of love and reconciliation. This same paragraph is a highpoint in Rolf's "Snapshots" speech, which appears in chapter 13 below.

6. Gompertz, *A Jewish Novel about Jesus*, xviii.

because they seem so absurd and impossible to carry out. Yet I keep them because, in spite of everything, I still believe that people are really good at heart."[7] Rolf Gompertz is not a world away from Anne Frank in this conviction, but he is not quite as optimistic as she was about the human heart, and he seeks to take full account of the dynamics of "persecution and oppression." This is evident in a variety of his writings, not least in his Jesus-novel, as shown below.

But in order to put that book into its historical context, we need to outline further Rolf's life, beginning from his days as a young adult. This is the task for Part 3 of this book, below.

7. Frank, *Anne Frank*, 237. The sentiment is completely different than that expressed by Kertesz, *Kaddish for a Child Not Born*. For instance, on p. 88 Kertesz writes: "Auschwitz . . . struck me simply as an elaboration of those [evil] virtues in which I have been indoctrinated since childhood." After the Holocaust, Kertesz loathes his Jewish identity, finds he has no love in his heart, and thinks that the world is best explained in relation to the supremacy of evil over good.

PART 3

Crafting a Contribution

8

Crafting a Jewish Life

On the morning after the horrific night of *Kristallnacht*, the *New York Times* reported that Herschel Grynszpan had spoken the following words to the German authorities that held him captive after the shooting of Ernst vom Rath:

> Being a Jew is not a crime. I am not a dog. I have a right to live and the Jewish people have a right to exist on this earth. Wherever I have been, I have been chased like an animal.[1]

Rolf Gompertz had similar experiences, and similar sentiments. But whereas Grynszpan died at the hands of Nazis, from 1939 onwards Rolf and his family now lived far away from Nazi Germany. No longer was his Jewish identity a crime. No longer was he chased like an animal. He now was set to do more than simply "exist on the earth"; now he was set to thrive.

It was not long before Rolf felt the rumblings of contribution growing within him. Having made a safe exit out of Nazi Germany, Rolf soon came to realize that his life was different from the vast majority of Jewish children who had been raised in Nazi Germany, and whose lives ended there so prematurely. Even before he was a teenager, he decided that he had to make his life matter. It was his responsibility to make a contribution that would help to counter the gravity of evil he had witnessed. His life was a gift. Others had died; he had lived. He didn't know how, but he knew that it was his

1. Reported in the article "Berlin Raids Reply to Death of Envoy," in the *New York Times* on November 10, 1938.

responsibility to make a contribution that would make a difference. So, in an interview conducted by Carolyn Howard-Johnson for the *Copperfield Review*, Rolf discussed the affect that his early life in Nazi Germany had on his development:

> [I]t affected me on the deepest level. For one thing, it turned me towards a spiritual search for meaning and for involving myself with the "big" questions: Who am I? What's it all about? Why am I here? I always felt that, since I survived, I had to make my life mean something.[2]

Making his life mean something took Rolf almost a whole lifetime to achieve. In this chapter, Rolf's life in the United States will be reviewed.

His life after arriving in the United States was fairly standard. He did not capture the attention of the public by holding a notable public office or by becoming a celebrity. He was never required to play the role of a hero. It is largely true that, even if the most rewarding, fruitful, and constructive years of Rolf's life were spent in the United States, his most intriguing years for the historian were his early years spent in Nazi Germany—precisely because they provide one of many windows into the horrific scenes that terrify the human conscience and torture the human imagination.

But those experiences became the ingredients in a mixture that was slowly but surely being processed in Rolf's continual reflections on life and its meaning. The mixture resulted in two separate but related outcomes: (1) Rolf's literary corpus, comprising five books (not including three classroom handbooks), spanning five decades beginning in the early 1960s, and (2) Rolf's life as a speech maker, which defined more than a quarter of a century of his later life. Each of these will be engaged in later chapters of this book. For now, the outline of Rolf's adult life provides the resources for understanding those outcomes within the context of his life.

$\ast$

If writing was to become a distinguishing mark of Rolf's life, it was also one of the threads through Rolf's early years in the United States.

After finishing at Virgil Junior High School, Rolf entered Belmont High School—both schools being in Los Angeles. Although he received an A in every subject except Chemistry, it was his high school "English

2. See the interview at http://copperfieldreview.com/?p=392; consulted on October 30, 2012.

and American Literature" course that fired him up the most, due to the influence of his teacher, Mrs. Marian Keyes, who brought the subject alive for him. In the meantime, Rolf began to write reflections on life in diaries; he wrote intermittently, but over the years, roughly 30,000 words would be recorded in three journals that spanned the years from December 8 of 1945 to December 29 of 1977.[3] The first entry began this way:

> Good evening diary. My name is Rolf Gompertz. You and I will see a lot of each other from now on, I hope. You see, there are so many things I want to tell you, and I want somebody to remember them for me. I'm a very strange character, you'll find out. It's too bad you and I didn't get acquainted with each other before. I've had many interesting stories to tell you.

After graduating from high school in January 1946, Rolf enrolled at the University of California at Los Angeles, or UCLA. "It was a disaster," Rolf has said of his time there, "a total disaster." Rolf had always been a good student, but he had never really been challenged in his pre-university days. So when the challenges of university academic life presented themselves, Rolf simply fell apart. He had never learned how to study, so he completed only one semester at UCLA, with barely passing grades.

Dropping out of university, Rolf considered various career options and finally landed upon the idea of joining the army—something denied to Jews in Nazi Germany from the year 1934. He had become a citizen of the United States in 1945 (when his parents became citizens after completing citizenship classes in evening school), and was eligible to join the United States Armed Forces upon the age of eighteen.[4]

The year was 1946 and the United States was no longer involved in wars on any front. Rolf's favorite book at that time was Friedrich Nietzsche's provocative advocacy of "the will to power" in the book *Thus*

---

3. The first diary dates from December 8, 1945 to April 9, 1953. The second diary dates from December 3 to December 10, 1966. The third diary dates from May 28 to December 29, 1977.

4. Rolf and his parents became citizens of the United States on April 27, 1945. A note from Anna Coffee Baer on that date was sent to Rolf's parents, and reads as follows: "Dear Oscar and Selma, We know that today is one of the happiest of your lives. We rejoice with you both and Rolf that you are citizens of this blessed land. I am proud that I had the privilege of bringing such noble and appreciative folks to America where you have found freedom and the pursuit of happiness. Too the joining of the Russian and American forces today sets *your* day apart, Oscar, so you truly can celebrate in fitting manner. We salute you as true and sincere citizens of the United States. Affectionately, Julius and Anna." The note was signed above the engraved words "Mrs. Julius Baer."

Spake Zarathustra. Besides announcing that God was dead, *Thus Spake Zarathustra* had greatly influenced Nazi ideology through the prospect that human will to power was the ultimate goal to which the human race was moving. The ideal human whom Nietzsche lauds is the *Übermensch* or "Over-man" who takes mastery over his situation and powers his way to influence, unrestrained by moral qualms that have for too long beset the human race—the fit with Hitler's construction of Nazi ideology being all too glaringly obvious. A fascination with the Nietzschean worldview testifies to a grappling on Rolf's part, even at the age of eighteen, with the big picture and the big questions in life.[5]

As a member of the army who was fluent in German, Rolf was posted in Washington DC and given the job of translating Nazi documents that, like him, had been brought to America from Germany. For eighteen months he worked in that position, unveiling Nazi Germany through documents that had survived its defeat. It was not the last time that words would be the focus of his efforts.

After his stint with the U.S. Army, Rolf tried his hand at UCLA once again in the fall of 1948. Rolf's time in Washington DC had stirred up his drive and determination, so his second attempt at earning a university degree was successful.[6] His time in the army qualified him for tuition support under the "G.I. Bill" as it was popularly called. That initiative spearheaded a sharp increase in the skills-base of the country for a decade from the late 1940s to the late 1950s, enabling those who had completed their time with the armed forces to develop their interests and skills through university tuition remuneration.

Rolf dug deeply into his university studies. His mind was brimming with ideas, and his creative spirit was overflowing. On October 9 of 1949,

5. In an email to me dated December 9, 2012, Rolf recalled his engagement with Nietzsche's *Thus Spake Zarathustra*: "I was introduced to the book by Steven Orey, a fellow soldier and refugee from Nazi Germany, who served with me in Basic Training while in the US Army. He was intellectually brilliant, and well read, a true scholar. . . . He challenged me about my beliefs and knocked the props out from under me and my superficial beliefs—he got me started thinking about the big questions. He found this book [*Thus Spake Zarathustra*] fascinating—and so did I, for a while." In 1954 Steven Orey became a professor in Probability Theory at the University of Minnesota. He speaks of his life (including his army days and his undergraduate studies having been paid for primarily by provisions laid out in the "G.I. Bill") at this website: http://dynkincollection. library.cornell.edu/node/1048 (consulted on December 10, 2012).

6. Rolf had stopped writing in his journal during his time in the Army, but began writing again in February 1949.

Rolf wrote in his diary how he felt his creativity to be in complete harmony with the creative spirit of America: "I love, I am in love with America. I feel that I understand it, that I am identical with it. I feel that America's Cultural Birth is here or shall soon come."

Majoring in English literature and minoring in philosophy, Rolf spent much of his time learning to appreciate good works of literature and reflecting on deep philosophical questions. His favorite books now were Walt Whitman's *Leaves of Grass* and two books by Herman Melville, *Moby Dick* and *Pierre* (also known as *The Ambiguities*).[7]

Although literature and philosophy operated out of separate departments within the university setting, Rolf excelled at merging them from an early age. This is reflected in many of his early poems, not least an early poem of choice, "The Search: A Song of Man and the Universe."[8] It is a poem in which Rolf rejected the Nietzschean philosophy that he had flirted with several years earlier while in the U.S. Army.

During this time Rolf had several other writing projects as well, and conceived of still others that might lie ahead. One was a novel that he completed but never tried to publish. It featured a character named Cornelius von Peck, who was himself an Army man.[9] On October 21 of 1949, Rolf made an entry in his diary in which he outlined his hopes for his next book. This is perhaps the book that Rolf spoke about in his 1952 diary entry of September 4, when mentioning that he had completed a novel the previous day, a novel that he had begun to execute only three weeks previously. His diary entry demonstrates how the whole process had invigorated him, to the extent that he felt "spiritually relieved" after having been "spiritually confused" prior to the experience of writing. Rolf imagined in his diary entry what its dedication would be: "To those whom Fate or Fortune robbed of their dream." Clearly his heady university days had not allowed him to forget the horrific days of his past.

7. In his diary of December 1 of 1951, he praised Olive Schreiner's *The Story of an African Farm* as the book that had touched him to the core, unlike any other. And on January 1, 1952, he praised James Michener's *Tales of the South Pacific*.

8. This poem, along with many others from his twenties, was first published in Gompertz, *A Celebration of Life*, 59–79.

9. The novel seems to have been written in 1949. In an email exchange dated to December 9, 2012, Rolf wrote this to me: "The novel was a typical first book, an autobiographical novel, of no further significance."

Rolf graduated with his B.A. degree in 1952, four years after he began. He graduated with the English Literature's award for Best Student of the Year and was admitted to the national honor society Phi Beta Kappa.

With his love of learning, Rolf stayed on at UCLA for a further year to receive a Masters Degree in 1953. But he then needed to get a job. He went to the Personnel Department of NBC (the National Broadcasting Company) and inquired whether the corporation was hiring. But he did not have the skills that they required. He could write sonnets, he told them, but they did not need sonnets; they needed typists, they told him, but he then failed their typing test.

Rolf did land a job not long after that, in 1953. He took a position as Editor of a weekly newspaper in Torrance, CA, seventeen miles out of Los Angeles. He remembers his experience in this way:

> What did the editor do? Everything. He was the editorial department. He was the reporter. He was the photographer. He was the makeup man. . . . He was the guy who went down to the print shop to read proofs . . .—he was it.

And then he adds in his usual manner of poking fun at himself, "And the only reason I got the job was because I came cheap. . . . I was a bargain, and worked fifty-six to sixty hours a week."

Four years later in 1957, Rolf married his sweetheart, Carol. He first met Carol Brown in October 1956, through the ingenuity of Carol's sister, who had spotted Rolf as a potential catch and made arrangements for Rolf and Carol to meet. "Are you more of an idealist or a realist," Carol asked him on their first date. Rolf the idealist had met Carol the realist, and the two of them started a loving relationship that would last the rest of their lives. In February 1957 they were engaged, and by April 1957, they were married.

When it came to choosing a rabbi to marry them, Rolf and Carol chose Rabbi Arthur Bluhm—the rabbi who had welcomed Rolf into the world back in Krefeld thirty years earlier and who had effectively saved his life eleven years after that. Rabbi Bluhm had been imprisoned at Dachau after *Kristallnacht* but was released after assuring Nazi officials that he would leave the country. He emigrated from Germany in 1939 and settled in Amarillo, Texas. Rolf remembers Rabbi Bluhm exhorting the newlyweds to "Live in the beauty of holiness."

Rolf soon found that his salary was not sufficient for a young married couple. So he began to look for a new position. With new skills, demonstrable experience, and renewed confidence, Rolf returned to NBC to seek employment. Bypassing the Personnel Department this time, he went right to the Press and Publicity Department to see if they would take him. He was hired there as a publicist not long after that, in 1957. He stayed with NBC until he retired in 1987. During those thirty years he dealt with the publicity for a vast number of television shows, movies, specials, and stars.

His experience with NBC gave him the credentials for an offshoot project that began in 1974, lasting until 2006. In those years, Rolf taught courses in Publicity and Media Relations with UCLA's Extension program.[10] And to service those courses, he also produced three "handbooks" on publicity, two of which he published through Word Doctor Publications—a publishing company that he established in 1974 and that published the first imprints of many of his published works.[11]

Both as a publicist for NBC and as a teacher with UCLA's Extension program, Rolf was never very interested in advertising *per se*; what grabbed his interest was the spinning of a story so that it caught people's attention and made them take note of the product on offer. In this way, his journalistic expertise from his days as an editor intertwined with his skills as a storyteller—skills that came to life in various forms as of the early 1960s.

In the meantime, Rolf and Carol raised three children—Ron, Nancy, and Philip. Two children were eventually born to each of Rolf and Carol's children, with six grandchildren now tracing their lineage through Rolf and Carol.

The importance of his family cannot be overestimated. In questionnaires returned to me from friends and associates of Rolf, the following comments were made. Wiebke Gruenberg wrote: "Family life is very important to Rolf. When I have letter contact to him, he often talks about the time he and Carol spent with their children and grandchildren." Bill

10. Four courses were the mainstay of his teaching over the years, entitled "Elements of Publicity," "Working with the Media," "Publicity: Writing for Television and Film," and "Media Publicity for Television and Film."

11. These handbooks include the following: *Promotion and Publicity Handbook for Broadcasters* (330 pages); *Publicity Writing for Television and Film: A How-to Handbook* (220 pages); and *Publicity Advice & How to Handbook* (148 pages). Rolf discusses the first in his third diary. On May 28 of 1977, he wrote about having received two letters that day: "One was from Tab Books notifying me that my 'Publicity Handbook for Radio and Television' is now out and copies (10) are on their way to me. This is the book that I turned over to the publisher in August 1974—and it is finally coming out in May 1977! Glad I didn't hold my breath or quit my job!"

Kiley, who shared an office with Rolf for many years at NBC, spoke of how he would see Rolf "beam or worry about his wife and children" whom he obviously loved dearly. Similarly Katrin Balzer mentioned this:

> Family life seems to be very important to Rolf. He talks about his wife and children with pride and happiness. My impression is that as a boy he experienced a strong solidarity in his family, and it gave him courage and hope to go his way with pride. I am sure he wants to give the same strong solidarity to his wife and children.

Tricia Aven had this to say: Rolf "sounds the happiest when he is looking forward to them [his children and grandchildren] coming to their home for the celebration of a birthday or a holiday." She continued by commending "the love and honor he shows when talking about his parents, and his love for and dedication to his wife, Carol, their three children and six grandchildren."

Rolf and Carol have been long-time members of the Adat Ari El Synagogue in Valley Village, North Hollywood. That synagogue was also to become the worshipping congregation for three members of the Meyers family—the family with whom the Gompertzes shared their Krefeld home in the aftermath of *Kristallnacht*, when the Meyer's home was destroyed. The Meyers family had managed to immigrate to the United States prior to the onset of World War II. The two daughters, now married, moved to Los Angeles with their mother, and the old friendship between the two families was reignited.

Along the way, Rolf kept a record of his experiences and reflections in his diaries. The final entry in the last diary was entered on his fiftieth birthday, December 29, 1977. In that entry, he registers his happiness, his sense of fulfillment and blessing, and his love for his parents, his wife, and his children. It ends with a prayer, which is recorded at the end of chapter 12 below, "An Appreciation."

🕊

When Rolf imagined early on that he had to make his life worth something, he framed that responsibility against the backdrop of Hitler and the Nazi pogroms against the Jewish people. Ultimately he would come to see his whole life, not just his contributions within it, as being an "answer to Hitler," a refutation and negation of all that Hitler and his Nazi collaborators had sought to achieve. More specifically, Rolf's answer to Hitler is found in his life as a Jew—in fact, a Jew who has not been beaten down by evil but who loves others as an expression of the presence of the divine spirit within him. Bill Kiley, when asked to encapsulate what he thinks of how Rolf has lived his life, said the following: "If this world could be filled with Rolf Gompertzes it would be a much, much better place."[12] Although Rolf would never say things in such self-referential terms, Bill's point echoes with the central theme of Rolf's literary works of prose and poetry—advancing toward a world in which people live in the divine spirit of love. And it is Rolf's literary corpus that now requires consideration.

12. Bill wrote this in a questionnaire returned to me, noting that he is saying this as an atheist.

9

Crafting a Literary Corpus

"It is my hope that this book may play its part in bringing healing to our hearts, light to our minds, peace to our spirits, and joy to our souls."

With these words, Rolf brought to a close the Postscript of the 2003 edition of his book, *A Jewish Novel about Jesus*.[1] It was his first book, and it was to be his most enduring and influential contribution to the public discourse about human identity, morality, religion, and God. It will be discussed later in this chapter, and in more detail the following chapter. But before that, Rolf's lesser-known works will be briefly surveyed.

*1. Sparks of Spirit (A Handbook for Personal Happiness):
How to Find Love and Meaning in Your Life 24 Hours a Day.*

Rolf advertises this book as a "personal development guide" and "a spiritual training manual" that is designed to help readers "develop and maintain a spiritual point of view" in life. Published by Word Doctor Publications in 1983 and reprinted by iUniverse in 2004, it received an endorsement from Norman Vincent Peale—the leading spiritual self-help guru in the United States and the author of the controversial best-selling book *The Power of Positive Thinking*. Peale describes Rolf's book as "inspirational, interestingly written, and contain[ing] many practical tools for developing and maintaining a useful and happy life."[2]

1. Gompertz, *Jewish Novel*, 175.
2. Cited in ibid., 185.

The book's origins lie in a comment that Carol said to Rolf one day in the 1970s. She acknowledged that Rolf had a "spiritual outlook" on life, but she wondered how she and others who did not share that outlook might work toward adopting it. Rolf took that as a challenge, and began writing. What emerged was a twenty-seven-chapter book containing reflections on nurturing one's spiritual health, along with citations from the Hebrew Bible that coincided with the themes of the chapters. Rolf considered the scriptural quotations to be an essential component of the book, gesturing to the fact that his insights were not novel but were part of a deep inherited wisdom that he was simply restating in a new fashion.

2. *The Messiah of Midtown Park: A Contemporary Comedy-Drama.*

In this screenplay written in the mid-1970s and published by iUniverse in 2004, Rolf offers a light-hearted analysis of what it means to be the messiah, or better, to have a messianic identity. In effect, he seeks to universalize the notion of "messiah" so that it pertains to each and every person who brings light where there is darkness.

This definition of messiahship expands on one aspect of Rolf's *Jewish Novel about Jesus*, as will be shown in the next chapter. But the screenplay correlates with that novel in another way as well. At one point in the screenplay, readers are shown the books that reside on the shelves of "the messiah"—the main character, Shlomo Hirsh (the last name being an abbreviated form of Hirshfelder, the doctor of young Rolf in Germany). On those shelves are books that Rolf relied on heavily when writing his *Jewish Novel about Jesus*. These include:[3]

1. A shelf of books about Jesus, including:
   Jesus of Nazareth, by Joseph Klausner;
   The Life of Jesus, by Edgar Goodspeed;
   Jesus, by Charles Guignebert;
   Who Crucified Jesus? by Solomon Zeitlin.

2. A shelf of books about the context of Jesus' day, including:
   Daily Life in Bible Times, by Albert E. Bailey
   A Social and Religious History of the Jews, by Salo Wittmayer Baron
   The Conflict of Religions in the Early Roman Empire, by T. R. Glover
   The Pharisees, by Robert T. Herford

3. Gompertz, *Messiah of Midtown Park,* 87–88.

The Sword and the Cross, by Robert McQueen Grant

Ancient Judaism and the New Testament, by Frederick Grant.

3. Three other books that all pertain to the messiah:

Messianic Speculation in Israel, by Abba Hillel Silver

The Messianic Idea in Israel, by Joseph Klausner

Messiahs, by Wilson D. Wallis.

In referencing these books, Rolf allows *The Messiah of Midtown Park* to gesture toward his *A Jewish Novel about Jesus*.

3. Abraham the Dreamer: An Erotic and Sacred Love Story.

Unlike some of his other books, this book had no precursor prior to its publication with iUniverse in 2004. Rolf wanted to turn his imagination to Abraham—the first follower of the God of Israel and one who lived surrounded by a pagan culture; perhaps it is not surprising, given Rolf's upbringing in Nazi Germany, that the dynamics of that situation fascinated Rolf. But what is most significant about this book is that it treats a foundational story from the Hebrew Bible much like Rolf's *Jewish Novel about Jesus* treats a foundational story from the New Testament. That is, it questions the moral configuration of the way the story is frequently interpreted. Here is what Rolf says in an interview about the book from 2012:

> The book deals, ultimately, with a profound human question, as symbolized by the *Akedah*, the Binding of Isaac. Abraham believes that God wants him to sacrifice his son, to demonstrate his faith in God. I challenge that view, as not worthy of either human beings or of our view of God. I believe that Abraham, in his attempt to serve and understand this new God, actually misunderstood God. I believe something else was at work here, which comes out in Abraham's final showdown with his wife, Sarah. What results [from my novel] is a much more humble and humbling view of God and understanding of God's will. This, for one thing, is crucial today, when some seek to justify cruelties and brutalities in the name of God and as the will of God.[4]

The importance of this will become clearer when considering Rolf's *Jewish Novel about Jesus* in the following chapter (although the book is first introduced at the end of this chapter).

4. Quoted from the *Copperfield Review*, "An Interview with Rolf Gompertz, by Carolyn Howard-Johnson" from April 28, 2012, http://copperfieldreview.com/?p=392; consulted on October 30, 2012.

4. To Life, To Love: In Poetry and Prose. A Spiritual Memoir.

Like his book *Abraham the Dreamer,* this book had no precursor prior to its publication with iUniverse, in this case, in 2005. It contains selections of literary works (poetry, short stories, articles, Sabbath reflections) that Rolf had composed over the years, comprising seventy in total. In it he identifies himself as a "Poet of the Foolish Heart." One reviewer, David Herrle, compared Rolf to "a Buckingham Palace guard who dares to grin and even stick out his tongue" while making serious points. Herrle continues:

> Rolf plays the humorist and teacher, the metaphysician and the fool, the studious speculator and the child who rejects his homework to race through flowery fields and loaf by brooks instead. Such laxness and boyish bravery might count as weakness in other writers, but Rolf's sincere and consistently intense insistence on resisting pretense treats readers to his flexible but strong-like-water core instead of some tightly guarded palace with nary a grin or forbidden stuck-out tongues.[5]

5. A Jewish Novel about Jesus (also titled My Jewish Brother Jesus).

This is the book that Rolf was born to write. If in later decades of his life Rolf used the phrase "my answer to Hitler" to refer to the whole of his life, that phrase was first pegged to this book in particular. And rightly so, since European anti-Semitism is the unseen backdrop against which Rolf's Jesus-novel is played out.

This novel is deserving of a much fuller engagement than the comparable space I have allowed to his other four literary pieces (all of which are notable in their own way), and for that reason I dedicate a chapter of this book to exploring it in more depth. But a general introduction to the book and its origins can nonetheless be included here.

The origins of Rolf's Jesus-novel go back to his days as a student at UCLA. In the spring of 1952 he had won the award for "Best Student of the Year" from the Department of English Literature at UCLA, and that award seems to have boosted his own confidence as a writer. So on December 9 of 1952, half way through his Masters program, the twenty-four-year-old Rolf wrote the following in his diary (pages 94–95):

---

5. David Herrle's review from August 2005, at http://www.subtletea.com/tolifeto-lovereview.htm, consulted on October 30, 2012.

> I think that I shall some day write a book to be called *Judas and the Messiah*. It will probably be my master-work. Anything that I would try to say about it now could not do justice to what I envision (only vaguely now) the work will be. But only an absolute love and compassion and sympathy and understanding for both individuals and both traditions which they represent will ever do full justice to them, to the human dreams, to life, and to God.
>
> Perhaps I shall continue studying at the university in order to devote my time indirectly to a study of the Biblical material since the dissertation topic on which I have settled is *Mark Twain's Use of the Bible*.[6]

Wanting to devote his time "indirectly" to studying the biblical material did not transpire until a decade later, however. The project languished in the 1950s, partly because of his heavy workload as the editor of a newspaper from 1953 to 1957, his adjustment to a new career in 1957, his nurturing of his marriage as of 1957, and his own uncertainties about the wisdom of undertaking such a project. But in 1962, Rolf experienced what we all experience at some point in our lives—an overwhelming sense of his own mortality. At the age of thirty-four, Rolf came to understand his impending death not as a theoretical prospect that lay far out in the future, but as an existential reality that could come crashing down upon him at any moment. Consequently, Rolf asked himself what he would regret if his life ended prematurely. His answer: he would regret having failed to write his novel about Jesus.

This new-found existential awareness of his own mortality followed in the wake of Rabbi Arthur Bluhm's death on July 16, 1962. The man who welcomed Rolf into the Jewish community had now departed this life. After Rabbi Bluhm's death, his widow Hanna gave his woolen coat to Rolf, along with a library of books about Judaism that Arthur had accumulated since immigrating to the United States. Now Rolf became, in a sense, the keeper of part of Arthur Bluhm's identity. This spurred Rolf to take further initiatives in shaping his own life in such a way as to make a contribution, and to make a contribution in relation to his own Jewish identity. The novel about "Judas and the messiah" was his way of making his life matter beyond the grave and contributing to the betterment of humanity.

---

6. Rolf mentions this project in his diary entry of January 8, 1953. Earlier on October 23, 1949, Rolf mentions in his diary an intention to write a spiritual biography of Moses and Jesus. Both of these diary entries are included in chapter 14 below. Rolf never wrote his project on Mark Twain's use of the Bible.

Now aware of his mortality and increasingly committed to his Jewish identity, Rolf's spare time between the years 1962 and 1966 was dedicated to researching and writing the book that had first sprung to mind as a bachelor in late 1952.[7] He delved into academic books on Judaism, Jesus, and the Greco-Roman world, taking copious notes on 4x6 notecards (a standard form of research back in those days). He started to conceptualize the intricacies of the novel's plotlines and characterizations, until finally he began writing. Four hundred and sixty pages later, he had a completed manuscript of his first published novel. He sat Carol down in front of him, held up the manuscript, and proudly announced to her, "This will be a bestseller within a year."

Rolf is not the first writer whose expectations for a book failed to materialize. The experience is widespread (especially in the days before the digital revolution in publishing). But the earliest indicator about the book's success was positive. Rolf had found a literary agent, Sylva Romano, who thought his manuscript was really very good.[8] She told Rolf to be "proud of the book for the rest of your life," confirming that she had been hooked by it, even though she was a Jewish atheist. She thought it showed "professional mastery" and expected to place it easily with a publisher. But after a year of sending it out and receiving rejection letters in return, Sylva apologized and said she could do nothing else for Rolf's manuscript.

So Rolf himself began approaching publishers about the book, but to no avail. In the end, *Judas and Christ* (the title that the novel bore at that time) was seen by approximately thirty publishers, none of whom were willing to add it to their list of publications.

In his fiftieth year, Rolf decided that he would go it alone. Establishing his own publishing company (The Word Doctor Publications), he published the novel himself in 1977, his printing press producing 1,000 paperback and 300 hardcover copies.

Several changes were made to the novel between 1966 and 1977. First, Rolf changed the title to *My Jewish Brother Jesus*, which enabled the Jewishness of Jesus to be advertised within the very title of the book.[9] He also ensured that the colors of the book's cover were blue and white, the colors of

7. The year he commenced the novel is sometimes said to be 1962, sometimes 1961, and sometimes 1963. I have gone with 1962.

8. Sylva Romano worked for the Mitchell J. Hamilburg Agency, which has represented people such as Robert DiNiro, Al Pacino, Jodie Foster, Wilt Chamberlain, Jackie Robinson, and Tom Brokaw.

9. Compare Richard L. Rubenstein's 1972 book, *My Brother Paul*.

the Jewish prayer shawl and the Jewish people. The title was placed on the cover in the shape of a cross, with the words "My" and "Jesus" forming the vertical stave and the words "Jewish Brother" forming the horizontal beam.

Second, the 1977 version was reduced in size by 40 percent. One comment that came back to him several times from publishers is that *Judas and Christ* was simply too long, especially for a first novel. Long novels cost more to produce, and virgin novelists usually do not sell well enough to merit the increased production costs. So what is currently a 200-page novel would probably have been published as a 340-page novel if the 1966 version had ever seen the light of day.

Third, the 1977 version cuts down on its depiction of sexual relations. Rolf realized that some readers were being put off by the erotic nature of his 1966 storyline (including his mother Selma, who could not get past an early chapter, due to its explicit eroticism). Rolf had thought it necessary to include a realistic portrait of Mary Magdalene within the book, whom he depicts as a prostitute (in common with traditional depictions, although perhaps wrongly). As the novel progresses, Mary Magdalene undergoes a transformation, emerging as a fulfilled character through Jesus' teachings about the love of God. But in order to show the extent of Mary Magdalene's transformation, she needed initially to be depicted as someone enslaved to sex in her unending quest for fulfillment. But the sex was probably too explicit, so the 1977 version includes a tamer depiction of things in this regard.

Rolf is quite open about this lack of publishing success during the 1960s and 70s—a fact that many authors might not have wanted their readers to know. Rolf mentions it even at the very start of the book (page xvii)—a move many might consider to be unwise, but one typical of Rolf in his desire to be utterly open and transparent. Rolf even wrote a little poem about his lack of publishing success, entitled "Immortality":

> Good books live forever.
> "I will write a good book," I decided.
> I didn't know about publishers.
> They only care about the here and now.
> Ha![10]

---

10. This poem appears in *To Life, To Love*, as well as in *Menachem's Mantras and Other Verses*.

In the year 2003, Rolf re-presented *My Jewish Brother Jesus* by publishing it with the print-on-demand publishing company iUniverse. Rolf found the print-on-demand publishing model to have many advantages, not least the fact that the book will remain in circulation in perpetuity, rather than being remaindered within a few years of its release. And so the novel reemerged, but under a new title, *A Jewish Novel about Jesus*.[11] That's when the book finally began to get some notice. Reviews of the book started to appear in literary venues. And anecdotally, I came across it in an internet search and subsequently included it in my undergraduate and Masters courses on "Jesus in Film and Fiction" as early as the 2003–2004 academic year.

But the book's various metamorphoses were not yet complete. In the year 2004 a Christian minister in Germany, Kai Schaefer, got in touch with Rolf about a matter having nothing to do with Rolf's Jesus-novel; when replying to Kai, Rolf sent him a copy of *A Jewish Novel about Jesus*. After reading it, Kai realized that the book needed to be translated into German and circulated within Germany. And within a few years, the novel was published by Aussaat Verlag (an imprint of the renowned German publishing company Neukirchener Verlag). Beautifully translated by a German Christian pastor, Carl Dieter Hinnenberg (who provided the translation free of charge, as a labor of love), the novel was published with a German version of the 1977 title, *Jesus, mein jüdischer Bruder* (*Jesus, My Jewish Brother*).

In a very real sense, then, Rolf's "answer to Hitler" had gone full circle, returning to the fatherland in order to have its full impact there. His voice was now being heard within the country that he had been born in, the country in which his life had been put under threat, the country that had been ravaged in his youth by an ideology of "the will to power." That ideology is paraded front and center in Rolf's Jesus-novel, where it is exposed and "answered" by Rolf's vision of "our common humanity."

That novel will be the subject of the next chapter of this book. But before turning to that topic, it needs first to be registered that Rolf's voice had been heard within Germany even prior to the publication of his Jesus-novel in German translation. This was in his role as a speaker about his experiences as a Jew living in Nazi Germany—a role that he increasingly

---

11. Rolf supplied the cover-work for this republication, which was again dominated by blue and white, this time supplied by a background photo of white clouds against the blue sky.

took upon himself after turning sixty. If in chapter 10 we examine Rolf's Jesus-novel in particular, it is also essential to highlight his important role as a speech-maker—a task carried out in chapter 11.

PART 4

The Gompertz Jesus-Novel

10

Corollaries of Violence

At this point we turn our attention in a dedicated fashion to Rolf's book *A Jewish Novel about Jesus*. For this chapter, however, I will usually refer to Rolf using his surname, "Gompertz," instead of his first name. This is simply because here, instead of speaking about Rolf and his life in familiar terms, I will speak about his novel's contribution, and assess its historical and ideological merits. For this exercise, the name "Rolf" seems too familiar; the name "Gompertz" allows a bit more distance from the person and a bit more interpretive freedom in relation to his novel. And so, to an assessment of *A Jewish Novel about Jesus*, by Rolf Gompertz.

Jewish Jesus-Novels

To begin, it is helpful to understand the Gompertz Jesus-novel in relation to other Jewish novels about Jesus. Such projects are not numerous, however. Beyond the Gompertz novel, two are worthy of mention: Sholem Asch's beautifully-written novel of nearly seven hundred pages, entitled *The Nazarene* from 1939,[1] and David Kassoff's much shorter novel of about two hundred pages, entitled *The Book of Witnesses* from 1971.[2]

1. Asch, *The Nazarene*. This was the first volume of a trilogy, with subsequent novels being *The Apostle* in 1943 and *Mary* in 1949.

2. Kassoff, *The Book of Witnesses*. Other Jewish Jesus-novels include Heym's *Ahasver* and Mossinsohn's *Judas*. A pseudo-narrative from a Jewish author is Neusner's *A Rabbi Talks with Jesus*.

The lives of each of these three authors (Asch, Kassoff, and Gompertz) straddle the Nazi period. Asch was born in Poland in 1880 and died in 1957. Kassoff was born in 1919 and died in 2005. Gompertz's life, which of course is outlined earlier in this book, stretches from 1927 well into the first quarter of the twenty-first century.

More to the point, for all three Jewish novelists, concerns about anti-Semitism play a significant part in their Jesus-novels. Asch published his novel at the height of the anti-Semitic pogroms in Nazi Germany; while several factors caused him to write *The Nazarene,* one of those factors was the hope that it might alleviate tensions between Jews and non-Jews in the face of growing anti-Semitism.[3] Gompertz's own experiences of Nazi Germany, and in particular *Kristallnacht,* set in motion a deep drive to contribute to the discourse about anti-Semitic sentiment. Kassoff, like so many Jews, experienced the anti-Semitism that drove the Nazi project despite the fact that he lived outside of Germany.

In fact, all three novelists make their intentions plain in this regard, explicitly linking their novels with their own experiences of anti-Semitism. Asch articulated it in this way: "Christian civilization is stained with blood and of that blood not a little came from the veins of my forefathers."[4] Kassoff's novel begins with a dedication recalling an event that occurred in 1927 or so:[5]

> This book is for my father, who died long ago.
>
> Once, when I was small, about eight, I was with my father, who was a loving man, in a narrow street in the East End [of London]. A huge labourer suddenly roared down at us that we had killed Jesus. My father asked him why he was so unhappy, and the fist lowered and the shouting stopped and he began to cry.
>
> We took him with us to my aunt for tea.
>
> This book is for my father, who was a loving man.

In Kassoff's storyline, Jesus is much like Kassoff's father, being portrayed as a man who extends warm and gracious love to counter the abusive intolerance that ingrains itself in uninformed cultural stereotyping.

3. This point is made by Siegel in *The Controversial Sholem Asch,* 137 and 141.

4. Rosenberg, *Face to Face with Sholem Asch,* 119, where he states: "I want to show in this book how far Christianity has departed from the original Christian faith, which was almost the same as the Jewish faith."

5. The excerpt comes from a numberless page at the start of Kassoff's novel. Kassoff was born in 1919, so his reference to being around eight years old puts this event in approximately 1927.

The theme of love also takes pride of place in Gompertz's novel—a novel shaped by his experiences of Nazi Germany. As he recalled in an interview with me, "I had Nazism in mind throughout the writing of that book." Gompertz highlights the novel's interface with Nazi ideology in the preface of the book:

> I am one of the fortunate ones who escaped the Nazi Holocaust with my parents. We fled Hitler's Germany after *Kristallnacht* (The Night of Broken Glass) and came to America as refugees in 1939, shortly before the outbreak of World War II in Europe. . . . I see this book as my answer to Hitler.[6]

In a sense, Gompertz's heart and soul is in this book. A narrative that breathes the same ideological air as Asch's *The Nazarene*, Gompertz's *A Jewish Novel about Jesus* is, in my view, his finest contribution.[7] This is less for its literary merits than its historical interests and subsequent challenges to ideological bias and to strategies of biblical interpretation.

Gompertz's Answer to Hitler

Gompertz's Jesus-novel seems almost to operate on two levels. First, the narrative that it recounts features first-century Jews in a struggle for survival and fulfillment in a world gripped by the violence of Roman power. But it resonates on a second level, one that does not have a foothold in the story itself but grafts itself onto the story, in a sense—that is, the story of European Jews in their struggle for survival and fulfillment in a world gripped by the violence of Nazi power.

Gompertz points this out in his note to his readers (cited above) that the novel is his "answer to Hitler." That note now deserves fuller citation here:

> As long as I can remember, I have wondered about the meaning of my life. I also have wondered why I survived. I have felt the need to give life meaning in the way I live it and in what I do with it. In its deepest sense, then, I see this book as my answer to Hitler. I see it as an affirmation of what he tried to destroy—the dignity and decency of Judaism and, by extension, Christianity. It is an

---

6. Gompertz, *Jewish Novel*, xviii.

7. Gompertz had read Asch's novel before undertaking his own, although the book that most engaged his imagination was *Jesus of Nazareth* by the Jewish scholar Joseph Klausner.

affirmation of faith and belief in the triumph of the spirit over persecution and oppression—whether in the form of pagan Rome or
Nazi Germany.[8]

Gompertz's "affirmation of faith and belief in the triumph of the spirit over
persecution and oppression" results in a Jesus-novel in which corollaries
of violence, persecution, and triumph arc from the first to the twentieth
century, and beyond. The bloodthirsty and megalomaniacal Roman Pilate
prefigures the bloodthirsty and megalomaniacal Nazi Hitler. Similarly,
Jesus the Jew, who was persecuted by the power-hungry Roman regime,
stands as a precursor of the Jewish Holocaust victims who were persecuted
through the power-hungry Nazi regime. The particulars of this correlation
need now to be noted.

Violence and Peace in Gompertz's Jesus–Novel

In his novel Gompertz does much to lay out two contrasting definitions
of reality. One version is articulated by Jesus and other Jewish rabbis, such
as Gamaliel (known to us from Acts), and the other version is articulated
by the Roman procurator, Pontius Pilate. Pilate's version in the Gompertz
novel meshes well with the depiction of Rome from ancient sources. So
Pilate states the following in Gompertz's novel:

> Life is a struggle for power—that's all it is, at the very center of
> its being. And power must be fought for—in the attaining, in the
> maintaining and in the regaining. You crave it, you gain it, you lose
> it, you crave it again! Death alone ends our hunger for power.[9]

It is this Nietzschean struggle—the craving and insatiable lust for power
at the very center of Roman reality—that Gompertz showcases at the very
beginning of the novel. In the first scene of the novel, we are shown the
crucifixion of a Galilean Jew outside the gates of the city Magdala. With its
"slow, inhumane torture" that testified to "the might of Rome," the practice
of slaughtering lives by means of crucifixion "was an abhorrence and an
abomination in the sight of God and man." But it signaled everything that
Rome stood for, since it "was the Roman way."[10] (And in these descriptions,

---

8. Gompertz, *Jewish Novel*, xviii.

9. Ibid., 137.

10. Ibid., 1.

one can easily hear subtle protests against the Nazi gas chambers and horrific executions performed in Germany's death camps.)

In contrast to the Roman way (i.e., the way of the inhumane and ab-
horrent abuse of power), Jesus articulates a different view of what lies at
the very heart of reality. For Gompertz's Jesus, reality is encapsulated in the
word "love," defined as the process of giving and receiving. Jesus states it
this way in the Gompertz novel:

> As you give, you receive; as you receive, you give. Love is the fun-
> damental nature of Life. . . . If love is basic to creation, then it is
> also basic to the Creator. . . . God is a God of Love, constantly and
> eternally giving and receiving Love![11]

In Gompertz's novel, this commonplace insight is woven into the deepest structures of the story of Jesus the Jew, who, in preaching love, simply
articulates the basis of the Torah's understanding of Israel's God.

Rather than depicting Jesus as a divine revealer who discloses new
insights about God (as Christian Jesus-novelists often do), Gompertz proposes that Jesus should be understood as simply having understood the
very heart of Israel's Torah, and so the very heart of God. He stands in line
with the great prophets of Israel.

The point is made explicitly in a scene in which Judas speaks to rabbi
Gamaliel about Jesus. Judas rejoices that Jesus "has brought us a new Truth."
But Gamaliel responds:

> No, Judas, not a new Truth, just an old, old Truth in new bottles.
> When the young discover Truth it is always new, like the world.
> . . . The prophets burned with God's Love! . . . [Love] is all God
> has ever talked about, it is all He has ever asked of us! To love the
> stranger, for we were strangers once in the land of Egypt; to love
> our neighbor, for he is as I am and you are; to have one manner of

---

11. Ibid., 27. Compare Judas's realization of the same, as a consequence of Jesus'
ministry (ibid., 63). Gompertz's novel is motivated in part by his understanding, which
came to him suddenly one day, that "the nature and meaning of life" is encapsulated in
love. "I saw this [i.e., love] as the dynamic principle underlying all of life. Human life,
the universe, God started to make sense to me. It was a momentous personal discovery"
(ibid., xvi). The same point is emphasized in his *The Messiah of Midtown Park,* 19, 96–98,
141, and throughout a vast array of Gompertz's work in general. For an important collection of insights into the primacy of divine love extending into human relationships in
religious traditions, see Levin and Post, *Divine Love.*

law by which all men are judged—rich or poor, high or low, strong or weak.[12]

The most excellent way advocated by the Jewish Scriptures is the way of peace, of *shalom*, of righteousness permeating every relationship. As such, it is a way that contrasts with the self-declared "way of Rome."

In Gompertz's novel, Judas notices that the way of Jesus (being itself the way of Scripture, of Judaism, of God) is on a collision course with the way of Rome. Wondering what might happen when Jesus takes a stand for the way of love in Jerusalem, Judas imagines that Jesus will bring his ministry to its glorious climax in a fashion that completely avoids the shedding of blood. There will be a glorious transformation of the world by means of divine power that overturns evil once and for all, but since divine power emerges from the heart of a loving God, the eradication of evil has nothing to do with the annihilation of evildoers. The universal exaltation of God and the overthrowing of evil will not involve human veins pouring their contents onto the soils of God's good creation. God's love itself contains the power of the universe within it, and as such, will create clean hearts within a transformed world. Judas says it this way.

> Jesus did not want bloodshed, Judas remembered. Jesus never called for bloodshed. . . . [Instead, Jesus realized that] Pilate . . . was the key to God's drama. He had to be convinced. He was the unbeliever, the instrument of power, the spear and the sword! Jesus had to confront him. Jesus would slay him with love, he would defeat him with the spirit of God. Not a drop of blood would be spilled. Pilate would die, only to be reborn; Rome would fall, only to kneel in worship! Pilate himself would lead Jesus to the holy Temple, Caiaphas would anoint him [i.e., Jesus], and all the world would come singing to Jerusalem!

Here, Judas has caught a glimpse of God from Jesus' mission of love, and completely realigns his understanding of God's ultimate victory as a consequence. Once a hotheaded youth eager to see the Romans slaughtered by the sword for their vicious abuses, Judas now understands God's character much differently, and so he envisages the ways and triumph of God much differently as a consequence. God's victory was not simply to be established by means of a grander version of the violent Roman way, with God sharing the same violent *modus operandi* as Rome but emerging triumphant through bigger swords and bigger clubs (in a sense). Instead,

12. Gompertz, *Jewish Novel*, 133.

Judas comes to imagine that God will absorb violence within himself, wrapping it within an all-engulfing cocoon of divine love, neutralizing it out of existence, and thereby destroying a violent world through its rebirth in love.

Judas comes to imagine that he himself might be called to play a part in this cosmic drama of God's redemption of the world. If he were able to orchestrate a way for Jesus to come face to face with the Roman and Jewish authorities, it would create a moment in which God's transforming initiative would simply engulf the world and establish God's loving peace once and for all throughout the whole of the world. Therein lies Judas's motivation for what is commonly known as his "betrayal" of Jesus.[13]

In Gompertz's novel, however, Judas is both right and wrong. He is right in his vision of how God will ultimately work to eradicate evil in a violently non-violent fashion—violently, because evil is ripped from its seedbed and extinguished; non-violently, because not a single drop of blood will flow from human veins, and not one life will be lost.

But Judas was wrong in imagining that Jesus was the one through whom God would ultimately work to initiate the overthrow of evil. Rome and its violence won out in this instance—and of course, the way of violence continued to win out long after the fall of Rome, as evidenced not least in the Holocaust. Hope, in the Gompertz narrative, lies not in Jesus' ministry of peace and love, even though Jesus rightly understood the very heart of God, along with the best of the prophets of Israel before him. While the love of the God of Israel will ultimately triumph over the cancerous abomination that Rome embodied in Jesus' day (and that Nazi Germany later would embody), the cocoon of all-embracing divine love is yet to manifest itself. The triumph of divine love will be accomplished through messianic initiatives, proposes the Jesus of the Gompertz novel, but not in the fashion normally attributed to him, as noted below.

Gompertz Redefines "Messiah"

With regard to the teaching of Jesus, the Gompertz novel depicts Jesus in much the same way that orthodox Christians frequently depict him. Jesus is shown to preach a message of love for others, since God is a God of love. But what makes the Gompertz novel distinct from Jesus-novels in the

13. Here again, Gompertz seems to borrow a page from Asch's *The Nazarene*, where Judas is similarly depicted.

orthodox Christian tradition is the estimate that Jesus was not, in fact, the messiah, precisely because the eschatological age of messianic peace had not been established by Jesus. This is what Gamaliel declares:

> Where is the new heaven and the new earth? Where do you see the wolf lying down with the lamb? Have the nations beaten their swords into plowshares, their spears into pruning hooks? Have they stopped hurting and destroying?[14]

As testified to most explicitly in "the Roman way" (and of course, the Nazi way), this world continues to be characterized by swords and spears and hurting and destroying. Consequently, the messiah has not come, for such things are not the ways of God or God's messiah, the peace-bringer.

Among Christians and Jews, debate about Jesus' messianic identity has revolved around precisely this point almost from the very start. The view of most Jesus-followers has usually been that the final age of peace has commenced but has not yet been completed, and will not be completed until Jesus returns again. At that point, peace will ultimately be established; prior to that point, we see it in incarnations of divine love within individuals and communities of peace and justice, even while evil remains rampant in God's world.[15] For non-Christian Jews, of course, things are seen much differently. The messiah could not have come already, since the world is so obviously out of joint.

Gompertz's Jesus novel, however, entertains a different notion about what messianic identity entails—a notion in which messianic identity is universalized rather than particularized. For Gompertz, *all* of humanity is called to live as the messiah (or messiahs) of the world by doing good in their indigenous setting. (And here, we remember the words of the ten-year-old who said, "Father, if they take you, I'm going with you"—the sentiment being indigenous and pseudo-messianic.)

This theme overshoots Gompertz's Jesus-novel, pervading virtually the whole corpus of his literary work. It even creeps into his diaries. His entry on December 9 of 1966 mentions it directly. It recounts Gompertz's conversation with Cantor Michaelson at his synagogue, as follows:

14. Gompertz, *Jewish Novel*, 132. See also Gompertz, *The Messiah of Midtown Park*, 130.

15. For discussion of Matthew's Gospel in the context of precisely this debate, see Stanton, *Matthew for a New People*, 185–90.

> His idea, among others, is that we [Jews] should all actively con-
> vert and evangelize. . . . I did agree with him so far as to say that
> the *messiahs* are sitting right out there in the congregation—that
> every man is a messiah, a redeemer of that part of life over which
> he has influence.

If in this conversation Gompertz was able to propose a universalizing notion to the concept of messiahship, the same was not the case for a conversation that he had fourteen years earlier, when meeting a fiery Christian
evangelist. Gompertz recounted the evangelist's ideas about the all-engulfing judgment that would transpire shortly when God's messiah finally visits
destruction upon the earth. So the evangelist propounded that "There was
going to be a big burst shortly. The day of the messiah was near." The fact
that "Judgment Day was just around the corner" made the evangelist "so
happy." This encounter is dated to February 23, 1953. It may have been a
formative encounter that filtered into Gompertz's reflections about how he
would grapple with the issue of messianic identity if he ever got around to
writing his novel about Jesus.

If the issue of messianic identity has a strong foothold in Gompertz's
early diaries, it takes on a life of its own in Gompertz's 1983 work entitled
The Messiah of Midtown Park (reprinted in 2004). That comedy-drama is
said by Gompertz to offer the reader "a messianic vision that is compat-
ible with our differences" and one that "can inspire our daily personal lives,
and . . . can strengthen or renew our faith in God and our fellow human
beings."[16]

The point is made in that work by its main character, Shlomo Hirsch,
who is in fact the "messiah" of Midtown Park. As early as page 18 of the
novel, the seventy-seven-year-old Shlomo articulates the point when he
speaks to another character, Nate Kaplan, in this fashion:

> Everybody expects the messiah to come and do everything for
> them. . . . Well, I came to tell everyone [that] the messiah isn't
> going to do it—you've got to do it. You're the messiah, Mr. Ka-
> plan—you, and everyone else.

Later Shlomo says the same thing again:

> I'm not the only messiah. There isn't just one messiah. There can't
> be just one messiah. Everyone is a messiah. . . . If all of us are

16. Gompertz, *Messiah of Midtown Park*, x.

human—if all of us are children of God—then all of us can be messiahs.[17]

According to Hirsch, when everyone takes on the mantle of the messiah, redeeming love will spread throughout the whole world (cf. 97–99). This is captured in the simple slogan "Bloom where you stand"—a slogan that hangs above the door to Hirsch's apartment and appears at key points elsewhere in the Gompertz literary corpus.[18] Again, the messianic Hirsch makes Gompertz's point by expanding the notion of "messiah" to universal proportions: "We're all here for one reason and one reason only: To improve the world where we stand, to hold the world together, to redeem the world, wherever we are, in place and time. We're all God's messiahs."[19]

If the 1983 *Messiah of Midtown Park* comprises Gompertz's full-blown exploration of messianic ideals, the same theme also has a strong foothold in his Jesus-novel of two decades earlier.[20] This is especially evident in Gompertz's depiction of Jesus in the Garden of Gethsemane.

In his depiction of that scene, Gompertz follows New Testament accounts that have Jesus going off to pray by himself on three occasions.[21] The first words of Jesus' three prayers are the same in each instance: "*Abba*, Father, all things are possible to Thee. If it be Thy will, take this cup away from me. Yet not my will be done but Thine be done." These words are familiar to the audiences of the canonical narrative, of course (see Matt 26:39, 42; Mark 14:36; Luke 22:44).

But in the Gompertz narrative, something novel happens. These words are heard by Jesus' three disciples who have accompanied him to his place of prayer—Simon Peter, John, and James. But after hearing these words, each of them falls asleep, on each of the three occasions. But because they fall asleep, they miss the rest of Jesus' extended prayer. This is a critical failing on their part, since it is in those three extended prayers that Jesus questions his ministry and its efficacy in ways that impact directly on the

17. Ibid., 144, 147.

18. Ibid, 101–2.

19. Ibid., 152. See also 193, for his final word on messianic identity in the novel.

20. Gompertz noted precisely this in the introduction to *Messiah of Midtown Park* (x): "After I had finished writing the Jesus book in 1966 I realized that I was not done with the messianic question and so I revisited it a couple of years later, when I wrote *The Messiah of Midtown Park*."

21. Gompertz, *Jewish Novel*, 151–53. See Matt 26:36–45; compare Mark 14:32–42. Luke 22:39–46 has only one occurrence of Jesus in solitary prayer in the garden.

messianic ideal. In Jesus' articulated but unheard struggle to comprehend his life and ministry, he ultimately comes to a new understanding of what messianic identity is. And notably, Jesus' new understanding of messianic identity corresponds wholly with that of Shlomo Hirsch in Gompertz's later comedy-drama about the messiah of Midtown Park. Here's what Jesus of Nazareth says about messianic identity:

> Father, were You to send a thousand messiahs, what more could they do? Or is that it, that one person can never do anything for another person, that each soul must reach out to You, just as You reach out to each soul? Is that it? Everyone must be a messiah? Is that the Kingdom of Heaven, the Day in the End of days when everyone everywhere at one time and with one heart sees the heavens open and Your spirit descend in the form of a dove and Your voice say, "This is my beloved"? Can the world be saved only by all, each one saving that portion on which he stands?[22]

If only the disciples had managed to stay awake to hear this important realization that dawned on Jesus in the final night of his life. If they had, the Gospels would have been written differently, along with the course of human history (not least the history of twentieth-century Germany).

Gompertz here almost takes a trick out of the playbook of ancient "gnostic" circles, which claimed to have secrets about redemption that failed to circulate among the populace. In Gompertz's intriguing narrative of Jesus in the Garden of Gethsemane, secrets about Jesus' true understanding of messianic identity are revealed to the reader, although those secrets run contrary to the officially recognized storyline of the Christian Scriptures, due to the fact that the three disciples could not stay awake to hear Jesus' dramatic development in understanding.[23]

The reader is subtly prepared to accept this definition of messianic identity because of the novel's depiction of another of Jesus' disciples earlier in the narrative. When the reader first encounters Matthew, he is shown to be a tax collector who is "spoiled" and "self-centered," but only until the time of his wife's premature death. At that point, "according to

---

22. Ibid., 152.

23. The slightly unexpected aspect of Gompertz's intriguing narrative is this. If Jesus had come to the view that all humanity is called to be the messiah in the Garden of Gethsemane (ibid., 151–53), it is curious that when he later stands before the priests and is asked, "Are you the messiah?" he does not say a word of this new understanding (ibid., 155). Perhaps Gompertz might have tweaked that situation slightly, to iron out this minor disconnect in the narrative.

the mysterious ways of the spirit, Matthew saw his life—past, present and future—in a new light." That is, he came to realize that his life up to that point had been marked out by "emptiness and hollowness." Accordingly, "Matthew's heart opened and reached out for his Father in heaven."[24] The novel recounts Matthew's transformation in this way:

> Once he discovered how spiritually parched he was, he started to drink deeply from the newly found fountain of his being. Night and day he meditated on God, learning how to pray, studying Torah, trying to walk in the ways of holiness, hoping to become acceptable in the sight of the Lord, yearning to become a blessing. He changed his business ways and levied fair and honest taxes, much to everyone's surprise.[25]

The novel reinforces the change in Matthew repeatedly. His friends, we are told, "could not help but notice the change that gradually was taking place in Matthew," since he was increasingly becoming a much "kinder" person to others. This resulted in him making new friends, such as James and John, the sons of Zebedee, who would later become followers of Jesus along with Matthew. They too, we are told, "detected a change in Matthew's life." Would the change result in Matthew being befriended by those higher up the ladder of socio-economic status? Matthew gave this some thought, but came to conclusions not unlike those of Shlomo Hirsch:

> Could it be that God wanted him to stay where he was? Could it be that God wanted him to be a friend to the least—the outcasts and the discards? Could it be that God needed him where he was?

In essence, what we see in Matthew is the coming alive of the messianic identity, as he began to "bloom where he stood," with the love of God spreading to places where it had not otherwise been. And notably, all this transpires even before Matthew meets Jesus for the first time. The messianic model propounded in the Gompertz Jesus-novel simply does not require Jesus to be God's one and only messiah for all time.

Of course, within the theological parameters of the Gompertz novel, it might be proposed that Jesus was the messiah after all, but only in the sense that all people are called to be God's messiahs wherever they are planted. If the lion does not lie down with the lamb, that is not because Jesus failed

---

24. Notice that the theme of the heart reaching out to God is shared in Gompertz's depiction of Matthew and his depiction of Jesus' prayer in Gethsemane.

25. Gompertz, *Jewish Novel*, 38.

in his messianic calling, but because the rest of us aren't playing our proper roles as messiah/messiahs. If we were, cruelty would disappear, the lion would lie down with the lamb, and the Isaianic vision of a world without cruelty and destruction would transpire (Isa 65:25; see also Isa 11:6).[26]

In Gompertz's novel, the leading Pharisee Gamaliel is shown to have too grandiose a notion of messianic identity (this being a problem that, implied by the novel, may have plagued much of human history). This is, in effect, what the High Priest Caiaphas says to Gamaliel in a conversation about Jesus. In this dialogue, the Sadducee Caiaphas is attempting to get the Pharisee Gamaliel to remove Jesus from the scene (i.e., to kill him), on some trumped-up charge. Caiaphas begins:

> "If it weren't for you, this [i.e., the Jesus problem] would never have happened!"
>
> "Me?" he [Gamaliel] asked.
>
> "You—all of you [Pharisees]! That's what comes of not leaving the Torah alone, as it was meant to be! No, you wouldn't listen to us. 'The Sadducees this' and 'the Sadducees that'—we were too strict, we were too literal, we refused to change with the times, we were so anxious to preserve the letter of the law that we killed its spirit! So what did you Pharisees do? You interpreted and re-interpreted and interpreted again! You bent and stretched and turned and twisted until you could find anything and everything in Scripture—including the messiah! You've infested the people with a Messianic madness! Their minds are on fire with fantasy, and there is fever in the land! Jesus is your madness, not ours! You breathed life into him!"[27]

In Gompertz's novel, what the Scriptures endorse is love, not messiah, at least if "messiah" is thought to be one particular historical individual that is eagerly awaited (= "messianic madness"). On the other hand, what the Scriptures speak of is love as messiah, or messiah as love, as long as the notion of "messiah" is not understood as referencing a single long-awaited individual but instead as referencing the whole of humanity and each individual within it.

If we follow Gompertz's lead, the notion of "messiah" needs to be universalized to include everyone; moreover, it needs to be extracted from a pessimism about human nature and, instead, filled with the notion of

26. This is the passage that Gompertz uses to conclude his article "The Messiah—Where Do We Go From Here?" 193–94.

27. Gompertz, *Jewish Novel*, 123.

ethical empowerment. What emerges from the Gompertz novel is a disinfected notion of messianic identity that is suitable to the dangerous world of the twentieth century (with its Nazis and nuclear bombs) and the twenty-first century (with whatever horrors might transpire within it). This is a messianic vision that proposes a way out of the holocaustic atrocities that have engulfed the past of human history.

Gompertz's Novel and the Charge against Jews as "Christ–Killers"

One of the reasons why Gompertz wrote his novel is to inspire peace between Christians and Jews. He says this explicitly in his introduction, framing the whole of his novel in this way:

> I hope to give Christians a better understanding of, and appreciation for, Jesus and his Jewish roots. I hope to give Jews a better understanding of, and appreciation for, Jesus in terms of Judaism. I do not wish to undermine the validity of Christianity or to convert Jews to Christianity. I wish only to create understanding, so that the two faiths may live side by side, respectful of one another, in dignity and peace.[28]

In accord with his expressed intention of creating understanding so that Christianity and Judaism "may live side by side, respectful of one another, in dignity and peace," Gompertz's narrative represents an attempt to "set the record straight about the pernicious Christ-killer charge [against the Jewish people], which resulted in Jewish persecution for 2000 years, culminating with the Holocaust."[29]

Many non-Jews rightly find this charge against the Jews to be, at the very least, embarrassing and despicable—not least because it has been used so often as an instrument for imposing violence, destruction, and terror against Jews personally and corporately. It is also an illegitimate charge. The pernicious charge that the Jews were/are Christ-killers is founded on

---

28. Ibid., xvi. Other Jesus-novelists have held similar goals for their Jesus novels. For instance, when I emailed Gerd Theissen on behalf of my students back in 2007 (the actual date is now lost from my records), I asked what he might do differently if he were writing the novel afresh. Responding directly to that point, he added that one of his goals in writing the novel would not change at all—that is, "creating understanding and sympathy for Judaism."

29. Ibid., 183.

a poorly-nuanced reading of the canonical Gospels, in which Pilate is depicted as a well-intentioned governor who seeks to implement justice but is manipulated, against his own better judgment, into crucifying Jesus by the Jews *en masse.*

The charge itself has perhaps its strongest roots (whether rightly or wrongly) in the Matthean depiction of Jesus' trial and crucifixion. So, Matt 27:24–26 reads:

> When Pilate saw that he could do nothing, but rather that a riot was beginning, he took some water and washed his hands before the crowd, saying, "I am innocent of this man's blood; see to it yourselves." Then the people as a whole answered, "His blood be on us and on our children!" So he released Barabbas for them; and after flogging Jesus, he handed him over to be crucified.

It is of interest that Asch, Kassoff and Gompertz do not give a foothold for this version of events in their narratives.[30] This is a strategy that academic scholars do not have access to—i.e., the strategy of omitting discussion of how to interpret ancient data. (And as a New Testament scholar, I offer in an appendix to this book my own proposals about how the problematic passage from Matthew is to be interpreted.)

But omission of the problematic passage from Matthew is not the only strategy for undermining the diabolical "Christ killer" charge within the Gompertz Jesus-novel. Others strategies include:

1. promoting respect for Judaism within the narrative; and

2. explaining the motivation of key players in the Jesus story in ways that either amplify or rework the New Testament data in order to bring to light historical dimensions that the New Testament does not bring to the attention of the reader.

We have already seen something of how Gompertz engages in the first of these strategies. Characterizing Judaism as a vibrant religion that incorporates at its very heart a double emphasis on love for God and for others, Gompertz repeatedly depicts first-century Judaism as being worthy of respect, and places Jesus firmly within that context. In that sense, he was well ahead of non-Jewish academic historians who, back in the 1960s, were still mired in the portrait of Judaism as an arid, legalistic religion of "works-righteousness," wholly devoid of the love of God (i.e., love for God and by

---

30. The people's shout is not included in Gompertz's *Judas and Christ* either—Gompertz's longer and original version of his Jesus-novel.

God). By contrast, Gompertz's Jesus was, in a sense, the best of Jews because he understood the best of Judaism and the heart of the Torah, which itself reflects the heart of God.

Much the same is evident in Kassoff's novel. If Jesus is all too often a Christian in the popular imagination, Kassoff reminds his readers early on that Jesus was a Jew—a notion that operates almost as a "given" and functions as a methodological control in most Jesus research of the late twentieth century and beyond.[31] But the point was not at all obvious in the early 1970s when Kassoff wrote his novel.[32] Kassoff makes the point by allowing one of his characters to speak about Jesus' role within his Jewish family: "Jesus had led the family in the same orthodox Jewishness always observed by [his father] Joseph. 'As a memorial,' he told me once, 'and because the religion is beautiful. My father loved beauty.'"[33]

Contrast these portrayals of Jesus the Jew with one that was popularized in the 1920s by Bruce Barton, the author of the widely read book about Jesus entitled *The Man Nobody Knows*. Barton's goal was to demonstrate Jesus' manly credentials—a commanding figure who was not in any way meek and mild, gentle or sissified; as Pilate pronounced, "Behold, the man!" The Jesus of Barton's pseudo-novel is a Jesus appropriate to the roaring 1920s—a man seen around town, popular, funny, engaging, pleasant to be with, a rugged outdoorsman full of great stories to amuse others with, and a keen businessman who could perpetuate success indefinitely with his razor-sharp eye for initiative and inventiveness. He was quick with "shrewd retorts" and "pointed jokes" and "loved it all—the pressure of the crowd, the clash of wits, the eating and the after-dinner talk."

But Jesus the Jew? How does that fit into Barton's picture? Quite blatantly, it is an embarrassment. Whenever the narrative veers toward it, Barton quickly steers his readers in a different direction. Here, for instance, is an instance of Jesus' Jewish piety being airbrushed out of the picture:

31. See for instance, Boyarin, *The Jewish Gospels*.

32. Compare the comments of Geza Vermes, an esteemed Jewish historian from Oxford whose 1973 book was published under the title *Jesus the Jew*. Vermes had this to say about that title in a 1994 interview: "When it came out, it sounded like a very provocative title. Today it is commonplace. Everybody knows now that Jesus was a Jew. But in 1973, although people knew that Jesus had something to do with Judaism, they thought that he was really something totally different" (see http://members.bib-arch.org/publication.asp?PubID=BSBR&Volume=10&Issue=3&ArticleID=12, consulted May 15, 2013).

33. Kassoff, *The Book of Witnesses*, 51.

> He loved to be in the crowd. Apparently He attended all the feasts
> at Jerusalem not merely as religious festivals but because all the
> folks were there and He had an all-embracing fondness for folks.[34]

Barton does not mention that the "religious festivals" were "Jewish religious festivals," but even if the reader is aware of that, Barton shuffles the deck quickly to pull out the card that he wants his audience to focus on—that is, Jesus' motivation for attending "religious festivals" was because that's where "all the folks" were and he had a "fondness for folks." There is nothing here about the "folks" being Jewish, or about Jesus identifying with the religion of fellow Jewish "folks." Instead, just as the roaring 1920s required people of repute to be seen in all the right places at all the right times, so too Jesus went to the big city (i.e., Jerusalem), because of his fondness for the "folks" among whom he mixed well. If Barton's silence about Jesus' Jewish identity is deafening, it is not out of character with popular conceptualizations of Jesus from Barton's day.

For people like Barton and the masses who were influenced by his portrait of Jesus, the religion of Judaism was a petty religion of rules. By contrast, Jesus's God "was no Bureau, no Rule Maker, no Accountant. 'God is a spirit,' He cried. 'Between the great Spirit and the spirits of men—which are a tiny part of His—no one has the right to intervene with formulas and rules.'"[35] It seems almost as if Jesus' Jewish identity, although never highlighted in the book, was simply something God might have begrudgingly allowed only in order to contrast the good way of high healthy living with the despicable foil that Judaism provided. You need a redeemer to drop into the worst of it in order for redemption to be seen for what it really is.

As a consequence of this way of setting the scene, Barton declares Jesus to have established "a new religion," one in line with the prophetic spirit of Israel's prophets, but one that enabled his followers "to substitute a new kind of thinking for all existing religious thought!"[36] And what is that "new kind of thinking" that had evaded "all existing religious thought" prior to Jesus? It is this:

> "God is your father," He [Jesus] said, "caring more for the welfare
> of every one of you than any human father can possibly care for his

---

34. Barton, *The Man Nobody Knows,* Kindle Locations 636–38.

35. Ibid., Kindle Locations 672–73.

36. Ibid., Kindle Locations 969 and 843–44.

children. His Kingdom is happiness! His rule is love." This is what He had to teach.[37]

It is little wonder, then, that Jewish Jesus-novelists from the 1930s (Asch), the 1960s (Gompertz), and the 1970s (Kassoff) found it imperative within their novels to reassert both the honorable reputation of Judaism itself and the essentiality of Jewish identity to Jesus of Nazareth.

These agenda items, which have predominated in New Testament scholarship since the 1980s, shape the Gompertz narrative of the early 1960s from start to finish. One example makes the point sufficiently. In Gompertz's storyline, the final words of Jesus from the cross are not "It is finished," as in John (19:30), nor "Father, into your hands I commend my spirit," as in Luke (23:46);[38] instead, after speaking these canonical utterances, Gompertz's Jesus repeats the first line of the Shema (Deut 6:4), the covenantal prayer recited daily by observant Jews: "Hear, O Israel, the Lord is our God, the Lord is one."[39] The final words of Jesus are the words that for centuries had been recited by Jews intent on affirming their covenant identity as Jews before their sovereign God.

By depicting Jesus as an observant and orthodox Jew immersed in a "beautiful" Judaism (using Kassoff's term here), the Gompertz novel disorients the normal perceptions of those who easily bandy about the unfounded accusation that Jews are "Christ killers." Quite simply, the double perception that (1) Jesus was a Christian (2) who was killed by Jews, becomes problematized in its first component. But what about the second component? If Jesus was a Jew, he was still the messiah (the argument would go) who was killed by the Jews. Against that accusation, the Gompertz novel also has an answer.

Gompertz's Depiction of Caiaphas and Pilate

If Jesus was a Jew, isn't Jesus' death simply a case of a Jew being killed by other Jews? Isn't the killing of Jesus simply an incident that unmasks Jews to be, at worst, zealous hot-heads quick to shed blood, or at best, a self-absorbed

37. Ibid., Kindle Locations 1415–17.

38. In fact, these words are said both by Jesus near to his death (*Jewish Novel*, 167) and by Judas at the point of his death (ibid., 163), and perhaps simultaneously in the novel's proceedings.

39. Gompertz, *Jewish Novel*, 167. Much the same thing was done by Asch in *The Nazarene*.

clique whose religion has left them mired in ridiculous (and therefore "un-wanted") patterns of thought and practice that hold back progress (as the parade outside Gompertz's house in 1936/37 depicted them)?

The Gompertz novel seeks to undermine the whole premise for assumptions of this kind. It does so by depicting key figures in the narrative in ways that sharply contrast with their common portraits in the popular mind.

In the Gompertz novel, the motivations of leading characters are brought fully to light, lest there be any mistake as to why they acted as they did. Since a single action can be attributed to any number of different and, at times, mutually exclusive motivations, Gompertz draws us into the motivational world of the leading characters, so that his readers' sympathies might be configured in ways he thinks to be historically legitimate. The following leading characters become key players in this exercise:

- Caiaphas the high priest;

- Pilate the Roman procurator; and

- Judas the "betrayer" (who, among some Christian circles, had come to symbolize the Jewish people *en masse* [as if "Judas" = "the Jews"], the ultimate betrayers whose damnation is deserved).

The recharacterization of all three figures is essential to Gompertz's project, as we will see.

One of the goals of Gompertz's Jesus novel was, as he says, "to set the record straight about the Trial and Crucifixion."[40] At the heart of this lies Gompertz's characterization of the fraught relationship between Pilate and Caiaphas.[41]

Gompertz's novel depicts Pilate as a despicable character (much like the way he is depicted by the ancient authors Josephus and Philo), intent on having Jesus killed. Because Pilate controls all the mechanisms of power, the Jewish leaders have no choice but to comply with his plan of having Jesus killed. Perhaps more than any other novel, the Gompertz Jesus-novel makes it clear that the responsibility for Jesus' death lies squarely on the shoulders of Rome, with only remorseful but compulsory complicity emerging from select Jewish leaders. If complicity with Rome is to be laid

---

40. From the publicity blurb "About Rolf Gompertz," published by Rolf Gompertz Communications and The Word Doctor Publications.

41. On this important issue, see further Bond, *Pilate;* Bond, *Caiaphas;* and Reinhartz, *Caiaphas.*

at the feet of Caiaphas the High Priest, it is complicity that Caiaphas regrets, complicity that is forced on him by a manipulative Pilate who uses Caiaphas as his pawn in the machinations of Roman power.

Caiaphas explains it this way:

> Rome . . . only wants two things—power and money. . . . So, if I cooperate, if I manage to maintain peace and tranquility in the land, we [Jews] are permitted "freedom" of worship. If I do not cooperate, if there is trouble in the land, Rome will find someone who will cooperate, or else Rome will choke us to death. . . . Something will happen, some final outrage, large or small, and the nation's blood will flow. I fear for us.[42]

Instead of allowing Rome to choke the Jewish people to death, and instead of losing his own position as High Priest through Pilate's dissatisfaction with him, Caiaphas finds it judicious to comply with the wishes of Rome. Through Caiaphas's repeated articulation of the point, the reader learns that it is Rome alone that wants Jesus killed.[43] For Caiaphas, handing Jesus over to Pilate is simply the prudent and required lesser of two evils. With the Roman way of violence hanging over the heads of the people, the Jewish leaders have no other choice. This is what Caiaphas makes clear to Jesus' disciple Judas (in words that resonate with the Nazi pogrom against Jews in Germany):

> [Pilate will] kill him anyway, one way or another! First he'll go after him and you and the others! Then he'll come after the rest of us and he won't stop until the streets run red with blood! Is that what you want? It will happen![44]

Further, Gompertz highlights an important exchange between Pilate and Caiaphas that has an air of verisimilitude about it, as a conversation that might have taken place prior to the Passover during which Jesus was crucified. The exchange encapsulates the political dynamics inherent within the relationship between Pilate and Caiaphas, and as such deserves our close attention.

42. Gompertz, *Jewish Novel*, 21. This emphasis, quite properly articulated by Gompertz, is replicated quite successfully (and perhaps in a slightly more balanced fashion) in the HBO/BBC production entitled *The Passion*, from 2007 (and not to be confused with the Mel Gibson film of 2004 entitled *The Passion of the Christ*).

43. Ibid., 120, 134–36.

44. Ibid., 130. In all of this, Gompertz sets out a portrait of Pilate that falls more in line with those of Philo and Josephus than the NT Gospels.

The exchange takes place over two occasions and pertains to the holding of the High Priestly garments. The garments that the High Priest was to wear on three festival occasions throughout the year (i.e., the Feast of Passover, the Feast of Weeks, and the Feast of Booths) were normally held by Pilate in the Antonia Fortress—the Roman fortress that was built in order to oversee everything that transpired within the Jerusalem temple. The Roman procurator (or his representative) would have turned the garments over to the High Priest (or his emissary) only after the procurator was satisfied that Rome's expectations during the festivals would be met (see Josephus, *Antiquities* 20.6–9). What Rome expected of the High Priest was his assurances that the *Pax Romana* would not be compromised, especially during a festival as politically charged as Passover.

Gompertz introduces the first exchange between Pilate and Caiaphas regarding the ceremonial garments of the High Priest in this way:

> Caiaphas was on his way to ask for his vestments which he needed to officiate during the Passover ceremonies. Pilate kept them under lock and key in the Tower of Antonia. It was his way of controlling the High Priest . . . so that he, in turn, would control the people— and do Rome's bidding. . . . Caiaphas felt keenly reminded of the truth and indignity of the situation. . . .
>
> "It is the time of the Passover," said Caiaphas [to Pilate]. . . . "I would like to respectfully request, if it please your Eminence, the release of my vestments so that I may officiate over this festival in the tradition of my people."[45]

The conversation between the two leaders is cordial, Caiaphas doing little more than cow-towing to Pilate (e.g., "I am glad to have enjoyed such a long and pleasant relationship with your country and I have tried to be of service to both our peoples").[46] They discuss the religio-political significance of the Passover—a festival commemorating Israel's deliverance and independence from Egyptian bondage. Although parallels between Rome and Egypt are noted by Pilate, Caiaphas depoliticizes the festival's significance. According to Caiaphas, "The main concern of our people is religious, not political, and, so long as we enjoy religious freedom, we are not concerned about the political conditions of the time." Gompertz roots

45. Ibid., 117. The Gompertz novel was among the first to highlight the importance of this historical detail (i.e., the holding of the High Priest's garments in the Antonia Fortress) for understanding the trial and death of Jesus. It has now been caught on the silver screen in the HBO/BBC production of 2007 entitled "The Passion."

46. Gompertz, *Jewish Novel*, 118.

this in the context of its day by adding "To be plain, we are grateful to Rome for permitting us religious freedom."[47]

Satisfied with this, Pilate turns his attention to his real concern: Jesus, a self-proclaimed king who has the affections of the people. The dialogue is as follows:

> "One small matter," Pilate interrupted casually.
> "Yes?" Caiaphas asked generously.
> "Jesus."
> "Jesus?"
> "Get rid of him!"
> Caiaphas stared in stunned disbelief at Pilate, who stared back with cold, stony eyes.
> "What do you mean?" Caiaphas asked, trembling.
> "You have four perfectly good ways—stoning, burning, slaying or strangulation," said Pilate emotionlessly. "Any one will do."
> "Kill him? How?"
> "I've just told you how!"
> "Why?"
> "Because I said so!" thundered Pilate. "I do not render an account to Jews—only to Caesar!"[48]

The narrative continues along these lines until Caiaphas departs without his vestments; instead, Pilate requires him to return for them the next day, only after Caiaphas has taken care of Pilate's Jesus problem. The episode concludes with these words: "He [Caiaphas] turned and walked out sadly. It was Passover, but his spirit was enslaved. He was in bondage to Pharaoh."[49]

The following day, Caiaphas returns to Pilate's court, and the narrative plays out in this way:

> "I have come to request the ceremonial robes," Caiaphas said artlessly.
> "Then you have taken care of the matter?" Pilate asked matter-of-factly.[50]

Pilate learns that Caiaphas has not engineered the death of Jesus. In anger, he screams at Caiaphas:

47. Ibid., 119.
48. Ibid., 120.
49. Ibid., 121.
50. Ibid., 134.

I ordered you not to come back until you took care of the matter as I commanded! . . . Doesn't Rome get any kind of respect around here? Well, I'll have to see to it that there'll be some improvements—if it takes a different High Priest every month for a year![51]

On hearing Caiaphas say that he was not able to convince any of the Jewish leaders that there were sufficient grounds to orchestrate the death of Jesus, Pilate shouts:

Grounds! . . . Some madman decides he's King of the Jews and he's ready to set up his kingdom, God's kingdom, I don't give a damn whose kingdom, and they say there are no grounds? I'll give them grounds! Rome has grounds! That's all the grounds they need![52]

Caiaphas proposes a plan that will result in Pilate's requirement being met. Caiaphas will orchestrate things in such a way that a non-religious body of Jews will declare Jesus to be a dangerous political threat, and will then hand Jesus to Pilate, who will then sentence and carry out the execution "as is customary with political offenders."[53] The narrative continues:

Pilate laughed contemptuously. "So," he thundered, "You want Rome to do the dirty work and take the blame, eh?"

"May I remind the Procurator that it is Rome that wants his death!" Caiaphas said, with ill-concealed anger.

"May I remind you of your position!" Pilate thundered.

---

51. Ibid., 135.

52. Ibid., 135.

53. Ibid., 136. Gompertz's postulate that there were two groups of Sanhedrin, a religious and a political Sanhedrin, allows the religious dimension of Judaism to be kept free from responsibility in the trial and crucifixion of Jesus the Jew. This reconstruction of things had some currency in the first two-thirds of the twentieth century (see for instance Bücher, *Das Synedrion in Jerusalem*; Mantel, *Studies in the History of the Sanhedrin*; Zeitlin, *Who Crucified Jesus?*; Lohse, "*sunédrion*"; Rivkin, "Beth Din, Boule, Sanhedrin: A Tragedy of Errors"). But the distinction has since been dropped and has no real currency in contemporary academic scholarship. What is most commonly envisaged in contemporary scholarship is not a single body of members that comprise the Sanhedrin, but an *ad hoc* collection of people called by the high priest to offer him their council, without a distinction between religious and political interests. See, for instance, Taylor, *The Immerser*, 175–76, 181–83; McLaren, *Power and Politics in Palestine*; Goodman, *The Ruling Class of Judaea*, 40–42; Cohen, *From the Maccabees to the Mishnah*, 103; Grabbe, *Judaic Religion in the Second Temple Period*, 144–47; Sanders, *Judaism*, 472–90.

"I'm sorry," Caiaphas apologized and bowed. "May I suggest that by my action I will share the responsibility, which will cause the people to accept the matter without . . . incident."[54]

By back-narrating the scene, Gompertz enables his readers to see that Caiaphas was, in fact, Rome's pawn in the machinations of Roman power, while also enabling readers to understand how a text like John 19:11 can identify *Caiaphas* (i.e., "the man who handed me over to you") rather than Pilate as the prime mover in orchestrating Jesus' death. The *public perception* will be that Caiaphas has initiated the proceedings against Jesus, not Rome. Since the public were set to be duped by this plan, Pilate is satisfied with it, and the deal goes through: Caiaphas gets his High Priestly vestments, and Pilate will end up with a dead Jesus, with Rome being seen as relatively innocent in the matter.

Having clearly traced the historical "line management" of the trial and crucifixion of Jesus, Gompertz adds one other narrative wrinkle to the mix. The Jews who call for Jesus' crucifixion at the trial before Pilate only do so because they have been paid by Caiaphas to do so.[55] For Gompertz, things are not always to be taken at face value. Sometimes appearances are deceiving. Sometimes historical situations need to be probed beyond appearances to ask about the larger picture, about how the actions of the smaller players simply flow from the expectations of the larger players. In the Gompertz novel, the smaller players are pawns of those higher up in the configuration of power, with the actions of the smaller players having been orchestrated by those larger players.

The point is not new, nor was Gompertz the last to make it among those who retell the Jesus-story. Much the same is depicted in the historically robust film of 2007 entitled *The Passion* (produced by HBO and the BBC). In episode three of that very responsible depiction, Caiaphas instructs the captain of the Temple Guard to have all of "the faithful" (i.e., ordinary Jews who were loyal to Caiaphas and had not been corrupted by Jesus' message) standing outside the gates of the Antonia Fortress; when those gates were open, Caiaphas' people (not simply "the Jewish people") flooded Pilate's trial arena, where they could be manipulated into shouting out whatever Caiaphas needed them to articulate. In that film, it is the ventriloquist Caiaphas who shouts "Barabbas" (when Pilate asks whom he should release, Jesus or Barabbas) and "crucify him"—not from his own

54. Gompertz, *Jewish Novel*, 136, with the ". . ." being original.

55. Ibid., 135.

mouth, of course, but through the mouthpiece of the people that he had orchestrated to be on duty in Pilate's trial arena.

The HBO/BBC film differs from the Gompertz novel in its distribution of responsibility for the trial and crucifixion of Jesus, but both agree that Jesus was not killed by "the Jews"; both depict that process as having been orchestrated by the elite. The HBO/BBC film lays the responsibility at the feet of a good and politically astute Caiaphas who, in his duty to preserve the Jewish people, saw the necessity of sacrificing Jesus, who was fast becoming a figurehead for political disorder. In order to smash an impending uprising that would be disastrous against the people, Caiaphas painted Pilate into a corner, causing him ultimately to carry out a deed that needed to be done, symbolically by Rome. Conversely, Gompertz tips responsibility for Jesus' death so far to the Roman side of the balance that the dynamics of the trial and crucifixion of Jesus are drastically realigned, with the Jewish players virtually absolved of all responsibility; they act as they do simply because Rome has backed them into a corner and they have no choice in the matter.[56] They are, in the Gompertz novel, characters worthy of readers' sympathy. The only despicable character in the novel is Pilate.

Readers of the Gompertz novel might dispute whether the author got the balance of responsibility for the death of Jesus absolutely right. But there can be little dispute that Gompertz was wholly right to raise Rome's involvement in the death of Jesus to a much higher level than had traditionally been the case.

In this light, the sign that Pilate hung on the cross above Jesus' head identifying him as the "King of the Jews" is shown to be not an indication of Pilate's true view of Jesus' identity (contrast those Jesus-novels that depict Pilate as converting to Christianity not long after the crucifixion of Jesus); instead, that sign was a way of mocking the Jews—as if to say, "Here's the kind of king that you deserve."[57] The four sentences of the novel's final paragraph reinforce the fact that Pilate is the true villain in this story:

> Pontius Pilate congratulated himself with the news of Jesus' death. He had suppressed a rebellion and kept the Roman peace. King of the Jews! God's Kingdom! Pontius Pilate knew and served but one King and one kingdom—Caesar and Rome!

56. Here Gompertz's storyline is much in sympathy with that of Asch's novel *The Nazarene*.

57. Gompertz, *Jewish Novel*, 164. For a similar view of Pilate's actions, see Rensberger, *Johannine Faith and Liberating Community*, 92–95.

And with that, the novel ends.[58]

Gompertz's novel is the first Jesus-novel to offer, in a powerful and relatively compelling fashion, an extended analysis of the intricacies of Roman and Jewish involvement in the death of Jesus. It may also be among the best in this regard as well. Although what Gompertz sought to achieve would have been fresh back in the early 1960s, not many of his narrative proposals are particularly unique within contemporary academic discourse.[59] (Of course, academic discourse is not monolithic in the debate about the weighing up of percentages for Roman and Jewish involvement in the death of Jesus.) But if the issues that Gompertz raised back in the 1960s are now relatively standard fare within the academy, that is because scholarship has, in a sense, caught up to where Gompertz already was (along with a few others) back in the 1960s.

Gompertz on How to Read a Gospel

If Gompertz's depiction of the relationship between Pilate and Caiaphas is an important watershed in the history of Jesus-novels, Gompertz draws out important implications about how to read the New Testament Gospels in a fashion that resonates with what many New Testament scholars have been saying in recent decades.

In his "Retire the 'Christ-Killer' Charge" article, Gompertz takes account of several important challenges for interpreting the Jesus story today. He writes:

> The Jews did not kill Jesus. The Romans killed Jesus. The most obvious evidence is the form of execution—ordered by Pontius Pilate. . . . Pilate saw Jesus as a dangerous messianic revolutionary, who had to be destroyed. Pilate was a schemer and manipulator.

58. This ending is not in the original 1966 version of the novel, which ends with Jesus giving a loud cry and dying only after saying the Shema as his final words.

59. As a simple case in point, compare the comments by Taylor, *The Immerser*, 180: "The high priest's garments were often kept in the Antonia fortress, headquarters of the Roman garrison in Jerusalem (*Ant.* 20.6–9). The dependency of the high priesthood on Rome could not have been more blatantly advertised." On Pilate's involvement in the death of Jesus, Stendahl's comment from his 1984 book *Meanings* was already somewhat passé at the time; he points to the "increasing evidence that the role of Pilate was considerably greater in the execution of Jesus than the tradition and even the gospels lead us to think. . . . The crucifixion—a Roman execution—speaks its clear language, indicating that Jesus must have appeared sufficiently messianic, not only in a purely spiritual sense, to constitute a threat to political order according to Roman standards" (205, 210).

He had full control over the Jewish High Priest, who held office at Pontius Pilate's discretion.

Recounting some of the points he makes in his Jesus-novel, Gompertz adds: "Pilate was not the confused, conflicted, considerate, stymied person pictured in the New Testament. He was a harsh, brutal and cruel ruler."[60] The implications of this are obvious with regard to how New Testament Gospels are to be read. Quite simply, "The New Testament suggests that Pontius Pilate was willing to release Jesus, but that the Jews wanted him dead. It was the other way around."

How can this be explained? What reason can be postulated for this "distortion of these details"? Gompertz offers this explanation:

> There was good reason for such caution in the telling and writing of the story. With the death of Jesus, his followers had to convince Rome that they had no issues with Rome, and that they did not hold Rome or Pontius Pilate responsible for Jesus' death. Above all they had to convince Rome that their "kingdom" was not of this world. . . . It was not a good time to be a Jew or a follower of Jesus, or to say or write anything that would have placed Pontius Pilate or Rome in a bad light.[61]

Resonating with a large volume of academic scholarship, Gompertz's conclusion is as follows:

> We cannot change the past. But we can avoid the mistakes of the past, now that we know better. It is time that we retire the pernicious Christ-killer charge and bury it forever. It has no legitimate place any more in decent, knowledgeable, responsible Jewish-Christian relations, teachings, or story telling.

Gompertz said much the same in the Postscript to his *Jewish Novel about Jesus:*

> We cannot . . . rewrite the Bible. The text is fixed. It cannot be changed. However, it can be reinterpreted in light of new information or new insights. . . . We need to do this in connection with

60. *The Copperfield Review* (www.copperfieldreview.com/non_fiction/time_to_retire.html; consulted on 1 August 2008).

61. He goes on to note, of course, that "[e]ven so, the Jesus followers were persecuted for years. Christians faced horrible deaths by crucifixion or in Roman arenas where they were fed to the lions for the entertainment of emperors and the public."

these issues, for the sake and integrity of history, humanity, our religious communities and God.[62]

As Gompertz shows, telling stories often includes a moral dimension, not least with regard to stories that have served the self-definition of corporate groups throughout the centuries. The challenge of responsible storytelling has never been more pronounced than in our dangerous world today. Gompertz's narrative choices might not be definitive for all novel depictions nor does it exhaust all narrative options, but he has notably crafted a storyline that takes account of certain neglected features of power relationships of the first-century Judean landscape and of historical realities of Jewish-Christian relations throughout the centuries.

Final Thoughts

Gompertz's own retelling of the Jesus story is a noble attempt to discuss issues about the effect of the Jesus-story within a contemporary context where power is all too easily abused, oft-times with morally dubious outcomes.

His vision is refreshing in many ways. This is true, not least, because he does not give in to the view that religion causes all the problems in this world—a simplistic view that all too readily lends itself to easy sloganizing. (That view has pride of place in the Jesus-novel *The Gospel according to Jesus Christ* written in 1994 by Nobel prize-winner José Saramago.)[63] Instead, Gompertz believes that Christianity and Judaism are religions of peace. They are not inherently riddled by divinely legitimated violence (a charge some have laid against all monotheistic religions). Irrespective of their differences with regard to messianic identity, both Judaism and Christianity are, in Gompertz's view, intrinsically enmeshed in a matrix of peace and love that the world desperately needs.

The problem of violence lies not in these honorable religions, but elsewhere. In the case of Jesus, the problem of the violent abuse of power for self-serving ends lies wholly with Rome; in the case of the Holocaust against the Jewish people, it lies with Hitler and his Nazi movement. Judaism and Christianity can live peaceably together. In fact, enacting the heart of God's love for the world, those two religions should be living for the world, each in its own way modeling divine love that transforms hardened

---

62. Gompertz, *Jewish Novel*, 174.

63. On that novel, see Longenecker, "The Challenge of a Hopeless God."

human hearts. It isn't inherent within Judaism for Jews to kill other Jews with whom they disagree; similarly, it isn't inherent within Christianity for Christians to slaughter Jews. It is only when political troublemakers enter the frame, intent to structure the world for their benefit over against that of others, that things go wrong between religions.

For Gompertz, a story of Jesus demonstrates the point perfectly—but only once that story has been reworked by avoiding certain controversial points in the canonical Gospels and by highlighting other historical dimensions that have been neglected within those Gospels.

PART 5

The Voice of Rolf Gompertz

11

Speeches of the Heart

Although Rolf's heart and soul are embedded within his literature, they also emerge in the speeches that became such a prominent part of his life as he entered the seventh decade of his life and thereafter. In fact, had he presented himself as a regular speaker prior to the late 1980s, Rolf may not have been as effective in the role. This is because events that transpired within the mid 1980s impacted significantly upon him and caused him to delve even more deeply into processing on a personal level the meaning of his experiences and the phenomenon of Nazi Germany.

Rolf had often given talks about his life, and had been an occasional speaker in a variety of venues throughout his life.[1] But it was only in his seventh decade and beyond that things fell into place in such a fashion that speeches began to take on a new significance in his life and his self-identity.

Mike O'Hara, who took Rolf's course in Publicity (late 1970s or early 1980s) and who later became his colleague at NBC, commented on this in his returned questionnaire to me, noting how Rolf's sense of identity and purpose began to change as of the late 1980s: "In his later years, his experiences as a young boy in Nazi Germany seem to have totally redefined him." This astute observation of Rolf's redefinition of himself requires

---

1. Even in his first diary, Rolf makes occasional mention of speeches that he has made or wants to make, including his very first entry on December 8, 1945, when he was seventeen years old; also on the following dates: December 11, 1945; December 28, 1945; January 20, 1946; January 25, 1946.

back-narration in the next section of this chapter, and explanation in the section after that.

The Birth of a Speaker

In 1984, a twenty-page booklet was published by the Society for German American Studies that was to change the shape of the last decades of Rolf's life. It was entitled *Krefelder Juden in Amerika—Dokumentation in Briefen: Beitrag einer deutschen Schulklasse zum Jubiläum 1983*—that is, "Krefeld Jews in America—Documentation in Letters: Contributions of a German School Class on the 1983 Anniversary." The "anniversary" referred to in the title was the fiftieth anniversary of Hitler's rise to power.

The pamphlet's author was Renate Starck, a religion teacher in a Krefeld high school who had tasked her students to contact some of the Jews who had survived the Nazi pogrom and were now living in the United States. Sixteen hundred Jews had lived in Krefeld prior to the Holocaust; approximately eight hundred of them lost their lives in Hitler's death camps, and the other eight hundred had been spread far and wide, some of whom were still alive in 1983. Renate Starck hoped that she and her students could document some of the experiences of Jews living in Nazi Germany and their subsequent lives in the United States.[2]

The first time Rolf heard of this project was early in 1986, almost two years after the letters had been published. Although he qualified to be included among those surveyed by the project, Rolf had been overlooked.

His exclusion from the project set things in motion for Rolf. He realized that instead of being annoyed or frustrated by being excluded from the project, he was actually relieved. Because he had not received an invitation to participate, the emotional scars of his past had not been able to invade the emotional equilibrium of his present. No wonder he was relieved. But that state of relief did not last for long. Instead, it rebounded into a spiral of inner struggles with demons he never knew he had.

Rolf had come a long way, of course. He had already come to terms with his ordeal as an artifact of history, and he had already used it successfully as a pivot-point for comparing the health of differing ideological perspectives. Moreover, he had for long raised a strong voice in advocacy of a universalized model of messiahship. And a few years earlier he had written "a spiritual training manual" designed to help readers "develop and

2. Starck, "Krefelder Juden berichten von ihrem Leben."

maintain a spiritual point of view." But had he ever fully dealt with the personal wounds inflicted upon him years earlier when the demons of Nazi Germany sliced away at the souls of the Jewish people while German Nazis incarcerated their bodies?

Toying with the idea of writing his own letter to Renate Starck, Rolf batted the idea away with reasoning like, "It takes me three times longer to write in German than in English" and "the project ended in 1983; they don't need a letter from me now."[3]

But Rolf recognized that these reasons didn't get to the heart of the matter. Something in him propelled him toward the idea of writing, while something else was keeping him back. At the heart of his resistance lay not the practical hurdles of language and timing, but an emotional impediment: fear.

Rolf was afraid. He feared opening up a "Pandora's Box" that could devastate his emotional, psychological, and spiritual equilibrium. He had constructed a life that protected him from the onslaughts of unwieldy and dangerous emotional missiles from the past. Life was safer when issues of the past were compartmentalized as issues of historical and ideological import. Life was dangerous when they were placed in an organic relationship with his own emotional, psychological, and spiritual wellbeing. For years, the permeable membrane between the historical and ideological, on the one hand, and the personal, on the other, had been managed by Rolf with utmost efficiency, ensuring that leakage into Rolf's personal space was kept to a minimum. The control that he had exercised over his memories was now in danger of being lost to an upsurge of emotion—hatred, fear, incomprehension. The simple act of writing a letter to Krefeld high school students might unleash forces that he thought he had long ago tamed but feared he had not.[4]

The letter that Rolf eventually sent to Renate Starck in 1986 was not, in the end, written for the benefit of her high school students; the real

---

3. Although Rolf's German had grown a bit rusty over the years, he never lost his ability to speak or write German. In fact, on October 29 of 1949, Rolf's diary entry was written entirely in German, and partially in German on September 19, 1951; November 20, 1951; and March 9, 1952.

4. This is how he expressed it in an interview me in May 2011: "[I didn't] want to open that door, you know. So I [didn't] know what was behind that door: . . . Fear, hatred, terror, trauma, dead relatives, murdered relatives. What do you do with that? How do you process all of this?"

beneficiary was Rolf himself. It began, "Dear Krefelder Friends. This is the hardest letter I have ever written."[5]

Later that year Rolf received a letter from Renate's husband, Helmut Starck, the pastor of a Krefeld church and the president of a progressive organization called "The Association for Christian-Jewish Cooperation." The Association and The City of Krefeld were extending an invitation to Jewish survivors of Nazi Germany to return to the city in 1987, as a symbol of repentance for offenses done against them in the past. It was billed as "Die Woche der Begegnung"—"The Week of Encounter." Many who received the invitation did not return to Germany for the "encounter" of June 29 to July 7, 1987. But Rolf returned.

Both his letter of 1986 and his return to Germany in 1987 put Rolf face to face with issues that he had not needed to deal with previously; the Nazi years were half a lifetime away, and Germany was half a world away. But making contact with Germans who saw him as a representative Jew stirred up a swarm of emotion. When he returned to Germany, what was he to say? Think? Do? Was he expected to forgive? Is that what "they" expected of him? Is that what he expected of himself?

Or was he expected to forget? These were different people than those who had colluded with Nazi pogroms in the days of his youth, but that collusion had been largely collective, with vast swathes of the people sharing in the Nazi program through their own complicity with evil. Would that collusion overshoot the generations? When he arrived, would he simply be a pawn in another German game—this time, a game of excuse and avoidance, a game in which Rolf would play the role of a token Jew in an exercise of German deception and whitewash? Did he need to protect himself by donning layers of emotional protection, or make himself vulnerable, in the hope that gestures of reconciliation would open redemptive moments for all involved?[6]

---

5. Rolf says in his "Snapshots" speech that the letter was sent in 1986, but in an interview with me in May 2011 he said it was sent in 1987. I take the former to be correct.

6. Katrin Balzer, a German who met Rolf in 2007, wrote the following about Rolf's inner conflict at this point in his life: "He told me about his inner conflict when he planned his first trip to Germany as an adult. I guess in his situation you can't go to Germany again without fears or thoughts about Germany's present generation, how much you can trust German people and how the political situation really has changed. Fortunately the Germany from today is very different from the one he got to know as a child. But I guess an experience of a persecution will always have a formative impact of the relationship one will have to his country of birth."

In his book, *Sparks of Spirit*, Rolf had linked spiritual wisdom for to-day with spiritual wisdom of the past—in particular, the Hebrew Bible. And so Rolf turned once again to his Bible (as his parents are depicted as doing, in chapter 2 above).

In listening for the voice of Wisdom in biblical texts, Rolf found rein-forcement for the view that reconciliation does not require the forgetting of evil (a view that he found reinforced in Deut 25:17 and 19). But if he was not expected to forget, was he expected to forgive?

In addressing that matter, Rolf found that several verses from Ezekiel 18 spoke to him. Some spoke of God forgiving the transgressor of his sins, with a new heart and a new spirit emerging.[7] Did this apply to the people of Germany? Was their divine forgiveness enmeshed with the flourishing of a new spirit within the country? Were they turning, or had they already turned the corner to choose life? Was he a small part of the process of their repentance and recovery, and a small part in the process of reconciliation among human beings? Was he, as Shlomo Hirsch would have said, being called to bloom where he was planted?[8]

The same passage addressed his concerns from a different direction: "The son shall not bear the iniquity of the father, neither shall the father bear the iniquity of the son" (Ezek 18:20). This verse, with its denunciation of collective guilt, got right to the heart of the matter.

If history (even his own history) had taught anything, it was that col-lective identity can become an instrument in the propagation of evil. One

---

7. Ezek 18:27, 31–32: "But if the wicked turn from all his sins and do what is lawful and right, he shall surely live, he shall not die. . . . Cast away from you all your transgres-sions, wherein ye have transgressed, and make you a new heart and a new spirit, for why will you die. . . . For I have no pleasure in the death of him who dies; . . . wherefore turn yourselves and live."

8. In retrospect, Rolf much prefers the word "transformation" over "forgiveness" when it comes to situations of evil. This is how he articulated the point in an interview with me in May 2011: "What can you do with evil? What can you do with pain and suf-fering? You can take them and you can transform them and make them serve life. And to me, transform is an easier way for us to handle traumatic stuff like that than [the notion of] forgiveness. . . . Some people . . . who've heard my story say, 'Oh, you've forgiven.' I'm always surprised when I hear that. . . . There are two forms of forgiveness. The traditional Jewish one: 'You can't forgive until the person asks you for forgiveness.' And the other one, which is also Jewish: 'Forgiveness is not for the other person at all; it's to release yourself from being enslaved to the other.' . . . I think I can reach people better with . . . the word 'transformation.'" In fact, in the questionnaire responses from people who know Rolf, the words "transform" and "transformation" recur repeatedly in descriptions of his handling of his experiences of Nazi Germany.

of the ways in which Nazi ideology penetrated into every fold of German society was through the demarcation of different people-groups and imposing a veneer of collective identity over all individuals within that group. Aryans were the supreme people-group; non-German intellectual culture was inferior to German intellectual culture; Jews, homosexuals, and others were all substandard and unwanted. Moreover, many moments in Christian history had seen the same collective approach applied disastrously to the Jewish people: they were all Christ-killers, they were all Judases. "His blood be upon us and our children!"

Collective identity lay at the root of the evils that Rolf opposed. He could not allow himself the easy route of tarring all the German people with the same brush. This new generation from among the German people could not be blamed for the evils done to him, his family, and millions of others in generations past. To do so would be to enlist one's self in the service of the same demons that seduced Germany during the Nazi years, and to perpetuate their destructive program in a different context half a century later. Rolf himself would be a victim once again to their pernicious sleuthing, with hatred gnawing away, with repressed memories freezing his soul. If God wanted new hearts and new spirits to flourish, Rolf's would need to be one of them.

Returning to the scene of the crime to face repressed internalized demons, Rolf found the experience to have a profound effect on him. Civic leaders, religious leaders, and everyday people made themselves available to ensure that Rolf and other Krefeld Jews were welcomed back with dignity and respect. The guests were wined, and dined, and given a cruise on the Rhine.

During his week in Krefeld, Rolf stayed with a German Christian family for the week—Reinhard and Ulrike Gruenberg and their two daughters, Wiebke (aged eleven) and Ulrike (aged ten). In 2011 both Wiebke and Ulrike (the daughters) wrote to me regarding their time with Rolf. Wiebke remembers this: "He was slowly feeling his way back into the German language. My parents and Rolf were having long and serious conversations, cautiously looking for the right words." Ulrike remembers things this way:

> Rolf stayed with us and our family for one week. It was one of the most impressive experiences in my life, because of the emotional impact this week had on the group as a whole and on Rolf as an individual in particular. Our relationship developed from day to day. At the end of the week I felt a close friendship to Rolf. He

was so amiable, friendly, humorous and respectful, sensitive to the needs and feelings of others.

She continued with reflections about what Rolf stands for:

> Rolf appears empowered by his visions and dreams of a better world. He knows that there will never be a world without wars, injustices, hatred, hunger, poverty. But he knows, too, that everybody can do his best to bring about change. And when many people in their own small surroundings try to change hatred into love, injustice into justice, war between countries and individuals into peace, then the whole world would become more human. I would describe the theme of Rolf's life as reconciliation between people, countries, and religions. And so he continues to try and build bridges, through his writings and speaking.

Clearly Ulrike has put her finger on the pulse of Rolf's motivational and ideological world.[9]

During the week that Rolf stayed again with the Gruenberg family, he was also able to visit *Bismarckstrasse* 118, where his family had made their home. Now a dental office, Rolf entered the familiar doorway, climbed the steps, explained that he had lived in the premises as a boy with his family during the Nazi regime, and asked if he could spend a few reflective moments there. Of course, the request was granted. Now almost sixty years old, Rolf reflected on the little boy and his family of fifty years earlier. If those walls encapsulated the one place in Rolf's little world that seemed secure, it was also a place that, like his own inner world, was not impervious to unwanted intrusions.

At the end of the week, Rolf was asked to say a few words to the group of people who had come together from different places of the globe and

---

9. Ulrike's insights are notable in other regards as well. I recount more from the same questionnaire returned to me: "I understand that until 1987 Rolf didn't want to be confronted with his German past. He neither wanted to speak nor to read the German language. The memories of his childhood in the Nazi time and of the Nazi-slogans must have been deep in his mind but hidden. I think he felt fear of Germany." And also the following: "I think Rolf was old enough to understand what happened in the thirties. He had to leave his school, many things were forbidden for him as a Jew, he experienced the events of Crystal Night, he was aware that Jewish people were deported. I assume that must have been a heavy burden for him as a boy. This, and the resulting emigration to America, caused a fundamental rupture in his childhood. If it had not been for the Nazi time, his life would have gone in a very different way. But, despite all that, Rolf's life turned out well and successful. He apparently found his way in the free world, and looked ahead, supported by the deep love of his parents."

walked together in their pilgrimage of spirit. Rolf didn't say much, but the few words that he spoke pointed to what he took to be the main lesson they had learned that week: that the answer to the world's problems can only lie in love and reconciliation. And with that, Rolf the speaker was born, having faced his demons and having begun to repel any unrecognized residual influence they might have had in his life.

The Emergence of a Speaker

On August 6 of 1987, only a month after "the week of encounter" had ended, Oskar Gompertz died at the age of ninety-seven. "Father, if they take you, I'm going with you," Rolf had said to him forty-nine years earlier. The man who had risked his life protecting Germany in World War I, the man who had risked his life protecting his family from Nazi invaders on *Kristallnacht*, and the man who had done everything in his power to enhance Rolf's life over the decades, was now gone. So too was Rolf's loving mother Selma who, at eighty-four years of age, had died four and a half years earlier (January 22, 1983). For the first time in his life, Rolf had no one near to him who had endured the painful experiences of Nazi Germany with him; there was no one who, having shared those experiences with him intimately and first-hand, was bonded to him in an unspoken connection. Now Rolf alone was the bearer of those experiences—their memory, their pain, and their meaning.

There was no longer a generational buffer between Rolf and death. The ticking clock of his life had introduced him to a new phase of existence— a "parentless" phase that was soon to take shape in relation to a letter he received from the Krefeld city council in the autumn of 1987.

The letter announced the city's intentions of commemorating the fiftieth anniversary of *Kristallnacht* in the following year, 1988, and included an invitation for Rolf to be the main speaker at the commemorative event. Rolf readily agreed, but then struggled to know what he might say. In particular, he needed to decide for whom he was speaking. Was he speaking for the Jewish people collectively? The Jews of Krefeld? The six million Jews who were murdered in the Holocaust? The Jewish survivors? His family?

In the end, Rolf realized that he would be able to speak only for himself. He could not write a speech that would have satisfied all the Holocaust victims. Even the survivors had vastly differing perspectives on fundamental issues, like God, meaning, ethics, survival. If he was to speak effectively, he would have to shed the responsibility of speaking for others and accept the freedom of speaking only for himself.

Rolf delivered the speech on the anniversary of *Kristallnacht* in his childhood city of Krefeld. He spoke in German for forty-five minutes. In it he talked of a realization that came to him when preparing the speech—a realization that had never crossed his mind previously but that crashed in upon him now. He came to realize that he might well have become a child advocate of Nazi ideology if he had not been born into a family headed by Jewish parents (parents now lost to him). He recounts the dawning of this realization in this way:

> How would I have acted, if I had not been born a Jew? I came to a terrifying, humbling conclusion: I didn't know how I would have behaved! I only hoped I would have shown character and strength, and remained human.[10]

Consequently, in his Krefeld speech of 1988 he made the following point about the potential for good people to drift off-course from their moral compass.

> We cannot forget *Kristallnacht* or the Holocaust. The threat is always there. Decency is not guaranteed. Goodness is not guaranteed. Our prejudices, our darker thoughts and feelings can always be aroused again against somebody. Yesterday it was the Jews. Who is it today? Who will it be tomorrow? . . . Something went wrong in the human soul. . . . Love, compassion, justice, sensitivity—these were shut off. People lost their humanity. After that, anything was possible.

Humanity can experience moral-drift. Rolf, like millions of other Jews, has experienced that crushing reality to his own personal detriment. But he does not allow that reality to foster despair; there is good in humanity, and there is God. Rolf says it best when he speaks these words: "I still believe in man, because Judaism requires that I do. But I must believe in God, because I cannot place my total faith in man."

After his return to the United States, Rolf's speaking roster began to grow, but only slowly at first. He found himself invited to the occasional gathering where he had been asked to speak about his experiences, but these were intermittent events without a coordinated presence in Rolf's life.

---

10. Gompertz, from his speech "Snapshots," from which the following two quotations are also taken.

In 2006, however, this began to change. Rolf was invited to speak about his experiences at his grandson's school in the state of Washington. Carol went with him and recognized that he was developing a real presence as a speaker. "I've never heard you speak so well," she said to him afterwards. "You should do more of that."

Rolf began to give consideration to whether he might adopt a role as a speaker. Gunther Katz, a friend of Rolf's who was also a Jewish refugee from Nazi Germany, frequently spoke at the Simon Wiesenthal Center and Museum of Tolerance in Los Angeles. So Rolf made contact with the Center, inquired whether they could use another refugee speaker, and in no time he was a regular in the Center's calendar of events. Roughly every other week, for the six years from 2006 to 2012, Rolf spoke to gatherings of twenty to ninety people. On those occasions, people of all ages and walks of life were able to see, listen to, and shake hands with someone who had actually experienced the traumas of living as a Jew in Nazi Germany.[11]

In the spring of 2011 (March 30 to April 12), Rolf returned for the third and last time to Germany. During the annual celebration of Jewish culture, Rolf spoke on fifteen occasions in a variety of venues. Newspapers covered his speeches, and a one-hour radio broadcast went out in which he was interviewed. He met again with the Gruenberg family, who had housed him on his first return to Germany back in 1987, and he went to church with them on the Sunday, where he delivered a short talk to the congregation. He also attended two Sabbath services, one of which was in the beautiful new synagogue at Krefeld, to which he later donated some volumes from Rabbi Bluhm's Jewish library. And since the occasion of his return coincided with

---

11. He also spoke at other venues as well, most recently to the Jewish Law Students Association at Southwestern Law School in May 2013.

It is interesting to ask whether Rolf's effectiveness may emerge more when he speaks in German than when he speaks in English. Notice, for instance, the observation of Katrin Balzer, a German producer who spoke to Rolf in 2007 about his childhood experiences (these comments taken from a questionnaire returned to me): "I spent 2 days with Rolf when visiting him in Los Angeles. The first day we mostly spoke in English when he told me about his experiences of Nazi Germany in his childhood. On the second day I made the interview in German, which he still speaks fluently. It was very touching to realize that something changed in his voice, it was like being much more close to his remembrance. It was a very emotional moment for me." She continues in this way: "It [was] also made very clear to me that, although Rolf found a new home country, . . . there is still a deep connection to his roots. Also there was something in his voice which I interpreted as sorrow and bewilderment . . . concerning the losses he had to experience as a child by fearing death and persecution."

the release of the German translation of his Jesus-novel, he enjoyed much favorable publicity about it as well.

The trip was very encouraging to Rolf. He found that his sentiments about the peaceful coexistence of Judaism and Christianity were shared by a good number of Germans whom he met. Moreover, Rolf could see first hand that his voice was now being heard, not only in his speeches, but also through his Jesus-novel that would continue to speak within the country that he had long ago fled from, even long after his life would end.[12]

12. Or, as Tricia Aven well states in her questionnaire returned to me, "With the invitation to speak in his home town of Krefeld on the 50th anniversary of *Kristallnacht* in 1988, the publication of *Jesus, mein jüdischer Bruder* in 2010, and his trip to Germany in the spring of 2011, Rolf is experiencing an ongoing fulfillment of the purpose of his life that may be far beyond what he had hoped and dreamed."

12

An Appreciation

The story of Rolf Gompertz is just one story flowing out of the days of Nazi Germany. Of other stories that do the same, many millions of them are tragic. Each of those life stories is a precious strand in the tapestry of our common humanity. It is a good thing whenever one of those stories is salvaged from the depths of the Nazi darkness and retold—out of respect for each individual life and, hopefully, for the benefit of future generations. Most of those stories, however, have been lost forever; much of the tapestry is in tatters.

Rolf's story is not among the most tragic of those stories; he was among the minority of Jews who were "fortunate." The adjective is meaningful only in relative terms, of course. It was not only the millions of murdered victims who were victimized. Psychologically, emotionally, and spiritually, Rolf was wounded and wronged. But even so, he was nonetheless fortunate by comparison with the majority of European Jews who were not able to flee from the Nazism that had engulfed Europe within its clutches.

Being among the minority of fortunate ones does not make his story any less significant, however. His is a story of how one man found his "voice," both in his literature and his speeches, in order to contribute to understanding among human beings.

Rolf, or "Rolf Menachem" as he began to call himself in his last years, rightly eschews the notion that his voice speaks for any of those Jews whose lives ended in a premature, horrendous death. His is simply one voice. In the same way, I cannot ultimately speak for Rolf, although I have done my best to bring his contribution to the attention of a wider audience. The best place to hear his voice is in his literature, his diaries, and his speeches.[1]

What does one find in those places? Perhaps not philosophical complexity, but a clarity of vision. Perhaps not sophisticated answers to nagging theological questions, but suggestive signposts to healthy routes forward. Perhaps not *the* answer to Hitler, but *an* answer to Hitler, an answer rooted in the bedrock of our common humanity.

And perhaps that is what the Nazi saw when Rolf's father held his Iron Cross in front of his face. For a brief moment, enough to turn him aside, the Nazi saw a speck of common humanity between them. In that fleeting moment, the recognition of a common humanity broke apart their differences and opened up a small space in which one of the "sparks of spirit" took hold.[2] That spark did not fan into a glorious blaze of reconciliation, and was soon extinguished, as the Nazi no doubt moved on to other Jewish residences to carry out the Nazi pogrom that night. But the torch had been passed to the son—the same son who had said to his father moments earlier, "If they take you, I'm going with you," and the son who spent a lifetime considering if and how a spark of spirit could be fanned into a flame.

That spark has played a curious role within Rolf's own thoughts, since it did not always ignite thoughts harmoniously. Early on, Rolf wrote in his diary about Hitler's evil ways, ending the diary entry with this sentence: "Justice cries for revenge and eternal damnation!" That was November 24 of 1949, eleven years after *Kristallnacht* and the only time Rolf ever mentioned Hitler in the whole of his diaries (other than a reference back to this one a year later, on November 15, 1950). But later he questioned the premise of this entry, when he wrote the following on March 22, 1951: "I perceive that some very significant problems in regard to my philosophic idea exist still, problems which need to find an explanation still, problems about whose solution I am gravely concerned." The first problem cited is this:

> If everything is possessed fundamentally and originally with divine goodness as I do strictly affirm (i.e., if everything, in short, is a part of God) can anything be permanently damned? Can

1. For the latter two, see the four chapters comprising Part 6 of this book, below.

2. Rolf has wondered whether the Nazi's actions arose out of a momentary respect for a fellow-soldier, or whether the sign of the cross tugged at whatever "Christian" morality may have remained in him. Either way, a point in commonality was momentarily traced in the Nazi's mind—either by way of military involvement or by the remnants of a Judeo-Christian morality.

anything be damned at all, since that would mean that God would be deprived of a part of Himself! Since this seems to be the case, what explanation other than mistaken reasoning (self-perversion) can be found for Evil and what effective argument can be framed to satisfy our sense of Justice in the face of Evil.[3]

Has Rolf ever found an answer to this dilemma? It seems not. With regard to the Hitlers of this world, Rolf says things very simply in the "Snapshots" speech that he has given repeatedly in the final decades of his life: "I leave them to history and to God. What will God do? God alone knows."

It does not bother Rolf that his questions are sometimes left unresolved. He does not perceive it to be his job to resolve all the great theological and philosophical riddles. His job, instead, is to involve himself in the divine process of giving and receiving love, and to do so on the basis of Zech 4:6: "Not by might, nor by power, but by my Spirit, says the Lord of hosts."

This is not some cheery world in which one is oblivious to injustice and simply thinks dreamily about happy thoughts.[4] Instead, for Rolf it is an intentional commitment of the will to make himself vulnerable to others through the joys and tragedies of life. As his friend Tricia Aven wrote in a questionnaire returned to me:

> in his writings, Rolf has repeatedly said, "Here lies the triumph: Take what's to you given, and mold of it your paradise, your heaven." This saying, combined with his favorite mantra, which is "bloom where you stand," illustrates foundational characteristics of his identity and his faith that not only make him tick, but empower him as well. . . . [I]t is his incredibly positive attitude towards life—incredible, considering his childhood experiences in Nazi Germany—which is rooted in his Jewish identity and faith that has empowered him and enabled him to accomplish all that he has accomplished in his life. . . . [I]f and when something happens to cause him to be either angry or disappointed, he

3. It is this point of view that Judas articulates toward the end of Rolf's Jesus-novel. Judas imagines that God will slay evil through his overpowering love, with the wicked Pilate being destroyed by God's transforming power and restored as a healthy, loving, worshipful human being. On this, see the section "Violence and Peace in Gompertz's Jesus-Novel" in chapter 10 above.

4. Compare also David Herrle's comment from a questionnaire returned to me: "His [Rolf's] faith in God is more than reverence. It is friendship that's not a matter of full-time contentment. Rolf acknowledges doubts, sadness, and low times, as well as love and joy. Only one who knows despair can truly appreciate the light."

would respond with the attitude expressed above—"Here lies the triumph: Take what's to you given, and mold of it your paradise, your heaven"—and he would take steps, through his attitude and/ or actions, to transform the situation.

Or as his friend Lester Garfinkel wrote in a questionnaire returned to me, Rolf "admirably lives out the precepts of the prophet Micah [6:8], i.e., to have compassion, do justice, and walk humbly with his God."

Correlating with these words is a perceptive entry regarding anger that Rolf inscribed in his diary on March 25, 1951:

> There is [an] attitude which I hope to cultivate as I go through life as perfectly as at all possible: I hope to try keeping a calm and even temper in the face of anything—great or small—to which I shall be exposed; uncontrolled anger and temper is so very unpleasant in its effect upon others, and even occasional indulgence in this will turn into habit unbelievably fast; a well-balanced temper is unbelievably pleasant and an achievement that's not to be under-rated. It symbolizes mastery of the universe and of all that could possibly befall.

In the meantime, Rolf has moved through life with the love of his family (his parents, his wife, his children, and his grandchildren), with the deep respect and affection of his many friends, and with his humor. Appreciating humor is often a highly personalized thing, but I imagine that there are only a few who cannot appreciate the gentle wit in the following diary entry from June 10 of 1977, which beautifully encapsulates something of Rolf's sparkle. Written when Rolf was forty-nine and a half, the entry speaks about the release of his first two books (one of which was his Jesus-novel) within a two-week period. The entry then reads:

> The two books and the joy resulting from them have affected and infected everyone in the family. Carol is happy, Ron, Nancy + Philip are happy. Only Princess [the family dog] isn't happy—she can't get in the garage anymore—she's been displaced by Jesus. I hope this won't turn her against religion![5]

5. Then he adds, "Poor Princess. Maybe I'll give her an autographed copy. Better yet—a bone! That's something she can relate to: Anyway, there's no light in the dog house—so how could she read at night?" This was Rolf's first and only dog, after wanting one so much as a boy. Rolf wrote in an email to me dated December 9, 2012: "I had wanted a three-colored beagle—brown, black, white, but I was asked to take a look at a nearby neighbor's beagle, which was about to be turned over to the pound. It was all black. I couldn't walk away from it. Moral: Don't ever look in a dog's eyes. If you do, it's yours."

⅍

The reader of this book can enjoy more of Rolf's diary entries and his "Snap-shots" speech in Part 6 below. But here, I close with one final quotation from Rolf's diary. In an entry written on his fiftieth birthday (December 29, 1977), Rolf completed his third diary with this prayer of thanksgiving:

> Thank you, God, for all my blessings. A poem I once wrote in my twenties comes to mind: "Let me live, love and suffer . . . nobly."
>
> We yearn in spirit. We reach upward. We want to give life meaning. We seek to be worthy of life. It is not always easy to be-lieve in the vision—or to maintain it.
>
> Help me, God, to be worthy of the dream and of the vision for whatever years you will grant me.
>
> I want to love. I need to love. Help me to keep on loving in all ways. Let me always see your love in my life. Thank you. Amen.

PART 6

Gompertz in His Own Words

13

Snapshots

What appears below is Rolf's "Snapshots" speech—which his friend Alla Renée Bozarth calls his "life poem." Rolf has delivered this speech regularly every other week from 2006 to the time of writing this book (except when he was recovering from a stroke in late 2012 and early 2013) in the Simon Wiesenthal Center and Museum of Tolerance in Los Angeles. It is, in a sense, his signature speech, and this book would not be complete without it. The speech was always a work in progress, with Rolf constantly tweaking it here or there to make sure it moved a bit closer to the ideal speech that most represented him. What appears below is the version that Rolf used as of the spring of 2014. Although he presented it as a poem, it appears here more as prose, in order not to add to the length of this book.

Before reproducing Rolf's "Snapshots," however, the reader will benefit from two literary pieces that Rolf wrote regarding encounters he had with people in the aftermath of reciting "Snapshots" late in his life. On August 20 of 2013, Rolf sent me an email containing "The Storyteller," a poem that he had written the previous day. "The Storyteller" seeks to capture a moving moment that transpired after he delivered the "Snapshots" speech four days earlier (on Friday August 16) at the Simon Wiesenthal Center and Museum of Tolerance in Los Angeles, when about sixty people were in attendance. Similarly, on April 5 of 2014, Rolf sent me "The Earring," in which he recalls an encounter with a student after he recited "Snapshots" before an audience of 129 students at the John Burroughs Senior High School in Burbank California on April 2, 2014. These two pieces poignantly set the scene for "Snapshots" by capturing something of how others have been influenced by hearing the speech. Again, these have been changed from poetry format to prose format.

The Storyteller

An older man sits at the far-end of a row, to my right. As I finish, he leaves. Moments later, he reappears. He is about my age. As he comes closer I notice that he is all choked up, with tears in his eyes. I wait for him to say something but he cannot speak. What should, what can I say? I move towards him and give him a hug. He hugs back. We hold each other.

"Thank you," he mumbles.

I look at him. "Holocaust?" I ask.

"Yes," he nods, then leaves.

What had touched him so deeply? I will always wonder, I will never know. But something I said mattered.

We are all messengers to one another. We touch souls. We matter. We make a difference.

The Earring

The teenagers listen quietly, respectfully. At the end there is extended applause. We have time for a question or two. Then the students leave for their classes. A few stay back and come to me. We shake hands, take pictures, say a few meaningful words to each other.

One student hangs back, then comes forward. "There is so much bad stuff all around," she says, with tears in her eyes. "You gave me hope again, you restored my faith."

"That means a lot to me," I say.

She gives me a hug.

"Thank you," I say.

She reaches for one of her petite earrings, takes it off, offers it to me, and says, "I would like you to have this." Hanging from it is a tiny silver cross.

"I am deeply touched," I say. "Keep the faith."

I return home, and head for the glass-enclosed, see-through display cabinet in my office. I place the precious earring on one of the shelves, among the diverse objects of faith.

SNAPSHOTS[1]

I would like to share with you. My special photo album. But there are no photos. The pictures are in my head. They are in my heart, mind, and soul. I show them to you, in words, separated by three camera clicks. Click . . . click . . . click . . .

I call them "Snapshots of a Life: *Kristallnacht* . . . and Beyond; Of Fear, Hatred, and Reconciliation." Click . . . click . . . click . . .

My name is Rolf Gompertz. I was born two-months prematurely, in Krefeld, Germany, December 29, 1927. My mother and I almost die in childbirth. But we survive.

"If you can keep him alive until he's seven," the doctor advises my mother, "he should make it to old age."

I am eighty-six years old. I think I've made it to old age.

Rabbi Arthur Bluhm, and his wife, Hanna, come to Krefeld a few months earlier. I am the first baby boy born into his congregation. Our paths would cross significantly through the years.

I am an only child. I tried to figure out life quite early. I found it . . . confusing. For instance, when I was still very young, I had the whooping cough. My mother took me to the doctor. He gave me a shot in . . . you know . . . my bottom. I turned to him puzzled, and said: "But, doctor, that's not where I have my cough!"

One thing I did know, though, when I was quite young. I knew what I wanted to be when I grew up: a chimneysweep. I had a good reason. It seemed that every time my mother saw me, during the day, she washed my face. One day I had an epiphany. I decided that when I grew up, I would become a chimneysweep. That way I could stay dirty and would never have to wash myself again for the rest of my life.

I love to read, especially the adventure books by Karl May. He was a German writer who wrote wonderful stories about American Indians, like Chief Winnetou. I decide that I would become an American Indian, like Winnetou.

My parents are very good to me. I get a lot of things I want, but I never got a dog. Instead, I got a chicken. It's hard to play with a chicken. It's really, really hard to take a chicken for a walk.

And then came Hitler, and life changed, because I was a Jew.

---

1. Presented at the Simon Wiesenthal Center, Museum of Tolerance, Los Angeles CA; copyright © 2014 by Rolf Gompertz; used with permission

1933 . . . Hitler comes to power. He rants: "*Die Juden sind unser Un-glueck!*" "The Jews are our misfortune!" It's now bad to be a Jew. It is bad to look like a Jew. It is bad to have a Jewish nose. I am five years old. Click . . . click . . . click . . .

1933 . . . 1934 . . . 1935 . . . 1936 . . . 1937. Signs posted everywhere—restaurants, swimming pools, theaters, public parks, stores, hotels: "*Juden unerwuenscht!*" "Jews not wanted!" The Nazis ban and burn books, any book, by a Jew or about a Jew, any book—by anyone and about anything—considered incompatible with Nazi ideology. Even a book about us, titled: "*Die Familie Gomperz,*" "The Gomperz Family," from the first one around 1600 to 1900, by which time there are 5000 of us. Click . . . click . . . click . . .

It does not take long to notice the changes, not even for a child.

"Please, do not come here any more," our barber tells my father, the last time we visit his barbershop. "But call me and I'll come to your house, at night." Click . . . click . . . click . . .

"We cannot see each other anymore," my mother's best non-Jewish friend tells her. "It's getting too dangerous." That goes also for her daughter and me. We cannot play together any more, in the sandbox, or on the swings. We never see each other again. Click . . . click . . . click . . .

As I go shopping with my mother, I am drawn to a newspaper spread out in a glass-enclosed display case. I break away from my mother and rush over to see "the funny cartoons" and read the stories. My mother rushes after me and pulls me away. She explains that they are not nice cartoons or nice stories. They are about us, Jews. The "bad" newspaper is posted everywhere. It is called "*Der Stürmer,*" "The Attacker." Click . . . click . . . click . . .

I am at home. I hear the sounds of a parade. I rush to the window and watch it coming. The men dance around and look like they're having fun. They are in black, with long coats. They are wearing head coverings—the kind we wear in the synagogue. And long prayer shawls. They carry prayer books and are singing. They even have a Torah. They do funny things with the head coverings, prayer shawls, prayer books, and even the Torah.

My mother sees me at the window. One look, and she gets the picture. She draws the drapes quickly.

"Why can't I see the parade?" I ask.

"It's not a nice parade," she says.

"They are Jews!" I say.

"No," she says, "They are Nazis dressed up like Jews. They are making fun of us!" Click . . . click . . . click . . .

"Herr Gompertz," a Gentile acquaintance tells my father as they meet on the street. "It's bad and getting worse. Get out of here before it is too late." Click . . . click . . . click . . .

We find what's happening incomprehensible. We are proud, loyal German citizens. We are Germans, by nationality. We are Jews, by religion. Click . . . click . . . click . . .

We belong to a synagogue. It is not Reform or Orthodox, but Conservative, with a few lingering elements of Orthodox Judaism. Men and women still sit in separate sections. My family is moderately observant. We light candles Friday nights. My parents bless me. We go to the synagogue Shabbat morning. We observe the Jewish festivals. We are not as observant as my friend, Hans, down the block. His family is Orthodox, really Orthodox. They don't come to our synagogue, where Orthodox Jews can pray in a special room. Hans, and his family, pray at their home, with a handful of other Orthodox Jews. Since we are not kosher, Hans cannot eat with us.

The Nazis make no such distinctions: Orthodox, Conservative, Reform, religious, non-religious, secular. A Jew is a Jew is a Jew.

For openers, Hitler passes a law taking away our citizenship. And everywhere the signs, every time I walk through town: "*Juden Unerwuenscht!*" "Jews Not Wanted!"

One day I notice a new swimming pool, I look it over carefully, on all sides. There is no sign! I am around ten now. It has been five years since I learned to swim. It was also the last time I was allowed to swim. I run home.

"Mutti, Mutti!" I call out excitedly, "Mommy, Mommy! There is a new swimming pool in town. It doesn't have a sign! May I go swimming?"

My mother thinks about it for a moment. "H'm," she muses. "I guess it'll be all right." She hands me my trunks and the money.

I run back to town, change, rush out to the pool, and jump into the deep end. That is a mistake. Instead of swimming, I am drowning. I forgot how to swim. I go down, down, down. I manage to get to the side of the pool, find the ladder, and pull myself up. I climb out, plop down, and pump water out of myself.

When I can breathe and focus again, I look up. There, straight across from me, sits the lifeguard. He has seen it all, without lifting one finger. Now he motions me to come to him. I hurry over.

"Didn't you see the sign?" he demands, his voice as cold as his eyes.

I was not about to argue. But one thing I knew now for certain, he would have let me drown. I leave quickly. Click . . . click . . . click . . .

We now live on *Bismarckstrasse* 118. Otto, my best friend, and I are two months apart in age. He lives just two blocks away. It is 1937.

German Gentile boys approaching ten years of age look forward to getting a snappy uniform and joining the Hitler Youth. Walking through town one day, Otto declares: "When I turn ten I'm going to join the Hitler Jews!"

"You can't!" I say, startled.

"Why not?" he asks.

"You're Jewish," I say.

"So?"

"It's not for Jews!" I inform him.

"Of course it is," he insists with absolute certainty. "That's why they call it the Hitler Jews."

"No!" I say. "It's the Hitler *Youth!*"

"It's the Hitler *Jews!*" he argues.

"Hitler doesn't want us!" I declare. "He hates us! It's the Hitler *Youth!*"

"It's the Hitler *Jews!*" Otto insists. Hitler Jews, Hitler *Juden*; Hitler Youth, Hitler *Jugend*. We continue to argue like that all the way home, like . . . like . . . almost ten-year-olds. It was the only real argument Otto and I ever had. Some few months later, Otto and his parents flee to America— just before *Kristallnacht*. Click . . . click . . . click . . .

November 9 to 10, 1938. *Kristallnacht*, the Night of Broken Glass. Krefeld, *Bismarckstrasse* 118. It's already two o'clock in the morning, the next day. All is calm, all is quiet, in this unholy night. We live on the second floor. I have a room, on the third floor. Another month, and I'll be eleven years old.

Now I am sound asleep. Suddenly there is a pounding, a loud, constant pounding and I wake up—a pounding, a terrible pounding at the front door.

"Open up, open up, or we'll break the door down!"

I run to the banister. I see my parents on the second floor below, frightened, hesitant. My father wants to go down, but my mother stops him. He just had an operation around his eyes and she does not want anything to happen to him. Before he can argue, she is down the steps.

"Open up, open up, or we'll break it down!"

"I'm coming, I'm coming," my mother calls out.

I am scared. I rush into my room, grab a small suitcase and rush out again. "*Vati, Vati!*" I call down. "Daddy, Daddy! If they take you, I'm going with you!"

My mother has reached the door. As she opens it she and the door are hurled against the wall. Nazis, half a dozen of them, with rifles, rush up the steps. My mother follows. I come down. We all meet on the second floor. They want to lock us into the kitchen.

"No, no," my mother screams, "we won't be locked up!"

We run around through the rooms, one after the other. As we come into the study, my father rushes to his desk, with the head Nazi close behind. My father opens a drawer, pulls out the Iron Cross, his medal from World War I, holds it up, and shouts, "Is this the thanks I get for having served the fatherland?"

The Nazi and he stand face to face. What now? Curses: "Damned, dirty Jew!"? The butt of the rifle in the face? Or an even quicker, final answer: a bullet in the head?

For a moment, a long moment, silence, deadly silence, their eyes locked for an eternity. Suddenly, the Nazi turns, signals his men silently, leads them down the stairs, out of the house, and into the black night, without breaking one dish.

Day breaks but it isn't over. They come to take my father away to the concentration camp along with all the other Jewish men of the city. He is at the doctor's. They never come back for him and let him go.

Kristallnacht . . . throughout Germany (and Austria). Nazis murder ninety-one Jews, destroy houses and stores, burn synagogues, send 30,000 Jews to concentration camps, abuse and torture them, murdering 2,500. Click . . . click . . . click . . .

Rabbi Bluhm is arrested and sent to Dachau. A few months later, he is released, on promise that he would leave Germany, promptly. He and Hanna flee to America, settling in Amarillo, Texas, as spiritual leader of a Jewish congregation. Click . . . click . . . click . . .

The Meyer family, with their two teenage daughters, has no place to live. The Nazis destroyed their house, during *Kristallnacht*. They come to us, looking for shelter. We know that we will leave Germany in just a few months, in April. We offer them our apartment. The Meyers, too, manage to get to America. Years later, the daughters, now married, move to Los Angeles, with their mother. We are reunited and become members of the same Jewish congregation. Click . . . click . . . click . . .

I go to a Jewish school all these years. Two months, before *Kristall-nacht*, I enter public school, a Gymnasium. Most of the students are Gentiles. During recess, I retreat to the farthest corner of the playground. I make myself as inconspicuous as possible. I am scared, constantly. The day after *Kristallnacht*, I am kicked out, because I am a Jew.

January 1, 1939. It is now law that Jews take on identifiable Jewish middle names: Israel for men and boys, Sarah for women and girls. I become Rolf Israel Gompertz.

The Jewish Star of David becomes mandatory in 1941. It must be worn on the outer garment, when outdoors. If not, you were shot on the spot, or arrested and sent to a concentration camp. By this time, we were in America.

1933, there are 66 million Germans in Germany. 500,000—less than 1 percent—are Jewish. 150,000 Jews flee Germany by 1938. 115,000 more flee following *Kristallnacht*. Click . . . click . . . click . . .

To come to America, you needed a quota number from the American government. We get such a number through Rabbi Bluhm. It does not go into effect until 1939. We also need an American sponsor who will assume financial responsibility for us for five years. Anna Coffee Baer, a distant relative, sponsors us, and saves our lives.

We flee to America, a few months after *Kristallnacht*, the dress rehearsal for the Holocaust. We arrive June 11, 1939. We kneel down, and kiss the ground. Three months later the war starts. We have escaped on the eve of the Holocaust. World War II starts September 1, 1939. It is now too late. Click . . . click . . . click . . .

We three come with $10 apiece. It is all the money the Nazis let us to take with us. Our relative lives in Beverly Hills. We learn quickly that with only $10 apiece, you don't live in Beverly Hills. We move to Los Angeles. Click . . . click . . . click . . .

America! We arrive during summer vacation. I try to play with the kids on the block. We cannot communicate. I run home. "It's no use!" I tell my mom, crying. "I don't understand them, and they don't understand me." She assures me that things will get better, and sends me back down to play. One day, I run home and declare excitedly, "*Mutti, Mutti!* Mommy! Mommy! I can understand them now, and I don't even have to look at their mouth anymore when they speak."

School Days, American-style. No sooner do I start school than there is a spelling test. Out of fifty words, I get thirty-five . . . wrong! The next week the teacher has us write a poem, then share it with the class. Everyone is writing furiously. I can't think of a thing to say. At the last moment, inspiration strikes. I'm called on to share my poem, I declare:

> A monkey and an elephant
> They played once in a zoo,
> There came a tiger and a lion
> And both of them said, "Boo!"
> The monkey was so scared at once
> That he jumped on a tree,
> From there he looked in the lion's face
> And laughed: "Hee, Hee, Hee, Hee!"

The class explodes with laughter. I feel accepted. "Welcome to America!" Click . . . click . . . click . . .

December 1940. I have my *bar mitzvah*, the Jewish coming of age. I chant the blessings over the Torah, I read from the Prophet Zechariah. The rabbi tells me to remember God's words: "Not by might, nor by power, but by My spirit." Click . . . click . . . click . . .

My father has a hard time finding work. He delivers cleaning, sells household goods door to door, works as a shipping clerk. But the money does not cover the cost of living. My mother becomes a masseuse, to help make ends meet. In time, my father gets an administrative job in a pottery factory, in Glendale. My parents can now manage. They also pay back every penny they owe our sponsor.

It is the War Years, we lose contact with our family. How are they? Where are they?

My parents go to night school to study for their citizenship. Five years after arrival, they become proud Americans. So do I (derivatively).

January 30, 1933. Hitler comes to power. He institutes the Third Reich. He declares that it will last a thousand years.

May 7, 1945. Twelve years later. Nazi Germany surrenders unconditionally. Hitler and the thousand-year Reich are dead.

Half of our family was murdered: My grandmother, Nanni Herrmann, Auschwitz, murdered. My aunt, Grete von Minden, murdered. My aunt and uncle, Irma and Siegfried Stern, and their three children, Werner, Kurt, Irmgard, and her baby, murdered.

Helene Herrmann, saved on a Children's Transport to Palestine, now Israel. My uncle and aunt, Max and Alma Herrmann, survived. My uncle and aunt, Otto and Ilse Herrmann, Theresienstadt, Auschwitz, survived.

I hate Germany! I hate Germans! I want nothing more to do with them! Click . . . click . . . click . . .

1946–48. I enlist in the U.S. Army. I am sent to Washington DC to translate captured German documents. Upon discharge, I receive Commendation from the Quartermaster General for my work.

1948–53. I start UCLA on the GI Bill of Rights, study English literature, American literature, philosophy; I write my first book of poetry, featuring "The Search: A Song of Man and the Universe." I receive my B.A. degree (1952) followed by an M.A. degree (1953).

1953. After college, I apply for work at NBC.

"What skills do you have?" the personnel manager asks.

"I write sonnets," I say.

"We're not hiring poets right now," she says. "Do you have any marketable skills?" I look puzzled. "Well," she says. "Can you—type?"

"Yes," I say.

"Would you consider joining our typing pool?"

"Yes," I say, eagerly.

I take the typing test—and flunk it! I cannot even get a job as a typist.

UCLA notifies me that a weekly newspaper in Torrance, CA, is looking for an editor. I apply. I find out that there is no editorial staff; I would be the editorial department, and would have to do—everything.

I need the job. I take the job. Then, I panic. I had only had one semester of high school journalism. I race back to my teacher and blurt out: "Miss Hov, you must teach me everything you know, in one week!" She has me come to her office every evening after work, for a week. She administers journalistic First Aid. I survive.

1957. Carol and I marry. Rabbi Bluhm, comes from Amarillo to conduct the ceremony. "Live," he says, "in the beauty of holiness."

I look for a new and better job. I try NBC, again! This time I have a marketable skill. I avoid the Personnel Department. I contact the Press and Publicity Department, directly. I am hired, as a publicist. In time, I become a publicity director. I stay thirty years. I also teach publicity and media relations, at UCLA Extension, for thirty-two years.

Carol and I raise two sons and a daughter . . . and I keep on writing, writing, writing, in my spare time.

July 16, 1962. Rabbi Bluhm dies. My mother and I fly to Amarillo.

"You welcomed me into the world," I say in my eulogy. "Now, as you leave the world, and go to God, I come to say good-bye."

On parting, Hanna gives me some of Rabbi's Jewish books, in Hebrew and German, and his dark blue, wool overcoat. *Zichrono tzadik liv'racha.* May his memory be for a blessing.

January 22, 1983. My mother dies, at eighty-four. *Zichronah liv'racha.* May her memory be for a blessing.

1983, Germany. Religion teacher Renate Starck inspires her public high school students, in Krefeld, to write to us, find out what happened to us under the Nazis, and what has become of us. The letters go out, the replies come back and are published in 1986.[2] Click . . . click . . . click . . .

1986. I find out about the Letter Exchange. They had failed to contact me! They had missed me! I feel a great sense of . . . *relief!* I am glad that they hadn't found me! I am glad that I don't have to write!

"You must write, too!" an inner voice whispers.

"No!" I say. "No!"

"Yes!" the voice insists.

"I don't have to!" I argue.

"Yes, you do!"

"The Letter Exchange is over!"

"So?"

"It's too late!" I say gleefully.

"It is never too late!" the voice declares.

"I can't!" I say. "It's too hard to write in German. My German isn't good enough any more."

"You still know German."

"It takes too long. It takes two, three times as long to write in German as to write in English."

"Then you take two and three times as long."

"But . . ."

"You're making excuses."

And then I face the real truth. "I'm afraid," I admit. "I'm afraid."

---

2. Note: The actual date of their publication was 1984.

You see, it's easy to deal with people at a distance and in the abstract. You can hate them, avoid them, ignore them. But what happens when you make contact again with actual human beings? How do you meet again? What do you write? What do you say? What should my attitude be? Am I expected to forgive? To forget? Click . . . click . . . click . . .

I check the Bible. I search my faith for answers. It is written: "Remember what Amalek did unto you; you shall never forget it!" (Deut 25:17, 19). We must not forget, from Amalek to Haman to Hitler.

But God also says: "Cast away from you all your transgressions, wherein ye have transgressed, and make you a new heart and a new spirit, for why will you die. . . . For I have no pleasure in the death of him who dies; . . . wherefore turn yourselves and live . . . (Ezek 18:31–32).

"But if the wicked turn from all his sins and do what is lawful and right, he shall surely live, he shall not die" (Ezek 18:27).

"Turn . . . and live!" (Ezek 18:32). Germans and Germany, too?

God also says: "The son shall not bear the iniquity of the father, neither shall the father bear the iniquity of the son" (Ezek 18:20). If I believe, then I must believe this, too.

1986. One, two new generations since the Nazi time. Innocent! Not guilty! Click . . . click . . . click . . .

But those who "did it," those who lived from 1933 to 1945, I can hate them, can't I? Most Germans participated, actively or passively. But there were those who didn't.

Aunt Alma, my uncle's Christian wife, is ordered to appear before the Gestapo, The Secret Police.

"So, when will you divorce your Jewish husband?" they demand.

"I have no intention of ever divorcing my Jewish husband!" she declares.

She is summoned again and again. Each time they ask the same question. Each time she gives the same answer. She senses that this won't go on forever. Sooner or later, something will happen, and it won't be good. She moves her husband into the basement of her sister's house where he stays all day, day in, day out, week in, week out. He comes out only at night, for fresh air.

That arranged, Aunt Alma heads to the Gestapo. "I have come to report that my husband committed suicide," she declares.

"Good riddance!" the Nazi replies.

Case closed. The cover story works. Alma and Max survive Hitler and the war.

Tom G., our German English-teacher, calls on us the day after *Kristallnacht*.

"What can I do?" he asks.

"Would you save some important papers of ours for the time being?" my father requests.

"Yes," the teacher says, and does.

There were those who resisted, there were those who helped, in ways small and large, individually and collectively, at the risk of their lives, at the cost of their lives.

Collective hatred is wrong, collective guilt is worse. Click . . . click . . . click . . .

But what about Hitler, Himmler, Heydrich, Goering, Goebbels, Streicher, Bormann, Mengele, Eichmann, Ilse Koch? What about all the eager Germans, all the participants, all the willing ones?

I leave them to history and to God. What will God do? God alone knows. Click . . . click . . . click . . .

1986. I write my letter. "Dear Krefelder Friends." It is the hardest letter I have ever written. Click . . . click . . . click . . .

1986. After three years, Pastor Helmut Starck, President of the Association for Christian-Jewish Cooperation, succeeds in getting the city, and the Association of Christian Churches, to invite us back to Germany. Click . . . click . . . click . . .

August 6, 1987. My father dies, at ninety-seven. *Zichrono liv'racha.* May his memory be a blessing.

1987. Krefeld. Some 1,600 Jews once lived here. Half were murdered, the others fled to the four corners of the earth. We are invited back. Some return. Others will not set foot on German soil again.

I return. I stay with the Gruenbergs, a Christian family. I tell our story to students, participate in encounter sessions, attend Christian and Jewish services. It is an intense Week of Encounter, a life-changing experience for me. In a city that once was a place of evil for us, I find good, decent human beings again. Click . . . click . . . click . . .

November 9, 1988. I am invited back to deliver a forty-five-minute keynote speech, in German, on the 50th anniversary of *Kristallnacht*. What do I say?

I face two new, startling questions. Whom do I speak for? The six million? I have no right to speak for them. Whom, then, do I speak for? I have no right to speak for anyone, not even my parents. I can only speak for myself, then and now. Click . . . click . . . click . . .

And then comes the question that has never occurred to me and that blows my mind: If I had not been born a German Jew, if I had been born a German Gentile, if I had been born a Christian German, how would I have acted during the Nazi period, as a young boy, as a teenager, as a young adult, as an older adult? Would I have been a conformist, or would I have shown courage? Would I have just gone along, or offered active resistance? Would I have participated, from the Hitler Youth to Auschwitz? I come to a terrifying, humbling conclusion: I do not know how I would have acted! We never really know how we will act, in a crisis, until we are tested. Click . . . click . . . click . . .

I write my speech. It is the hardest speech I have ever written. It is the hardest speech I have ever delivered. I recount the facts, fears, feelings, and thoughts that brought me, us, to this moment. Finally, I declare:

> We German Jews and German Gentiles are now bound together by *Kristallnacht* and the Holocaust for all eternity.[3] But our story should not and must not end there. We are human beings. We stand here together now. We regard the past. We cannot forgive, we must not forget, but we can transform. We can, we should, we must transform the past for the sake of life. That is *our* triumph.
>
> And if there is a central truth to be snatched from the flames of *Kristallnacht* and the Holocaust, it is this: That we must always remember our common humanity. In case of conflict, in case we are forced to choose between ideology and our common humanity, we must choose humanity!
>
> Can we build bridges again? Yes, we can, we must, because after all is said and done there is only one answer left: Love and Reconciliation.

Click . . . click . . . click

November 9, 2008. The 70th anniversary of *Kristallnacht*, The Night of Broken Glass. Isn't this ancient history? I wish to God it were! But genocides are still with us, all over the world, threats to and violations of human rights and civil liberties are still with us, here, and all over the world. Jews,

---

3. In its early version, this speech mentioned "Jews and Germans," which Rolf later corrected to "German Jews and German Gentiles."

too, are targeted again, in vile and shameless ways, for hatred, defamation, and death. It could drive us to despair, but despair is not a good answer.

Martin Niemoeller found the answer; he learned it the hard way. He was a famous German U-boat commander, a hero of World War I. An ardent admirer and follower of Hitler in the 1920s, Niemoeller became a Protestant minister. Hitler had great plans for him. In 1933, Hitler comes to power. By 1934, Pastor Niemoeller realizes the big mistake he has made in supporting Hitler. He now preaches against him and the Nazis. By 1937, Hitler has had enough. He has Niemoeller arrested, tried for "abuse of the pulpit," "crimes against the State," and sent to concentration camps, one after the other. Niemoeller survives. After the war, whenever he spoke of these matters, he said:

> They came first for the Communists, and I didn't speak out, be-
> cause I wasn't a Communist. Then they came for the Social Demo-
> crats, and I didn't speak out, because I wasn't a Social Democrat.
> Then they came for the Trade Unionists, and I didn't speak out,
> because I wasn't a Trade Unionist. Then they came for the Jews,
> and I didn't speak out, because I wasn't a Jew. Then they came for
> me, and, by that time, no one was left to speak out.

Niemoeller has given us the answer. We must speak up, speak out, and act, in whatever ways we can, small or large. We must speak up, speak out, and act against genocide, for human rights and civil liberties, especially on behalf of individuals and groups who are different from us. We must do so for their sake, and we must do so ultimately for the sake of our own souls. Click . . . click . . . click . . .

What can we do when bad things happen to us? What can we do with pain and suffering? What can we do with evil? We can transform them.

2004. I am contacted by a young pastor, Kai Schaefer, from Krefeld, who works with youth at the local occupational college (Berufskolleg Krefeld-Uerdingen). We have not met before. He is teaching about the Ho-locaust and he wants a connection with someone from his hometown.

I am now a writer, with five books in publication. Pastor Schaefer and I correspond by phone and e-mail and quickly become friends. Since he speaks and reads English, I soon send him a copy of my book, entitled, *A Jewish Novel about Jesus*. I tell him that I wrote this book for several reasons:

- to give Christians a better understanding of Jesus, the Jew, and of Ju-daism, which inspired him and out of which he came;

- to give Jews a better understanding of Jesus;

- to put to rest once and for all the pernicious charge of Christ-Killers leveled against all Jews, then and for the last 2,000 years, laying the groundwork for the Holocaust and Hitler's "Final Solution";

- I explain that I do not wish to undermine Christian faith or convert Jews to Christianity;

- I say that I wrote the book so Jews and Christians could live together, side by side, respectful of one another, in dignity and peace;

- I say that, at its deepest level, the book is my answer to Hitler, *Kristallnacht*, and the Holocaust.

After reading it, he calls me: "This book must be published in Germany. I would like to try getting it published here, with your permission."

I give permission, gladly and gratefully. I first considered writing the book in 1952, while still in college, and then wrote it from 1963 to 1966. It was published in English in 1977, under the title: *My Jewish Brother Jesus*.

In 2010, it is published in German under the same title, with the words reversed: *Jesus, mein jüdischer Bruder*.

Spring 2011. Germany celebrates Jewish Culture Days (*Jüdische Kulturstage*) in fifty-two cities, and, for the fourth year, in Krefeld. The Culture Bureau (*Kulturbüro*) of Krefeld invites me back to speak about my life, and to present readings from my Jesus novel. I deliver fifteen speeches, readings, and conversations in Krefeld and other cities, at churches, schools, and the new Krefeld synagogue and community center. (On my return home, I send Rabbi Bluhm's books, which I had received, to the rabbi of the new synagogue and congregation in Krefeld.) I begin each of my German readings and presentations with the following words:

> It is a wonder that I am here. It is a wonder that I, a Jew born in Germany, am here. It is a wonder that my parents and I were able to flee to America. It is a wonder that I am now here for the third time. It is a wonder that my book, *My Jewish Brother Jesus*, has been published in Germany. It is a wonder that there are Jews again living in Germany, that there are these Jewish Culture Days in Germany, and that I was invited to participate in them.

Now, at eighty-six, in the winter of my life, I ask myself: "Menachem ben Shimshon v'Sarah, Rolf, son of Oscar and Selma Gompertz, what did you do, as a survivor? What was your transformative answer to Hitler, *Kristallnacht*, and the Holocaust?"

And I reply: "I lived as a Jew, I wrote books, about Love, I bore witness." Click . . . click . . . click . . .

So, finally, what's it all about? Life?

It starts with a miracle, birth! It ends with a mystery, death! And all points in between are miracle and mystery!

My friends, my friends, we are more than we think we are! We are more than men and women, husbands and wives, parents and children, strangers and lovers! We are more than our jobs and our job descriptions! We are special, we are unique, each one of us! We are sparks of spirit, sailing through the universe, stopping here and there for a momentary connection.

But we have only one permanent connection: The Divine Connection. We are here to improve the world, to redeem the world, to hold the world together, wherever we stand, however we can. We are here to serve, and to reflect, the image of God! Then every act, every act, can be offered as a service to God, and every life, every life, can be lived as a service to God!

What greater role can we play, what greater value can our lives have than to love and serve God, in whatever way we can, through the love and service of our fellow human beings.

God said: *Lo v'chayil, v'lo v'koach, ki im-b'ruchi.* "Not by might, nor by power, but by My spirit" (Zech 4:6). That spirit is Love. Love is reciprocal: Giving and receiving, loving and being loved . . .

Give, and you shall receive. Love, and you shall be loved. Law and Justice are also Love. They are the fairness of Love . . .

And when human beings fail us, God is still with us and there for us.

Where was God from 1933 to 1945? Where was God—at Auschwitz? That is not the question. We have free will. The question is: Where was humanity?

Keep the faith. Love, blessings, and Shalom. Click . . . click . . . click . . .

One more thing: a Jewish blessing, chanted in Hebrew, spoken in German, now in English:

Baruch atah adonai, elohe'nu melech haolam, sh'heche'yanu, v'kiyi'manu, v'higi'yanu, las'man haseh.

Gelobt seist du, O Gott, unser Gott, Gott der Welt, der uns hat am Leben erhalten, der uns hat bewahrt, der uns hat erreichen lassen diese Zeit.

Praised are you, O Lord, our God, God of the universe, who has kept us in life, preserved us, and enabled us to reach this time!

Shalom.

14

Rolf Gompertz's First Diary, Extracts

At three points in his life between the years 1945 and 1977, Rolf kept a diary or journal, allowing him to reflect upon what was going on in his life. Those diaries provide valuable resources for understanding the contours of Rolf's life and appreciating his multifaceted character. Extracts of those diaries appear in the next three sections of this book.[1]

This first diary, a very long one of over 20,000 words, was begun on December 8 of 1945, just before Rolf completed high school. It was completed on April 9 of 1953, just before Rolf took his first job as editor of the newspaper in Torrance, CA.

Spanning the seven-and-a-half year period when Rolf was seventeen through twenty four, the entries in this journal change noticeably from start to finish in one way—that is, there is a certain enchantment with girls at the beginning which, toward the end, loses some of its poignancy. The early heady days of naiveté give way to a more settled and staid Rolf. This is probably due to the fact that the excited nervousness about the opposite sex early on gives way to steadier and deeper relationships with women later on. Whereas a little heart-flutter is recorded in some detail in the early entries, in the later entries a stable relationship simply appears on the pages in a fashion that surprises the reader for its lack of back-narrative—a girlfriend simply appears on the pages in a matter-of-fact, taken-for granted

1. The full diaries, along with other literary memorabilia, are available in the "Rolf Gompertz Archive," held in the Simon Wiesenthal Center and Museum of Tolerance in Los Angeles.

fashion without the reader knowing who she is or how the long-established relationship has taken root.

The obvious constant throughout these years is the allure of literature. Rolf had an obvious love of literature that, in good Shakespearean fashion, was both his strength and his weakness. On the one hand, it drove him to immerse himself in his studies of literature, to the extent that he excelled and stood out from the rest of his peer group in both his high school and his undergraduate work. On the other hand, having crafted a solid reputation as someone with a bright future, during his time as a Masters student at UCLA Rolf began to delve into extensive writing projects of his own that he felt passionate about but which inevitably distracted him greatly from his university requirements. This resulted in a downturn in his academic performance and a change of direction in life, with his shift into the world of newspaper editing after his completion of the Masters degree in 1954.

Along with this, another constant is his desire to be a writer, to be involved in the beauty of literature and to make a contribution to the world. In these years, Rolf seems to have undertaken the writing of a novel and an extensive amount of poetry, some of which ended up in *To Life! To Love!* Some poetry is included in the journal itself.

What is perceptible within this journal is his growing commitment to developing his Jewish identity, alongside a deepening philosophical pursuit of truth and meaning.

The following are extracts comprising approximately one third of the journal.

December 8, 1945

Good evening diary. My name is Rolf Gompertz. You and I will see a lot of each other from now on, I hope. You see, there are so many things I want to tell you, and I want somebody to remember them for me. I'm a very strange character, you'll find out. It's too bad you and I didn't get acquainted with each other before. I've had many interesting stories to tell you. . . .

I'm a dreamer, diary. I see everything so clear and beautiful. I have no real worries. Fairyland is my home and all the people with whom I associate are citizens of my realm where I am king. . . .

I'm often very worried of what will become of me. I am so idealistic—I am a dreamer. I . . . often wonder whether I'll be successful. I'm so impatient, diary; I want everything to happen at once. I take everything so serious and am often deeply hurt because of it. . . .

Sometimes it worries me that I can't think of marriage until ten years hence. I have plans for me, for my profession. I think I have a message to give the world. I must not let anything get in the way. I have to think of my family. I wonder if I'm right by saying that it is detrimental to my ideals to consider anything else but my purpose here for the next decade. If only my family were secure, I would not worry about myself and my future so much. Maybe it is meant to be this way. Maybe this is the path to my creation, maybe. . . .

I have so many conflicting natures. I try to take everything lightly, to regard things lightly, but I ponder too much. This makes me often very unhappy. I try to cover it up as best as I can, usually by appearing free and easy, joking, and pretending not to have a care in the world. It is only I who know how hard that often is.

Now that I am about to graduate, I am a bit uncertain. According to the teachers and my class, I am the one most likely to succeed. Yet I have strange forebodings. I am undecided, I am half as sure of myself as they think I am, as far as I am concerned, my future looks still very hazy. But I am happy today. I shall not worry. Life is young, I am young—the future, maybe, is still bright. Good night, diary, you've made me happy.

December 11, 1945

Remember when I told you about that most beautiful girl I had taken to the ball? [At this point, Rolf talks about how that came to nothing.] . . .

Miss Keyes, the most wonderful and intelligent English teacher I've ever had or will have, told me today she'd love to meet my parents and wants to invite us over for dinner. I think she is the image of Geoffrey Chaucer.

December 28, 1945

When the sun comes out, Jerry will take pictures of me dressed in my Indian costume. I'll have them taken when I make fire . . . and a few posed with my Yucca pole. I'll probably wear just Levis, my war bonnet and ermine skins, a pearl necklace, crocodile tooth, shell necklace, aluminum bracelet, cow's horn, war-paint, and maybe a blanket. It really looks good.

I don't know what's the matter with me, diary, but at times my imagination is very active. Last night, dressed up as an Indian, I performed a Spear Dance which I originated. I sang my own rhythm and words to it, and it made me feel very good . . .

I wonder whether I'll ever be able to make use of my imagination? . . .

Diary, do you think I am a dreamer or putting on an act? I often have this feeling but I tell myself that is my business. You know, I often find it very interesting to study myself. That is the reason I'm telling you about me. I want somebody to remember me so that many years from now when I have settled down, I'll remember exactly what I acted and felt like.

January 1, 1946

I am so confused. Am I supposed to be that way? Sometimes I think that because of this, I'll someday write my greatest book. But then, when I try to analyze myself and this book, I have not the slightest idea of how to go about it. Often I think I'm just acting this way to be interesting and create attention. Maybe that's true. There is conceit involved in it—I'm almost sure. I seem to love to act, to put on a show. . . .

One of the greatest hardships I endure is the constant reminder by teachers, friends, and relatives that there is not a doubt of my success. They place such great confidence and hope in me. I, myself, am so, so doubtful often. I'm afraid mine is just an empty dream, out of a fairy book. Everything I do, everything I have planned is like a drama, like something which I want badly, yet feeling that life is never meant that way. Today, for the first time clearly, I can compare my life, thoughts, and deeds to something describable. I am living in a fairy world full of drama. Everyone I know is an actor in it—I am an actor and the producer. Life is often hard but never ultimately tragic. That is the world I live in now. It is the world I love. That is the world that starts my imagination going, that gives my pen words, that fills my soul with happiness. (That is the world I turn to whenever I am discontented, when I am in need of an understanding heart.) I am lost without that world. It is so beautiful to me. I want to dream, all the time, dream and in these dreams, I am the actor and that world is the stage. . . . There are times when I am separated from this world. . . . All I know when I live in it is that it is beautiful and that, if ever I shall write, it can only be about this world. Often I long for an understanding heart. I know my parents always have it. But there are times when I want to share my feelings with someone my age, somebody with as much imagination as I have, somebody who will want to listen and understand. I am often afraid to want to have a person like that. I take things too serious. . . . I could not ask anyone to be true and patient with and to me for such a long time; I know in case anything should ever happen to separate us, it would hurt me too much—I take things so serious. I know I could never think of marriage until I had finished my studying and proven myself worthy of a wife. I could not ask anyone to live with me when I had not yet established myself—and be happy. I often long for just a friend and companion. . . . I could not expect a sacrifice so great from anyone. I think that it is for this reason that I am often sad, dissatisfied, although I lack no material thing. My head often dreams such fantastic dreams—thus hurting my heart. . . . I have everything I want; only I am a bit lonely.

January 5, 1946

I have come to the conclusion, that if I am ever to write anything of a creative nature, a pleasant friend is as necessary to me as is food itself. A decent girl eases my spirits and makes me happy.

As concerns other subjects, I believe I am also too much of an idealist. . . . There is too much make-believe, too much fairyland with me. I have everything planned. It never happens that way. This, too, often leaves me very sad and disappointed. It is hard, very hard, at times to ease my mourning spirits. Outwardly I appear cured. . . . Inwardly, however, I feel a pain, I feel very much alone. . . .

To put it into a short phrase, the thing that will work toward any success I wish to reach is an understanding heart.

January 20, 1946

. . . I have always been rather bashful of girls, and not until recently have I overcome this feeling. A few years ago, just the thought of talking to a "female of the opposite sex" sent goose pimples up and down my spine and heat waves would follow this. My first date was in 1943—the time I graduated from Jr. High School. (I must say, although I was bashful to ask girls for a date, once I overcame this fear, I'd always ask good-looking girls. It must be the beast in me.) I asked her to go to the show with me, and she accepted. You don't know how nervous I was from the time I asked her until it was all over. I spent exactly 35 cents on her and really felt as if I had accomplished something. I don't know whether she trusted me; we turned around and there, in back of us, was her brother. She needn't have been worried. I was more nervous than an actor is at his first performance. . . . That was the last time I took her out. I had a strange feeling that R.G. [Rolf Gompertz] was not too welcome, and made my exit silently. This was my first active romance! . . .

It was the night of the Prom (not the last, but the next to last—June 1945). I had asked a girl whom I didn't know too well, but who was a nice, decent, intelligent, girl. To make matters short, after the dance we rode with another couple whom we knew and after stopping in at a restaurant, the fellow (20 years old) decided to show us Los Angeles from a mountain top. We arrived up there listening to the radio. As you can probably guess, I was scared stiff. We sat there holding hands (which, by the way, was a rather new experience having done it for the first time only a week previous on a date with Hannah). The girl was bending my fingers back and forth and to all other directions. She told me to relax and feel more at ease. I told her I was very comfortable listening to the beautiful music. Occasionally she would lean her head against my shoulder, but I would ignore all advances. I was a perfect gentleman! If I had wanted to, I guess I could have (to use a very awkward and slangy expression) necked with her. (I don't like that expression.) There were two reasons why I didn't. First and foremost—I was scared stiff! It was all I could do to keep my heart from jumping out of my mouth, much less indulge in that. My five wits (or are there six) were running around in circles in my head, and my blood vessels were working harder than Xavier Cougat's band. I was miserable. The other reason, which is probably the higher as far as morals is concerned, is that I was primarily concerned with the girl's and my reputation. Her reputation was more important than momentary pleasure—and so was mine. As far as I'm concerned, I could not have accounted for any other actions than I took that night to my conscience. It would have haunted me. It just didn't seem right to me to sit there kissing and smooching away. What helped me resist temptation whatsoever was that I regarded myself as a young Indian brave who was not allowed to kiss a girl until he had proven himself to be a warrior. I thought if a girl is the kind I want, she'll respect me for this attitude; if she is angry, she is not my type! (The couple in the front seat did not smooch.) . . .

I often tell Mother that what I miss most here are real friends who are more than just acquaintances, friends who understand each other and are open with each other. The trouble here is, I have friends but who in turn can't offer the spiritual understanding. . . .

Add to the description of a perfect girl that she should be religious and know a bit about Jewish customs. This is one of my shortcomings and I want my children to be brought up with a good religious background.

January 25, 1946

Today I received my diploma from Belmont High School. I have experienced every type of sensation within the past twenty-four hours. It was impossible to sleep the night before the graduation. The opening words of my speech constantly repeated themselves in my mind. I was very tired the 24th and felt as if butterflies kept flying around in my stomach. This day was one of the most nervous I've ever spent or will spend in my life. I was afraid of my speech, recalling that once before at an oratorical contest I'd stumbled and lost my memory for a few seconds. This is one of the worst sensations that can come to you. You begin to think too far ahead of your place and all at once your mind goes blank. You stand there, while all kinds of thoughts enter your mind—why did you do this, what will the audience think, how did it happen? Even if you continue again, this accident will haunt not only the rest of your speech, but also your mind.

This was the greatest fear I had. Would I stumble again. I told myself I would not and could not. But you might. . . . How embarrassed and discouraged I'd be! It happened once before, it can happen again!

How happy I was when, for the first time in my speaking career, I recited my oration without a single mistake. Every sentence, every word was repeated as I had written it. This gave me the greatest satisfaction I could have. It was worth everything to me. It seems that once I stood before the mike, I had completely ignored all thoughts of fear; and trying hard to keep my mind solely on the speech, I succeeded in doing this. This was the happiest graduation present I could have received because I knew now that I could talk without notes and without errors. If I had failed, it would have left a great complex in my mind. . . .

For the first time in a long time, I enjoyed myself that night. Irene and I went to the Coconut Grove and spent a most lovely evening there. She looked like a picture out of fairyland—lovely as a rippling stream.

What also left a lasting impression of beauty upon me was when we sat on a bench in front of her house—the scenery was perfect. It reminded me of a little village scene—a small hillside dotted with trees and bushes, a primitive bench, and twinkling stars gazing peacefully upon two lonely yet happy people. There was something of restful beauty there which I hated to disturb—something sweet and lovely which my heart had been craving for a long time. Yes, I felt contented and could have sat on endlessly doing nothing. It was a beautiful feeling. I don't know what Irene thinks of me—I wouldn't blame her if she thought I act rather childish. I think I do. I account for that by saying that that is the way I ease my spirits. It is a hard thing to stay serious and scholarly day after day. Whenever I have the opportunity then to relax, I try to make up for the leisure pleasures I miss while engaged in my work. This, I believe, accounts for my carefree and often silly actions when at rest. . . .

It is seldom that I have felt so humble as I do today. It was a rather sad day for me. Not only was I awarded great honors by my teachers, but what they said left me greatly awed. I feel so overcome by their high hopes for me that it is difficult to write of it without a strange feeling in my heart. I feel so utterly worthless of all their elaborate praise—they place such great confidence in me. Imagine—they count it an honor to have known me. But after all, is it not their example and efforts which brought this about? Is it not their willingness to help where the need was greatest which won my admiration? If it be counted an honor to know me, it is nothing but that which they have helped plant. How can I ever feel myself greater than those people who have helped me steer a straight course. Is this sentiment not another proof of their greatness? They are willing to credit me with that which they themselves have earned. Is that not friendship?

I feel humble today. I wish I could stay where I had to leave. Parting from this heritage is like losing the greatest friend on earth. I shall miss their kind advice and understanding smiles ere many moons have passed. Whatever happens in the future will happen because of a result of their teaching. If I should succeed or fail, their message will be constantly borne within my heart. They, to my knowledge, succeeded to educate me—that is, they have drawn out of me the forces which they so deeply planted. It is not I who deserve honor, but rather they without whose guidance I might never have reached the position I so humbly accept.

January 27, 1946

[Here Rolf recalls the evening with Irene, first recorded on January 25.]
The happiest moment I've ever had was when she invited me to sit down a while on that crude little bench. It still makes my spirits soar thinking about it. I regard that action as one of reciprocal friendship—it was such a beautiful gesture. I would have liked to kiss her that night, yet refrained—partly for fear and partly for courtesy. I hope to sit on that little bench again—soon, it is so beautiful.

February 8, 1946

My greatest strength is my greatest weakness—I take *everything* too seriously!

March 23, 1946

The dreamer travels down a lonely, deserted road—a road of many, countless dreams. No matter what it is that makes him dream—whether it be love or hate, laughter or sorrow, life or death—he must travel his road alone. At times a friendly wanderer will glimpse in shortly upon his pondering (thoughts)—'tis nothing but a fleeting glimpse.

The dreamer is not happy, not contented. He sees that which he dreams [about] but cannot have. He feels that which he desires yet is withheld from him. Never is he happy, because he dreams. Whether this changes with love, I cannot say. Ere this should be, he will have dreamed a thousand dreams, and loved a dozen loves, and lived a dozen lives. (Yea, suffered that which but his dreams unveiled.) Then, maybe then, will he find life upon a deserted road. This is the penalty, the destiny of dreams.

> See I a vision? See I the sky?
> Seems like the heavens are drifting by.
> Feel I a kindness? Feel I your glee?
> Seems like the stars 'gain are smiling at me.
>
> Are you of mortal born or but a dream
> Radiant as sunlight? Bright golden beam!
> What hallucination, what foolish farce,
> brought back the darkness, brought forth the stars?

What? Have we met but to be torn apart?

Soon you will leave me, soon we must part.

You tear out my senses, you've captured my heart.

In glen and in forest, on land or on sea,

My heart I'll recover when you'll come to me.

April 17, 1946

He who is dissatisfied will presently take actions. What the result will be is usually the difference between good and evil.

July 22, 1949

I arrived at the end of the novel today! I began it with Monet's return, on the 16th July, and finished today! The rest of the novel is still greatly in outline or poor form due to a lack of fluency in writing and integration of thoughts when I began. In the meantime, since having finished "The Search," the title poem, I have acquired much knowledge and experience in the harmonizing and integrating of ideas. However, I was particularly amazed by my progress with this section. Within seven days I completed it, an amount of writing equivalent—if my calculations were correct—to 9,300 words, i.e., about 1,300 a day! I could not help but recall Thomas Edison's comment regarding creative work that it was 99% perspiration and only 1% inspiration. I think that my performance of the last seven days was the closest I have ever come to pure unalloyed inspired writing. The thoughts just seemed to flow on paper and even the various transition periods—when one part had been written and the next one had to be thought about—seemed to glide into the shadows with a minimum of friction. I know that it must have been the subject matter that did it. The impressions were so powerful, so lasting, so beautiful that is seemed truly as if the gods sang!

I think that there shall hardly be any revisions necessary as a result. All the other parts of course need a great deal. The poem needs some refining and some additions in places, but it is pretty good as it stands. It will not take much work. The novel, however, needs quite a bit of work still and it is that project that I want to concentrate on for the rest of the summer. Some other poems which I have fairly well in mind—or at least thought about—still must be written. They are short enough to hold over for the period when my time is more limited. The discourse on poetry and the poet still must be written.

July 23, 1949

[Here Rolf speaks of meeting with an old friend, Steven Orey, whom he had known two years earlier when they had been in the U.S. Army together; see also footnote 36 in chapter 8 above.]

. . . Two years ago my beliefs were rightly shaken at the foundations by this remarkable person. I was on the defensive throughout, uncertain as to Right and Wrong, Good or Bad, God or no God. The tables, I feel, are turned. For the first time in my life I feel that I hold true, unshatterable convictions. I feel as if I have pierced the very depth of darkness and come up with answers which still seem fantastic to me because of the profound clarity and universality of application which they represent. I feel that there is no ambiguity of values, that there are definite principles, that there is such a thing as Truth, and that in my theories—and in my major theory from which all others are derived—there lies the Simple Answer, the type of answer that, because of its simplicity, is far superior to and far more valid than the complex. How these theories shall stand in relation to future theories I do not know. Maybe they shall be as Newton's is to Einstein's. That alone would justify them. Perhaps even these theories and Theory shall remain established for even a longer period of time.

I have not discussed these theories—these my most personal possessions, these, my Self!—with Steven. I cannot! They are mine and they must and shall not be expressed until they are ready for expression, until the finished opus is ready. Then, only, can I talk freely because then I know that the contemplation of the mind and the urgings of the soul are fully and unambiguously and indisputably recorded. . . .

On the topic of God we differed again. I have come ever closer. So a belief in something corresponding to all ideas concerning God—some Creative Being, Purpose, Cosmic Urge, even "Infinity," is a synonym for God!

August 5, 1949

. . . I have a great respect and love for all my characters. Each one of them plays a significant role. I have tried to picture them according to my two principles underlying my writing: Beauty and Truth. Truth has forced one to write the story as it is; Beauty has forced me to write the story.

September 4, 1949

I am not certain of the validity of this thought, but I want to keep it in mind as I begin my study of Shakespeare this semester: Shakespeare mirrored nature but did not interpret it. [In a note added to this entry and dated May 6 of 1950, Rolf wrote "incorrect, unjustifiable."] . . .

At the moment I am reading, among other things, Faurset's *W. Whitman, Poet of Democracy*. Whitman holds for me an extraordinary interest, and as I read I am frightened, elated, and awed at coming inevitably to the conclusion again and again that my thoughts are the clarification of his imperfect, though magnificent and prophetic, visions and that my work is the divine answer to his pleas. Wherever I look, whatever I read—from the dark and floundering notes of the literary magazine to the profound reflections of the Bible—I see my thoughts, my analysis of human needs, my reflections covering Man and the Universe verified! It is a very strange, triumphant, and immediately humbling experience. . . .

Perhaps I shall have to wage a continued and relentless battle of self-assertion until my energies are spent, perhaps my public obligations shall overwhelm me. I am not worried yet about that. I have learned that time brings its own solution.

October 9, 1949

. . . I feel now intensely that I must not stop here. I feel that I must know the literature of the past as a foundation to understand clearly the evolution of Man's nature and poetry, which express Man's emotional and intellectual development. I feel that I cannot dwell in the past, that I cannot identify myself with it that I am not and cannot be an antiquarian. I feel myself a part of the spirit of this New Age, this New World. I love, I am in love with America. I feel that I understand it, that I am identical with it. I feel that America's Cultural Birth is here or shall soon come. I feel, earnestly, passionately, intensely, that America's Cultural Declaration of Independence is about to be issued to, and acknowledged by, the world. America shall not, cannot divorce itself from the Past. Yet, the European Muse shall be like a mother. We owe to her our birth. She has guarded us and guided us, taught us and inspired us, chided us, praised, and loved us, and we love her and esteem her, and shall ever love and esteem her, with all the devotion, gratitude, and respect that a noble, virtuous, and courageous mother deserves. She and we are, in all respects, inseparable. But I think that the time of the American Muse is here! I think I see her! I think America sees her or will shortly see her! She is beautiful, animated, independently dependent, humbly proud, proudly humble. She is new, different, unique, and yet within her and about her are the beautiful, virtuous, courageous traits of her mother.

I love her, and America loves or shall love her. I must seek her, I must serve her, I must follow her, I must woo her, I must be wedded to her. I must leave the care, the protection, the safety of the mother's hearth to wander forth independent, free, alone—with her, my love—even as it is written in the earliest laws of the Bible.

I want to, and I think I can, participate in the interpretation of America, the New World, the New Age, and God.

October 17, 1949

. . . I have come to the realization now that I can write, that I have become aware now of that fact, and that I am filled with the great satisfaction that I have something to say, and a manner of saying it, and that I shall say it independent and regardless of what success or failure shall otherwise accompany it.

October 21, 1949

I think I have just definitely received the inspiration for my second book. [Here he describes the book in three sentences, then adds the following.] It shall, I think, bear the following dedication: "To those whom Fate or Fortune robbed of their dream."

October 23, 1949

There are two other poetical works which, in time, Monet Southwell [the pen-name that Rolf expected to adopt in publications] hopes to write. They shall represent the mental and spiritual development toward self-realization of Moses and Jesus of Nazareth.

November 24, 1949

I am amazed and thankful at the flashes of inspiration which have come to me lately with regard to future creative works.

In addition to the Moses- and Jesus-poems, I have decided and hope to be able to write a Hitler-poem as well. It shall serve as a glaring example of all the forces of Evil and the utterly hateful, despicable, corrupt effect upon the self, mankind, and the universe of a Perverted Ego. With these works finished, I hope to incorporate them in one volume, to be called: *Between Heaven and Hell*, the first section containing the Moses poem, the Jesus poem, and the Search, the second section containing the Hitler poem. I am using Hitler because of the intense unconditional hatred with which he must be regarded by all the forces of the universe and with which I have only now come to fully, understand and despise him. Justice cries for revenge and eternal damnation!

January 15, 1950

I know what true creation means. It means that for which one would, at any moment, pay with his life.

March 22, 1950

I perceive that some very significant problems in regard to my philosophic idea exist still, problems which need to find an explanation still, problems about whose solution I am gravely concerned. These problems are as follows:

If everything is possessed fundamentally and originally with divine goodness as I do strictly affirm (i.e., if everything, in short, is a part of God) can anything be permanently damned? Can anything be damned at all, since that would mean that God would be deprived of a part of Himself! Since this seems to be the case, what explanation other than mistaken reasoning (self-perversion) can be found for Evil and what effective argument can be framed to satisfy our sense of Justice in the face of Evil.

[Rolf then enters a problem pertaining to the issue of Death, then adds the following:] I think that in the way answers can be found to these two points there will also lie a better understanding of the Nature of Paradise and of the God of Love.

This is by no means an admission that I am doubting the truth of any conclusions. On the contrary, I am no more certain of anything as to their absolute veracity. The problems here mentioned are of the same nature as scientific problems are. A new truth—a more general, universal truth—has been discovered. There are still many questions left requiring solution. They will be solved in time. Some questions take a short time; a long time; some may evade solution until the very End—the time of Cosmic Self-Realization.

November 15, 1950

The Moses-Jesus-Hitler project is unnecessary [see entries for October 23 and November 24, 1949]. The real records (esp. the Bible) are much more dramatic, much more meaningful, much more lively, fresh, and authentic than any superficial and artful reconstruction I think. Besides, my poetic interests are leading onward in the Common Quest, and thus I hope to concentrate on and try to discover new insights.

March 22, 1951

I feel fundamentally that I want to give.

March 25, 1951

. . . I hope to try keeping a calm and even temper in the face of anything—great or small—to which I shall be exposed; uncontrolled anger and temper is so very unpleasant in their effect upon others, and even occasional indulgence in this will turn into habit unbelievably fast; a well-balanced temper is unbelievably pleasant and an achievement that's not to be underrated. It symbolizes mastery of the universe and of all that could possibly befall.

May 1, 1951

Dr. de Seda said today, "Your work is like discovering the first composition of Mozart."

January 9, 1952

... As to Dad, there is something strongly resembling the nature of the Old Testament about him. There is that sense of Absolutes, that feeling of an unclouded, unquestionable sense of Right and Wrong; there is a seeming dogmatism and harshness at times, though basically the harshness is a protective coat of an extreme sensitivity that has received many rude shocks. There is a certain element of hardheaded realism in evaluating human beings. My sympathies I find in a large degree opposed to these often. This is due to a large part because I like to think in terms of what is potentially present in all human beings. It is so essential to remind ourselves eternally of this. There is nothing unpractical in emphasizing realistic qualities that may not always be visible. The mistake that we are guilty of too much is ascribing non-existence to qualities and things which may simply not have appeared. Because I have not seen the other side of the moon does not mean that this planet has but the side which I had heretofore observed.

March 9, 1952

Dad mentioned an interesting German proverb the other day. "Besser ein Ende mit Schrecken als Schrecken ohne Ende." [Translated: "Better an end with terror than terror without end."]

June 7, 1952

Dreaming is the poor man's substitute for television.

September 4, 1952

I finished my novel yesterday—Wednesday, September 3, 1952. The whole writing—except for the natural and constant strain of creative effort—was almost a very delightful task. I felt thoroughly happy and I progressed at almost a constant rate daily. It was in a sense thrilling—the ideas and the whole pattern of the work just flowed out with gratifying ease. I really felt as if I could write! I hope the work is good. I personally am enthusiastic over it and feel as if I have caught a big fish. I feel spiritually relieved once more....

These three weeks I really submerged myself in my thoughts and works, and ate, slept, and drank almost nothing else. I didn't read anything almost, and I didn't partake of any other activity, except go out on a date occasionally.

I hope that I will be able to make the few revisions that have to be made and retype the whole work soon. Just now I must concentrate on my M.A. orals which I have knowingly neglected. I just had to write. I couldn't carry the creation inside me any longer—I was getting spiritually confused and I had to give expression to the vapor ghosts floating around within me . . . .

September 27, 1952

Idea for dialogue:
    "But that which you are about to do is dangerous!"
    "So is Life itself—one can die from it!"

November 15, 1952

I believe that finding the meaning to life in all its aspects is kids-stuff compared to finding one's true Love. I have already done the former and I am not yet twenty-five—but as for finding the true life-partner, what a Herculean task that turns out to be! What pains, what disappointments, what self-criticism, what uncertainties, what skepticism, what loss of confidence, what conflicting factions within the soul! Wow!

December 9, 1952

I think that I shall some day write a book to be called *Judas and the Messiah*. It will probably be my master-work. Anything that I would try to say about it now could not do justice to what I envision (only vaguely now) the work will be. But only an absolute love and compassion and sympathy and understanding for both individuals and both traditions which they represent will ever do full justice to them, to the human dreams, to life, and to God.

Perhaps I shall continue studying at the university in order to devote my time indirectly to a study of the Biblical material, since the dissertation topic on which I have settled is *Mark Twain's Use of the Bible*.

December 31, 1952

[Having written much of his "novel," Rolf then states the following.]
. . . There is only one other fundamental and much more deep-rooted problem which I still haven't answered satisfactorily to myself: am I morally justified in publishing this story? Will it hurt anyone?

January 8, 1953

I am again beginning to vibrate slowly, and I am terribly thrilled as the creative pattern begins to emerge in the gradual and fragmentary bit-by-bit way that it always assumes. The novel that I hope to write some day—I wonder when it will finally be written. I already hold my breath as I gradually visualize its scope and I think of Sandburg's *Lincoln* and the modest roots from which it grew and its original humble pretensions.

Judas and the Messiah will be the epic of the Bible and, as I see it unfolding, I see how the whole rich beauty and grandeur and timelessness of the whole Bible will form the background chapters against which this central story will be played out. The book shall do for the Bible what *Moby Dick* did for whaling and what the Michener novels did for the South Pacific. Oh, what work will be ahead for me! At least now I see a focal point towards which I can direct my whole life. It is good to have found the lodestar!

February 10, 1953

[Rolf begins by saying that he has several interests, then lists them.]
. . . First and foremost, I want to write . . . I wonder what will come of all this! Fifty years from now the story will be told! The Great Author is a master at suspense, conflict, and plot structure.

February 17, 1953

Prof. Griggs suggested on the 16th that being the only son, my parents are betting everything on me. Yes, I seem to be the family's dark horse. I hope that I won't turn out to be its black sheep.

February 23, 1953

Spoke to picturesque evangelist. Walked into Bible House publishers and walked into nest of somewhat frantic but kind evangelist missionaries.

He received messages—one at 4 o'clock in morning, which resulted in his editing of St. John's gospel. I had the good fortune to see him receive a "message" before my very eyes. Something about three "r's" resurrection, remission, and (?). He suddenly forgot what the third was. One of the others suggested "retribution." He thought it would do.

He gave me a little pep-talk—it lasted a full hour. All I had to do was be attentive and listen sympathetically. I did. He read the most remarkable things into the Bible. I think he was familiar with every comma in it. There was going to be a big burst shortly. The day of the *Meshia* (messiah) was near. He was so happy. Judgment Day was just around the corner.

Fascinating fellow—he has some really brilliant ways of explaining the touchy points of Christianity. He darted from one problem to the next with such rapidity that I've only retained the impression, not the argument.

[The following is the penultimate entry in Rolf's first diary, entered on the same date as the above, before the final entry on April 9.]

The End of the Old;

The Beginning of the New;

My life as a Newspaper Editor with all the trimmings.

15

Rolf Gompertz's Second Diary, Extracts

This short diary of just over 2,000 words was written over the course of a week in 1966, being comprised of only three entries (December 3, and two on December 10). The first concerned his eagerness to hear good news from publishers about their willingness to publish his book "Judas and Christ." The second pertains to Rolf being asked to develop the adult education program in his synagogue. The third describes his participation in the Sabbath service of the synagogue that he and his family had recently joined. His responsibility was to interpret Torah for the congregation. The date of this event corresponded to the date of his *bar mitzvah* back in 1940, which led him to describe the joyful day as his "second *bar mitzvah*." The following are extracts from the third entry.

December 10, 1966—Shabbat Chanukah

This, my second *bar mitzvah*, was a great moment in my life—one of the greatest moments.

It began Friday night when . . . the children presented me with a new *Kippah* from Ronnie and a *Tallit* clip from Nancy—and a shiny [illegible] from Peegee (Philip). . . .

This was followed by the greatest surprise of my life—a beautiful, wool, Israeli *Tallit* from Carol. The kind I always yearned to have. We discussed this once and it was decided that it would not be right to replace the

Tallit my parents gave to me on my *bar mitzvah* and which I was still using. But I must say that emotionally I was thrilled to receive the new *Tallit* from Carol. She said, "You are no longer wearing the same suit you wore on your *bar mitzvah*, so you can also have a new *Tallit*. I just felt like I wanted to give you a *Tallit*—from me."

I am thrilled. . . . This *Tallit* represents our spiritual life together and our dedication to Judaism—as children of the commandments.

The day was a beautiful, [illegible], thrilling event. I picked up Dad to attend services. . . . [Mother is ill, so her] condition prevented her regrettably from attending. Carol and Ronnie sat with "Pappa." . . .

This was the day of my official spiritual commitment. . . .

When we had circled with the Torah, Rabbi Aaron M. Wise introduced me. He said, "Rolf Gompertz is a recent member of the congregation but he has quickly found his way into the inner circle of our Temple. It is a great joy to have his family join with ours."

I prefaced my address with the statement from my *Haftarah* which had been given to me: "Not by might, nor by power, but by my Spirit, says the Lord." I had not written it into the text—but I felt I had to say it.

As I talked and as I finished, I knew I had reached the congregation. [Rolf recounts the comments given to him by many, including a comment by Ruben Lazar to Carol: "He was much better today than in Hebrew class." Then Rolf mentions his family's responses.] Dad, I am told, was several times moved to tears. Ronnie said though he did not understand what Daddy said, he felt like yelling, stomping, and applauding at the end. . . . Poppa couldn't get over it—he couldn't figure out "where you got it from." He was emotionally moved. He suppressed tears at the table. He probably thought also of mother who couldn't be present (she said she was present in spirit all that time—and she appeared pleased and in good spirits). Later *Vati* asked how long the sermon took to write. I said "10 hours and 39 years." . . . Anyway, the next 40 years belong to Judaism.

He wants to discuss his concepts further. He said I would be able to express them better than he. His idea, among others, is that we should all actively convert and evangelize. . . . I did agree with him so far as to say that the messiahs are sitting right out there in the congregation—that every man is a messiah, a redeemer of that part of life over which he has influence and thus influences others. . . .

It was a beautiful, beautiful day. It was good to be home.

16

Rolf Gompertz's Third Diary, Extracts

This medium-length diary of almost 7,500 words was written in the last seven months of Rolf's forty-ninth year, concluding on his fiftieth birthday on December 29, 1977. It deals with Rolf's exuberant days in the aftermath of getting his first two books released within a two-week period in late May and early June of 1977—first his *My Jewish Brother Jesus* (which he received from the printers on May 31) and second his *Promotion and Publicity Handbook for Broadcasters* (which he received from Tab Books on June 8). It describes his inexhaustible efforts to market and sell the books, some of his successes, and some of his failures. The following are extracts of approximately a third of the journal.

May 31, 1977

[Here Rolf describes opening the package containing the first printed copies of his *My Jewish Brother Jesus*.]

I tore open the package—and just looked and looked and looked. It was beautiful. . . . I looked the book over for all major details—the way a mother looks over a new-born baby to make sure all the main features are there and healthy. I drove back to the office feeling a tremendous glow—finally, finally it had happened. A book. My book. *The* book.

June 2, 1977

[Here Rolf describes his parents' reaction to having received a copy of the book the evening before.]

"I seldom have seen you so animated," Dad sad to me. "You were so happy." It was of course not only because the book was out—but because I was able to share this event with both of them. While they were alive!

This has been one of the greatest satisfactions of my life—perhaps the greatest—in terms of my relationship with them as their son. Dad had just turned 87 on May 15, and Mother turned 79 on March 25.

About five weeks ago Dad was hit by a car as he stepped off a curb. It had been the driver's fault—Dad suffered a shattered right elbow which had to be operated on. It was a traumatic experience for all of us. The accident could have been worse—Dad pulled through. His arm is functional again. It was a difficult time for him and Mother, and all of us. I am doubly grateful, therefore, to have been able to share this moment with him.

June 8, 1977

I had lunch today with Cynthia Jessup and Bill—which was a true celebration, since we are so attuned to each other on a deep level. I said: "I feel like the actor who has talked about himself and then says: Now that we've talked about me, let's talk about you. What did you think about my latest picture?—Today I want to talk about myself unashamedly," I told them. They laughed and indulged me. . . .

I have turned this project, which is so much bigger than I, over to God. "Not by might, nor by power, but by my Spirit."

June 10, 1977

The two books and the joy resulting from them have affected and infected everyone in the family. Carol is happy, Ron, Nancy & Philip are happy. Only Princess isn't happy—she can't get in the garage anymore—she's been displaced by Jesus. I hope this won't turn her against religion! Poor Princess. Maybe I'll give her an autographed copy. Better yet—a bone! That's something she can relate to: Anyway, there's no light in the dog house—so how could she read at night?

Yesterday, the 9th, was a lovely day. I go around all day and can't stop smiling. I feel like Alfred E. Newman of Mad Magazine!

June 20, 1977

It's been 10 days since my last entry. Everyday has had its special surprise.

The most significant thing that has happened in this period is the letter from Rabbi Wolf. He put his finger on what I want to be the true significance of this book—he zeroed in on its meaning and essence. I felt so understood and so grateful that the book could be approved and praised from a Jewish point of view. His endorsement lets me know that Jewish support of the book is possible.

I felt relief on this point for the first time in the 25 years since I envisioned the book—particularly in light of the strange non-reaction the book received on the two previous occasions when I submitted it to Jewish scholars/theologians (*not* Rabbi Rothblum, who, too, was very complimentary).

July 11, 1977

[Here Rolf speaks about his need to market the books with booksellers.]

I find that I don't particularly enjoy doing this—but do it because I know it has to be done if the book is to survive and succeed. . . . I really don't like having to "sell" myself and my product in person—I prefer to let the product speak for itself and do my own "selling" in writing. But I do what I have to do, and learn how to do it, and for the sake of the book. . . .

Personally I feel very satisfied. I see myself now as I always wanted to see myself—a writer. I feel justified in this now and I do take satisfaction from being so regarded by others. I don't know why this should seem to be so important to me—it just is. There is something about being a writer that just does something for me. Others have to be doctors or lawyers or ballplayers or scientists—I have to be a writer.

July 22, 1977

I ran into opposition in two Christian stores. One . . . rejected it outright because I *personally* do not believe in Jesus as divine and the son of God, the Virgin Birth. He was very gentle about it, even cordial, but found this a matter of conscience.

July 27, 1977

[Here Rolf speaks about difficulties in getting major distributors on-board in distributing the book.]

Distributors find it unprofitable and logistically difficult to work with independent presses, especially when only one title is involved. His advice [i.e., advice given by a distributor]: contact stores individually and place it. . . . "The book business," he said "has gone the way of the supermarket. Only the big ones can make it—the little ones, and the little publishers are being driven out of business. Everyone's become too greedy."

August 10, 1977

[Here Rolf speaks about a Book Fair that had taken place on September 23, where he had a table advertising and selling *My Jewish Brother Jesus*.]

The greatest value was having made contact with Jack [a literary agent dealing with marketing publications on the foreign market]. . . . I asked him to exhibit the book ($60, Frankfurt & London) & act as my agent (10%). He asked to read the book first (Saturday night). Sunday morning he asked me to take a walk. I thought he'd probably try to let me down easy. Instead he revealed that he had been a priest, felt [called to] the monastic life, was in Israel recently where he was deeply moved—and that the book had the same effect. He thought it would be hard to find a publisher but that European publishers do look for quality—he could not promise anything but would try. He personally felt the book was a classic and would last a long, long time.

I told him what he said made the weekend worthwhile, and that even if he were not to represent the book, that was worth more to me than anything he could accomplish. It was a thrilling moment.

November 1, 1977

Met with Trude [Dr. Trude Weiss-Rosmarin, editor of *The Jewish Spectator*, who had already published several of Rolf's short stories and articles, including "The Day of the Messiah" (Sept 1973), "The Regulars," (Fall 1975), and who would later publish "The Messiah—Where Do We Go from Here?" (Summer 1993); Rolf had sent her a copy of his Jesus-novel, and met with her on this day to discuss the book in her Santa Monica apartment].

She was warm and cordial. Bad news: She hated the book. Good news: she wouldn't review it.

Her main objection: "Jewish Brother Jesus" is what Jews for Jesus claim. This book plays into their hands. She sees no redeeming value—other than my talent as a writer. "Why don't you apply this talent to something more worthwhile," she said. She said I have Jesus out of my system now. She was curious as to my attraction to Jesus (felt it was conditioning of Christian society). She did not see at all that I was making a Jewish statement with the book. She sees no need for Jews to comment on Jesus, apologize for Jesus, "explain" the trial or crucifixion. . . . Christians are not concerned with the historical Jesus at all—just the Christ of Faith.

[Also] Temple Sinai . . . turned the book down for Temple Book Fair. It's apparent that book is encountering resistance in Jewish community.

December 5, 1977

[On] Monday eve, November 28, Arthur . . . took me to the Comedy Club. I sat across from David . . . who became interested in my book. He belongs to Hollywood [Temple] Beth El . . . and asked if I'd be interested in speaking there. I said "yes." He said he would speak to the rabbi. A couple of days later David called and invited me to attend services and meet the rabbi. I took a book along. [This happened on December 2.] We met before service.

"I heard you on the radio," said the rabbi. "I usually don't listen and at first I thought it was a Jewish Christian program, but then I realized you were talking about the Nazi period and you didn't sound like a Jewish Christian—and I continued to listen. I remembered the title of your book." During the service he mentioned my presence, held up the book, announced its title and said I would be invited to speak.

After services we went in his office. . . . He asked briefly about my book—I explained its aim (Jewish roots), its "mission" to the Christian world, its relationship in terms of the Holocaust (statement of Jewish faith), its value for Jews (a Jewish interest of Jesus), indicated I'd be pleased to receive an invitation to speak—and will await his response. It would be my first synagogue appearance (I did not say this). I keep feeling that I am being led from person to person by an invisible hand.[1]

1. Note: This episode implies an openness to Rolf's ideas that failed to transpire. Rolf wrote the following to me in an email received on December 25, 2012: "After meeting with the rabbi, who was fully sympathetic, interested, and who announced during the service that he had invited me to come and speak, I got a call, after Shabbat, Sunday or

December 4, 1977

I stopped at the House of David—its owner, David, kept two copies for sale, lent one to Rabbi Martin Pauker, because he is involved in ecumenical relations in the [illegible] Community. He heads the small orthodox synagogue (storefront) next door.

David kept saying—since September—he'd get me together with the rabbi. As I walked in the backdoor this morning, a man came walking out. "Shalom!" he said "Shalom!" I answered. I'd say he was in his 40s, pleasant, tall. David looked up, quickly called him back. "This is the person who wrote the book on Jesus!" David said. The man was Rabbi Pauker. . . .

"I enjoyed your book," he said. "I am very much involved in this area. I'd like to get together with you." "I would like that too," I said. "Here is my number," he said, writing it down for me. "I don't have a card with me." I gave him my card. "Call me," he said. . . .

David told me Rabbi Pauker had been in before to get *Chanukah* candles (it was *Erev Chanukah*) but returned to give them back—since he found his own. If it hadn't been for that, we would not have met that moment. Another moment—guided by an invisible hand. "Not by might, nor by power, but by my Spirit, says the Lord of hosts." 37 years ago—*Shabbat Chanukah*—this saying from Zechariah was given to me, to remember. Today was *Erev Chanukah*.

Monday, from the retired rabbi emeritus, who spoke in a friendly voice, soon getting to the issue, about the invitation from the current rabbi to come and speak about my Jesus book. Said the rabbi emeritus: 'You were quoted in a newspaper article as saying "Jesus is the ultimate Western symbol of love." You must have been misquoted. I'm sure you may wish to deny that.' [The quote is from *The San Fernando Daily News*, "Out of the Holocaust, a Jew, and His Brother Jesus," by Brian Alexander.] 'I was not misquoted,' I said. 'And I do not deny what I said.' 'Well,' said the rabbi politely, 'you can understand then why we cannot have you come and speak and why we must uninvite you.' 'Yes,' I said, finding further conversation pointless.'

Other rabbis read the book early on and proved to be sympathetic and supportive of what Rolf was attempting to do. This included Rabbi Moshe J. Rotbluhm (from Adat Ari El synagogue), who provided him with an endorsement published on the front cover of the book; Rabbi Allen Freehling (University Synagogue, Los Angeles), who invited Rolf to speak at a Friday night assembly and who supplied an endorsement for the book; and Rabbi Allen S. Maller (Temple Akiba, Culver City), who invited Rolf to speak to his congregation about it.

December 29, 1977

This was my 50th birthday. It was a happy day. I felt fulfilled. I appreciate all my blessings. I feel a sense of satisfaction in all areas. . . .

I am grateful that my parents were alive to enjoy this day. They wrote me a beautiful letter [and went out for a meal with Rolf]. . . . Ron, Nancy, and Phil gave me a beautiful digital watch. Carol is giving me a big family party Sunday. They have been so good to me. I am grateful for this love.

Thank you, God, for all my blessings. A poem I once wrote in my twenties comes to mind: "Let me live, love and suffer . . . nobly."

We yearn in spirit. We reach upward. We want to give life meaning. We seek to be worthy of life. It is not always easy to believe in the vision—or to maintain it.

Help me, God, to be worthy of the dream and of the vision for whatever years you will grant me.

I want to love. I need to love. Help me to keep on loving in all ways. Let me always see your love in my life. Thank you. Amen.

APPENDIX 1

Who am I to Write This Book?

SOME MIGHT ASK WHY a non-Jew has written a book about a Jew who survived years of Nazi oppression. Some might question whether it is even proper for a Christian to write about a Jew who was nearly forced to join six million other Jews in the murderous death camps of a "Christian" country.

I do not write as one who is able to do justice to the task. The emotional and spiritual trauma that intertwined with Jewish identity during the years when Nazi ideology ensnared Germany is something that will always lie beyond my scope of experience and beyond the limits of my comprehension.[1] Despite these inadequacies, I have nonetheless undertaken the writing of this book in appreciation of what Rolf represents. I also have written it out of a ten-year friendship between Rolf and myself—a friendship that has nurtured both of us, a Jew and a Christian, in our common humanity.

I first encountered Rolf in 2004. I was teaching a course on Jesus-novels at the University of St. Andrews in Scotland, where I had been based since 1999. In an Amazon search that included the keywords "Jewish," "novel," and "Jesus," I of course spotted Rolf's Jesus-novel. Not knowing anything about the publisher of *A Jewish Novel about Jesus,* I decided to

---

1. Nor could I ever comprehend what it would be like to live as a Christian under Nazi reign. See, for instance, the experiences of Christian New Testament theologian J. Christian Beker, who was taken prisoner by the Nazis, as recounted by Ollenberger, "Suffering and Hope: The Story behind the Book." My failure to comprehend the experiences of those who suffered was brought home to me in the late 1980s when, for five years in succession, I made it a practice to read Elie Wiesel's *Night* on "Good Friday."

contact Rolf by email to see whether he could supply copies of the novel if the publisher's stock ran short for my class of two dozen students. A cordial relationship took root from that point, and grew into a friendship over the next few years.

By the time I moved to take a position at Baylor University in 2009, I had already agreed to serve as Rolf's literary executor upon the time of his death. I agreed to this arrangement on two conditions: first, that all members of his immediate family approved of it, and second, that I would receive no financial remuneration in undertaking this role.

Being Rolf's literary executor, I received from him several boxes full of documents and materials—resources that are now included within the "Rolf Gompertz Archive" held by the Simon Wiesenthal Center and Museum of Tolerance in Los Angeles.[2] In spare moments, and with the help of student assistants, I began to piece together the puzzle of his life, to the point that it seemed right for me to undertake the writing of this book in due course.

With that in mind, I asked Rolf for a list of people who knew him well, which he duly supplied me, along with their contact details. With the invaluable help of my undergraduate assistant, Tyler Davis, I sent out questionnaires to some of Rolf's friends and associates. The questionnaire was not very long, but asked simple questions that were broad enough to allow personal reflections to emerge. The twenty-six questionnaires that were returned gave me valuable glimpses into Rolf's relational world, and enabled me to triangulate my research, ensuring that my impressions of Rolf were earthed in perceptions from a variety of people whose lives have crossed Rolf's path at some point along the way. The returned questionnaires will ultimately be housed in the "Rolf Gompertz Archive."

I also asked Tyler Davis to transcribe the diaries that Rolf had kept between the years 1952 and 1977; excerpts of those transcribed diaries appear in Part 6 of this book, above.

In May 2011, I visited Rolf and Carol in their home in Los Angeles, spending three days with them, during which time I interviewed Rolf on four occasions, totaling 292 minutes, or almost five hours. I also was fortunate to be in attendance when Rolf presented his "Snapshots" speech to the

---

2. That archive includes (1) the original and much fuller manuscript of what he would later reduce in size and publish as *A Jewish Novel about Jesus*, (2) his three journals, (3) more than two dozen questionnaires about Rolf returned to me from people who have known him over the years, (4) a number of Rolf's literary works, and (5) miscellaneous correspondence and other memorabilia.

Simon Wiesenthal Center and Museum of Tolerance in Los Angeles. The speech is included in Part 6 of this book, while the interviews are available on the website of the Institute for Oral History, Baylor University, both as a streamable audio file and in transcript format.[3]

Our friendship has continued since then through regular email exchanges. I never receive emails from Rolf on the Sabbath, but we usually converse a dozen times a month, often more than that. These email exchanges stopped abruptly on Monday, October 8, 2012. That was the day that Rolf had a rather severe stroke—as reported to me in an email from Rolf's friend Tricia Aven on October 19. As a result of that stroke, Rolf struggled primarily with an extreme loss of mobility and other motor skills, and impaired speech. But by the beginning of 2013, the eighty-five-year-old Rolf was undergoing a remarkable recovery. Emails between us started to pick up again, and soon he was back to his old self, with virtually no noticeable damage remaining from the stroke.

At the time of writing, Rolf is eighty-six years of age and continues to live a productive life with his wife Carol. Moreover, for the past year and a half he has returned to the Simon Wiesenthal Center and Museum of Tolerance every other week to bear witness about love.

3. These digital resources can be accessed through this portal: http://www.baylor.edu/oralhistory

APPENDIX 2

A Reading of Matthew 27:25: "His blood be on us and on our children"

ROLF GOMPERTZ's *A JEWISH Novel about Jesus* offers an occasion to rethink how to interpret certain passages within the New Testament canon. For instance:

1. When Pilate washes his hands of the crucifixion of Jesus, it is not because he is really innocent of Jesus' death (which is the public line) but because, behind the scenes, he has already orchestrated a "fall guy" to take the blame instead—Caiaphas.

2. When Pilate puts a sign on the cross above Jesus saying "King of the Jews," he was not (as in some later Christian traditions) expressing an incipient belief in Jesus which would later blossom into a full-blown conversion to Christianity; instead, he was taunting the Jews about what they were worthy of.

3. When Judas "betrayed" Jesus, it was not because he was malicious and had been overwhelmed by the forces of evil (again, the public version runs this way) but because, unknown to most others, he thought he was doing what God wanted him to do in setting forth the kingdom of God through Jesus himself.

Retelling the story in a fashion that gets us behind the public version of the story and into the motivations of the characters allows Rolf to explore possibilities of this kind.

My own view is that the first example above (i.e., Pilate's manipulation of events) has enough merit to permit plausible scenarios to be proposed along such lines; if Pilate did declare his "innocence" publicly, it might well have been because the script had already been written (largely by him) and he could step back from responsibility for that matter and watch the events unfold. The fact that Jesus was crucified on a Roman cross means that any declaration of "innocence" is unlikely to have been wholly genuine on Pilate's part.

Similarly, there is good reason to think that, if Pilate did have the sign fixed to the cross, it must have been derisory in some fashion—either derisory of Jesus himself or of the Jewish people, or both.

With regard to Judas handing Jesus over to the authorities, we will never know his motivation for doing that.[4] The New Testament texts are fairly uniform in pointing in a certain direction on that score, but there might be some forcefulness in the retort "But they would, wouldn't they!" And Rolf was neither the first nor the last to imagine alternative explanations.[5]

Rolf relies heavily on this strategy of reconfiguring the motivations of characters through back-narrating the story of Jesus along non-traditional lines. But the strategy he uses in relation to the words uttered by the Jewish crowd in Matthew is omission; that is, the cry "His blood be upon us and upon our children" has no foothold in the Gompertz novel, presumably on the premise that it is wholly unhistorical.

While that might be, the Matthean gospel is configured in such a way that another strategy for interpreting this phrase also presents itself. In order to recognize this, attention needs to be given to the way the characters serve certain of the evangelist's narrative purposes, with a differentiation between the Jewish leaders and the Jewish people playing a critical role in the interpretation of Matt 27:25.

In what follows, then, I will present a relatively simple reading of a few key passages from the Matthean gospel that pertain to this thesis. In doing so, I will articulate certain aspects of that gospel's theology, not in any way as a means of scoring theological points or setting out a theological agenda, but simply as a way of placing the cry of Matt 27:25 into its larger narrative

---

4. Here I by-pass the suggestion that Judas is merely a fiction created by Jesus-followers; on this, see Maccoby, *Judas Iscariot and the Myth of Jewish Evil*.

5. For other alternatives, see Kazantzakis's *The Last Temptation* and Archer's *The Gospel according to Judas, by Benjamin Iscariot*.

context, where its significance functions in a much different fashion to the way it has often been interpreted throughout Christian history.

For our purposes, it is necessary to start at the beginning of Matthean gospel. The genealogy in the first seventeen verses might look dull to contemporary readers, but to ancient audiences it would probably have served to capture their interest from the start.

Knowing that the three parts of the genealogy are comprised of fourteen generations, the first-century audiences would ultimately be drawn to ask whether the number fourteen has any interpretive significance. For those who knew the "gemmatric" values of Hebrew letters, a moment's reflection would reveal the matter, focusing on the figure of David. Prominence is given to King David, both in the genealogy itself (see the pivot from the first to the second part of the genealogy in 1:6–7) and in its interpretive key provided by the evangelist at the end (1:17). With the number fourteen being highlighted throughout the genealogy, ancient audiences that could calculate the Hebrew name "David" would have an "Aha" moment in store for them, since that name has a numerical value of fourteen ("d" = 4 [twice]; "w" = 6).[6] In this way, the Matthean evangelist has constructed an enchanting connection for his audience between the historic figure of King David and the central character of his gospel. The Jesus of this gospel should be a leader of the people. The evangelist imagines that a rightful leader will benefit the people. But will that transpire within the narrative?

This question serves as a backdrop against which the evangelist's depiction of certain characters is best understood. He wants his audiences to evaluate the legitimacy of particular characters in relation to this baseline identity of Jesus—those characters being the Jewish leaders, the religious elite.

The first mention of Jewish leaders in the story is in 2:4, where "all the chief priests and scribes of the people" are called to King Herod to inform him of what the Scriptures foretell regarding the birthplace of the Messiah. They know the Scriptures well, the evangelist implies, as they recite for him Micah 2:6, which references Bethlehem—the city of King David. Of course, King Herod eventually slaughters all the children under the age of two in Bethlehem and its environs in order to wipe out his potential competitor as ruler over the Jewish people. This is something of a "Gompertzian" moment—evil has been set in motion by powerful people (because power has

6. An informed presenter delivering the narrative orally could easily have alerted first-time audiences to these features.

corrupted their common humanity), and ordinary people are harmed as a consequence. But this episode also depicts the Jewish leaders as closely aligned, even if unintentionally, with the abusive misuse of power for personal gain. Will this contagion of self-interested abuse of power with disastrous impact on the people play a further role in the narrative? Will the Herodian cancer spread to those whose task is to lead the people through their discernment of the divine will?

The next time Jewish leaders appear is in the wake of John the Baptist's ministry to "the people of Jerusalem and all of Judea" (3:5). For reasons that are not back-narrated, John identifies a different configuration of leaders (i.e., the Pharisees and Sadducees) as a "brood of vipers" (3:7). This is the first in a series of rather brutal attacks against the Jewish leaders in the Matthean gospel—the Pharisees in particular, who are repeatedly described as "hypocrites" and "evil."[7]

We might ask why the level of bitterness against the Jewish leaders is so high in this gospel. Why, for instance, are there are no favorable or friendly Pharisees, unlike Luke's Pharisee-friendly stories (e.g., Luke 7:36; 13:31; 14:1)? Or why are there no stories in the Gospel of Matthew that link the synagogue and laudable faith, as there are in the Gospels of Mark and Luke?[8]

The answer seems to be that, from the Matthean perspective, the Jewish leaders were deficient leaders of the people, having led the people astray from God's will. Two of the best examples of this are evident in the two episodes in which the Pharisees charge Jesus with being a sorcerer in league with Beelzebul.

7. Throughout the Matthean gospel, the Pharisees are repeatedly said to be "hypocrites" (see 6:2, 5, 16; 15:7; 22:18; 23:13, 15, 23, 25, 27, 29; 24:51). They are portrayed as evil (12:34), having evil in their hearts (9:4), and being the foremost examples of an "evil generation" (12:39, 45; 16:4), which is infested with "evil spirits" (12:43–45). Jesus picks up John the Baptist's charge that they are a "brood of vipers" (12:34), in resemblance to the satanic serpent of archetypal myth. Presumably, then, they are also the "weedy seed sown by the enemy" in the exclusively Matthean parable of the wheat and the tares (13:24–30), in which the weeds that grow up among the wheat are said to represent "the sons of the evil one, and the enemy who sowed them is the devil" (13:38–39).

8. Contrast, for instance, Mark 5:21–43 (esp. 5:22, 35, 36, 38) with Matt 9:18–26; Luke 7:1–10 (esp. 7:5) with Matt 8:5–13; contrast the favorable relations Jesus has with a scribe in Mark 12:28–34 // Luke 10:25–28 with the Matthean depiction of the same episode in Matt 22:34–40; contrast also Joseph of Arimathea's depiction in Luke 23:50–52 and Matt 27:57–59.

In the first, a mute Jewish demoniac is healed by Jesus (9:32–34). But whereas "the crowds were amazed" and said "never has anything like this been seen in Israel," the Pharisaic leaders say the following: "By the ruler of the demons he casts out the demons."

Precisely the same pattern is evident in another episode, in which a mute and blind Jewish demoniac is healed by Jesus (12:22–24). Whereas "all the crowds were amazed" and ask whether Jesus might be "the Son of David" (which, of course, corresponds with the evangelist's view, as we've seen from his genealogy), the readers are told that "when the Pharisees heard it, they said, "It is only by Beelzebul, the prince of demons, that this man cases out demons."

In each of these episodes, the Matthean evangelist depicts the Jewish people as developing an embryonic fascination for Jesus, which is quickly eradicated by the Jewish leaders that were on hand—in these cases, the Pharisees. The people's positive reaction "we've never seen anything like this" is undercut immediately by the leaders' spin, "Look out, he's an agent of Beelzebul." The people's key insight that Jesus could be the Son of David is quickly trounced by the same interjection. In each case, the leaders of the people disadvantage the very people whom they're meant to lead by leading them away from the one who would be "Emmanuel, God with us" (1:23). From a Matthean perspective, the Jewish elite are at fault, and the people are trapped under the leaders' influence. And therein lies the tragedy.

These two episodes set up the relevant dynamics and characterizations that ultimately should inform our understanding of the passage that concerns us—that is, Matt 27:25, and the cry from the people: "His blood be on us and on our children." Here's how that should work.

All through the narrative, it is the leaders (*not* the people) who have concocted the view that Jesus must be removed, and that characterization of the leaders plays out in the Matthean trial scenes as well. It is, for instance, "the scribes and the elders" who gather at the house of the High Priest (26:57); it is there that Jesus is treated abominably (26:67); and it is "the chief priests and elders" who make the official accusations against him to Pilate (27:12–13). If the leaders are the ones who are orchestrating things, their machinations all come to a head when Pilate mentions that he can release Jesus or Barabbas to the people. At that point, the Matthean audience is told the following, in the most important interpretive guide to how Matt 27:25 should be understood: "Now the chief priests and the elders persuaded the crowds to ask for Barabbas and to have Jesus killed" (27:20).

What we are witnessing, then, is the same Matthean pattern reemerging that we have already seen in the two "Beelzebul" episodes. The Jewish people are manipulated by their leaders, who impose onto them what is, in the eyes of the evangelist, the worst situation for the people themselves. (And the same pattern repeats itself a fourth time, in 28:11–15.) Consequently, the narrative simply writes itself from that point. When Pilate asks whom he should release, the crowd shouts "Barabbas." They are the mouthpiece of the Jewish leaders, even against their better interests. When Pilate asks what he should do with Jesus, the crowd shouts, "Let him be crucified!" When Pilate washes his hands of the ordeal, the Matthean audience hears that "the people as a whole answered, 'His blood be on us and on our children!'"

Is this a moment of Matthean loathing of Jews, "the people as a whole"? I don't think so. The narrative has been configured in order to draw out the utter tragedy of the situation, with the people having been stage-managed against their better interests by their line-managers, who had only their own interests in mind. How do we know this aspect of their character? The Matthean narrative tells its audience precisely this only a few verses prior to this dreadful outcome. Pilate, we are told, "realized that it was out of jealousy that they [the Jewish leaders] had handed him over" (27:18). Jealousy? Why jealousy? Because (in the evangelist's view) Jesus was winning the affections of the people and jeopardizing the leaders' power-base. In Matthean perspective, the religious elite sought to get rid of Jesus in an effort to protect their interests; in order to accomplish that goal, they used as pawns the very people whose interests they were supposed to enhance. Narratively speaking, the situation is virtually Shakespearean in its dripping irony and tragic outcome. And narratively speaking, it is a variation on the theme established toward the beginning of the narrative, when Herod, jealous that another might usurp his power, acted in self-interest and slaughtered the innocents.

In its context, then, the cry of Matt 27:25 is anything but anti-Semitic, and nothing if it is not anti-elite. The Matthean evangelist does not intend his audiences to brutalize the Jewish people on the basis of that verse; they have already been brutalized by their leaders. Therein lies their national calamity, in the eyes of the Matthean evangelist.

Consequently, when Walter Wink says that it is "damningly true" that Matt 27:25 "call[s] down everlasting guilt on the Jewish people for their part in the execution of Jesus," it is not quite true after all.[9] For the Matthean evangelist, the Jews are not "Christ-killers" *en masse*, and the cry of Matt 27:25 is not a valid testimony to the truth of the situation. The "Christ-killers," at least in Matthean perspective, were the Jewish elite of the early first century of the Common Era, not the Jewish people for all time since then.[10] Now, of course, we need to go some way to put Matthew's narrative in a much more nuanced historical situation—that much is true. But narratively-speaking, Matt 27:25 is not intended to foster anti-Semitism; instead, it is a moment of heartfelt tragedy in the narrative, a moment that was ironically manipulated by the very elite who should have had the people's best interests in mind.[11]

In making this proposal, I cannot pretend that the Matthean gospel is a template for healthy inter-faith relations today. Regarding historical matters, its presentation of Jesus' trial and crucifixion requires added nuance in

9. Wink, *Engaging the Powers*, 123.

10. For this reason, the view articulated by Carroll and Green (*The Death of Jesus in Early Christianity*, 47) requires some slight tweaking. They write: "Clearly, this dimension of Matthew's narrative . . . reflects the later experiences of Matthew's community within first-century Palestinian Jewish culture. Through these words placed by Matthew on the lips of the chorus at Jerusalem, the author [writing in the 80s or so] casts light upon the dark episode of the fall of Jerusalem to Roman armies in 70. What meaning does Matthew assign this catastrophic event at the close of the generation of Jesus? It was divine retribution for the violent death of the Messiah." This estimate is probably correct in all that it says, but falls short in what it fails to say. It is true that the Matthean evangelist sees the events of 70 CE to be a form of "divine retribution"; this emerges from the Matthean "Parable of the Great Banquet" (Matt 22:1–10), where the king destroys a city for the murderous actions of the invited guests. But the Matthean evangelist demonstrates in both the slaughter of the innocents and the crucifixion of Jesus that murderous actions are ultimately inspired by the leaders gone bad. The people are, at best, manipulated pawns in the service of the powerful, and at worst, those who undergo personal misfortune as a result of the machinations of the powerful.

11. The fact that the people are manipulated pawns of the powerful connects two other aspects of the Matthean storyline. Matthew 28:11–15 depicts the Jewish leaders suppressing the storyline that the evangelist wants his readers to adopt; this suppression shapes the options of the Jewish people in general, who end up being the pawns of the Jewish leaders in a further round of suppression—depicted in Matt 10:17 as the flogging of Jesus-followers in local synagogues. In Matthean perspective, this tragedy results not from a virus in the heart of an ethnic people, but from a cancer in the heart of the powerful who "jealously" seek to protect their own self-interests and use the people as a mechanism for propping up the leaders' power-base. This aspect of the Matthean narrative is thoroughly Gompertzian in its interpretation of power gone wrong.

relation to Rome; the Matthean version lets Pilate "off the hook" for reasons that Rolf is probably right about (i.e., the early Jesus-movement was not wanting to alienate the ruling authorities).[12] Its fierce rhetoric against the Jewish leaders as "whitewashed tombs" (and the like) is best understood not as legitimate historical descriptors about the true character of first-century Judaism but, instead, as polemical tags that enhance the evangelist's definition of the boundaries of acceptable thought and practice. And underlying all this is a supersessionistic perspective that originates in a conviction that "the law and the prophets" have been fulfilled in the life, death, and resurrection of Jesus and are being fulfilled in the lives of those who follow him.

If the Matthean gospel is not a paradigm of inter-faith relationships for today (and more could be said along these lines), two points nonetheless need to be registered. The first has already been argued for—that is, it runs contrary to the configuration of the Matthean storyline to read Matt 27:25 as a blanket condemnation of the Jewish people throughout the ages.

The second is this: where the Matthean gospel is most foreign to interfaith relations in the twenty-first century is precisely where it is most like some of its counterparts in the first century. It is not the case, for instance, that supersessionistic theology was necessarily and inevitably a form of anti-Judaism or anti-Semitism (although it clearly can be one or both, and all too often has been). If that was the case, then whole swaths of Early Jewish literature would need to be characterized as anti-Semitic—a bizarre

---

12. When depicting the Pilate-Caiaphas relationship, there is one historically viable option that gives Caiaphas a fairly strong hand. If Jesus' trial took place in the year 33, for instance, Pilate's power-base might have been weakened two years earlier, and his relationship with the Jewish leaders might have precariously altered as a consequence. Sejanus had been Pilate's mentor in Rome, and presumably he initiated and sponsored Pilate's procuratorship in Judaea. Sejanus himself was widely known to have been anti-Semitic, and it might well be that Pilate saw no reason why he should foster a healthier attitude towards the Jews prior to the events of 31. But early in that year, Sejanus' power-base crumbled, with the emperor Tiberius growing weary of Sejanus' conniving and power plays, to his own (i.e., Sejanus's) glory. On October 18 of 31, the Roman senate arranged for Sejanus to die by strangulation, and the sentence was carried out that day. Whereas Pilate had previously fitted in with Sejanus' anti-Semitic policies, at this point he now had to be extremely cautious when dealing with Jews of Judaea, not least Caiaphas. In this scenario, Caiaphas may well have had more leverage than is credited to him in Rolf's Jesus-novel. This reconstruction is articulated in Hoehner, *Chronological Aspects of the Life of Christ* and is explored narratively in Monhollon, *Divine Invasion*, and in Bruce Chilton's pseudo-narrative *Rabbi Jesus* (esp. 204–7 and 241–42). For my part, I do not adopt this strategy, since it puts interminable pressures on Pauline chronology, which is more robust than the more speculative chronological options pertaining to Jesus. I put the year of Jesus' crucifixion at 30, give or take a year.

result, itself indicating that something is wrong in the house of supersessionist studies. As historical research has increasingly recognized, Judaism was an overarching genus containing a variety of species within it, of which the early Jesus-movement was only one. Supersessionism lay at the heart of many species within the umbrella of Early Judaism, with various groups often defining what it means to be "the people of God" over and against other Jewish definitions of that same notion; Matthew's supersessionism is simply one alongside many from that Jewish stable.[13]

Matthew's rhetoric, for instance, is not a world away from the polemic evident in the Dead Sea Scrolls, which have come to special prominence in the decades after Rolf wrote his Jesus-novel.[14] Some of those scrolls polemicize against the temple authorities in ways that outstrip Matthean denunciation of them, but for much the same reason: they have led the people of Israel astray from true worship of Israel's God.[15] According to the great War Scroll, for instance, God's angels will soon swoop down, destroy the Jerusalem temple, and wipe out "the Sons of Darkness"—a designation that includes the Romans, the Jewish leaders, and all the people of Israel who have been misled by the Jewish leaders; once all that is accomplished, a new temple will be built, with "the Sons of Light" (i.e., the Dead Sea community) serving God there in priestly holiness for all time.

There are, then, some parallels in the way that the Jewish leaders are denounced in the Matthean gospel and in the Dead Sea Scrolls. There is, however, one significant difference between Matthean polemic and the polemic of the War Scroll—that is, the Matthean gospel became part of a movement that was later to become a religion wholly separated from Judaism, where its polemic began to take on a life of its own in despicably anti-Semitic ways. The difference between the Matthean gospel and the Dead Sea Scrolls, then, hinges on "the partings of the ways" between Judaism and

13. The point has been well made in relation to Paul, for instance, by the Jewish scholar Daniel Boyarin in *A Radical Jew*. He notes (205) that there is a supersessionist dimension in Paul's thinking, but he also insists that "Paul's [supersessionistic] doctrine is *not anti-Judaic*," maintaining that "Paul's discourse [is] indigenously Jewish."

14. Although the Dead Sea Scrolls were discovered in the late 1940s, Qumran studies have blossomed only since the 1980s or so.

15. So too, just as the Jewish elite are depicted in Matthean terms in the evangelist's gospel (rather than speaking for themselves and in their own terms), the same is much the case in the Dead Sea Scrolls as well, which at times denounce the temple authorities for collusion with Rome without entertaining any nuance in that denunciation.

Christianity and the reception history of texts that began in one context and ended up in another.

For that reason, in the aftermath of the partings of the ways between Judaism and Christianity, the interpretation of the Matthean narrative inevitably requires careful handling when it comes to its depiction of these relationships.

Where, then, might this leave us with regard to the Jesus of history—especially his ministry in relation to the Jewish authorities and to Rome? Very briefly, in order to capture those dynamics most credibly we need to recognize aspects of both "collusion" and "collision." It seems best to imagine that, in Jesus' perspective, the Jewish leaders were on a "collusion course" with Roman power, and that his own vision of God's kingdom was on a "collision course" with the upper echelons of power within that society. Jewish elite and Roman elite—both figure into the most likely scenarios of shared responsibility for the death of Jesus. It is not anti-Semitic to say, as the Jewish scholar Albert I. Baumgarten rightly does, that a "purely Roman explanation of the death of Jesus seems unlikely."[16] What lies behind this conglomeration of responsibility shouldered by the Jewish elite and the Roman elite together is not "Judaism" *per se* nor "Rome" *per se*, but instead, as Walter Wink has capably defined it, "the System of Domination"—a system in which the powerful colluded and collided in their own quest for power.[17]

It needs only to be noted at this point that such a view of things coincides fully with the outlook of Rolf Gompertz, in his efforts to prioritize "our common humanity" over against the hijacking of ideology in the quest for blatant self-interest and the dangerous manipulation of others for selfish gain. At times, religious leaders have been far too complicit with power to serve the purposes of justice. According to some Jews of the first century (such as the Dead Sea covenanters at Qumran), the Jewish temple elite were among their number. The Matthean evangelist seems to have built parts of his narrative on this sentiment. Tragically, one passage within that narrative has been understood by Christians as reflecting badly upon the Jews

16. Baumgarten, "Setting the Outer Limits," 96. Baumgarten is a member of the Department of Jewish History at Bar-Ilan University (Ramat-Gan, Israel), and specializes in the Second Temple era. Note too that Talmudic traditions mention the need for the Jewish leaders to have silenced the Nazarene and his followers, on the basis that they were misleading the people of Israel; see, for instance b. *Sanhedrin* 43a–b.

17. Wink, *Engaging the Powers*, 123. As Wink has rightly observed, "[T]ruth is not served by denying . . . that Jewish religion in first-century Palestine was corrupt at the top [i.e., the elite purchased the high priesthood to perpetuate their self-interests, etc.]."

collectively when, in its narrative context, it was intended only to reflect badly upon the religious elite who had colluded with power "out of jealousy" for their own positions of power. If Jesus of Nazareth was himself critical of the abuse of power by the elite (as was likely the case), then Rolf Gompertz had every reason to entitle his 1977 Jesus-novel *My Jewish Brother Jesus*.

APPENDIX 3

Further Reading

ALTHOUGH I AM NOT a historian of the Holocaust, the process of writing this book required me to familiarize myself with the context of Rolf's early days in Nazi Germany. Digging into a variety of resources reconstructing aspects of early twentieth-century life in Europe, I was able to catch a glimpse of historical currents and of individual lives within those currents. I offer here an overview of some of the resources that proved to be most helpful in that regard and that interface to a certain extent with the narrative of Rolf's own life.

In his book *My German Question: Growing Up in Nazi Berlin,* Peter Gay recounts his assimilated existence as an anti-religious Jew in Nazi Germany, the growing realization within his family that they would have to emigrate, and the thorny issues surrounding the family's emigration out of Nazi Germany. Gay's is a valuable account that helps to fill in the details of what the process of Jewish emigration from Nazi Germany entailed. See also Michael Schäbitz, "The Flight and Expulsion of German Jews."

Another personal account of a different sort can be found in George Clare's *Berlin Days: 1946–1947.* On page 6 of that book, Clare recounts his family's experience of *Kristallnacht* in this way:

> On 9 November 1938, . . . we were still in Berlin in the Jewish Pension Lurie on the *Kurfürstendamm.* With the other guests, we sat in fearful silence in the lounge listening to the howls of the organized mob smashing the windows of Jewish shops. We all had but one thought. When would the SS come and take us away?

In Clare's case, he and his family were able to flee to London not long after that. Just as Rolf Gompertz and his family kissed the ground upon reaching land in a free country, so too Clare recounts how he "more skipped than walked along Finchley Road to Swiss Cottage and then down the whole of Wellington Road and back, singing softly with every step: 'I'm free, I'm free, I'm free!'"[18]

The atrocities of Nazi Germany are widely documented. For an astonishing account, see The Hamburg Institute for Social Research's publication *The German Army and Genocide: Crimes against War Prisoners, Jews, and Other Civilians, 1939–1944*. For photographic horrors, see Barbie Zelizer, *Remembering to Forget: Holocaust Memory through the Camera's Eye*.

For experiences of Jewish children who lived through the Holocaust, see especially Allan Zullo, *Survivors: True Stories of Children in the Holocaust*. For the account of another boy whose character was shaped so that it could never acquiesce with Nazi ideology, see the intriguing letters of "Gerhard G." in *Youth at War*: Feldpost *Letters of a German Boy to His Parents, 1943–1945*.

On popular perceptions of the Jews and persecution against them, see especially Ian Kershaw, *Hitler, the Germans, and the Final Solution*. On the long roots of European anti-Semitism prior to the rise of Nazi Germany, see especially Enzo Traverso, *The Origins of Nazi Violence*. On the attitude of Henry Ford, Sr., to "the international Jew" (as noted in chapter 1), see *The International Jew: The World's Foremost Problem*. Ford's attitudes had currency with the other leading car manufacturer of the time, General Motors; see Henry Ashby Turner, Jr., *General Motors and the Nazis: The Struggle for Control of Opel, Europe's Biggest Carmaker*.

On resistors to the Nazi regime, see the documentary *The Restless Conscience: Resistance to Hitler within Germany 1933–1945* by Hava Kohav Beller. On the varieties of responses to the Nazi program within Germany, see Pierre Ayçoberry, *The Social History of the Third Reich, 1933–1945*.

On the re-socialization of the German population in progressively adopting Nazi values, see Kressmann Taylor, *Address Unknown*; William Brustein, *The Logic of Evil: The Social Origins of the Nazi Party, 1925–1933*; Henry Ashby Turner, Jr., *German Big Business and the Rise of Hitler*; and, in novel format, C. David Baker, *The Seduction of Eva Volk*. In the Baker novel, well-intentioned people undergo an imperceptible creeping erosion of their moral compass. I sent a copy of Baker's novel to Rolf and received

18. Clare, Berlin Days, 7.

his comments about it on December 15, 2009. He had nothing but praise for it, including the following comments:

> It is outstanding and totally chilling! He's done a brilliant job of capturing the totality of what Nazism was all about—on every level of life, and in every nook and cranny of Germany, in the lives of individuals and conflicting ideologies in Germany. Furthermore, the quotes at the beginning of every chapter capture the horror of it all. . . . I am so impressed with the big, detailed picture which he painted. He accomplished what he set out to do superbly. His Preface says it all. He is a remarkable writer. . . . David really captured the all-pervasive mood and spirit of the country, which was also evident to me as a kid, but from a kid's experiences and perspectives.

And on the phenomenon of willful blindness within a society, we might compare the plight of the Native Americans, the ethnic cleansings in Rwanda and Kosovo, and even the North American banking system prior to the economic collapse of 2008—although the moral deficits of that latter situation cannot compare to the moral atrocities within ethnic cleansings. The point is simply that the phenomenon of willful blindness overspills a variety of contexts.

Bibliography

Archer, Jeffrey. *The Gospel according to Judas, by Benjamin Iscariot*. London: Macmillan, 2007.

Asch, Sholem. *The Apostle*. New York: Putnam's Sons, 1943.

———. *Mary*. New York: Putnam's Sons, 1949.

———. *The Nazarene*. New York: Putnam's Sons, 1939.

Ayçoberry, Pierre. *The Social History of the Third Reich, 1933–1945*. New York: New Press, 2000.

Baker, C. David. *The Seduction of Eva Volk*. Mill Hall, PA: PrestonSpeed, 2009.

Barnett, Victoria. *For the Soul of the People*. Oxford: Oxford University Press, 1992.

Barton, Bruce. *The Man Nobody Knows*. 1925. Reprint. Hal-Far, Malta: Lewis Press/Amazon Digital Services, 2013.

Baumgarten, Albert I. "Setting the Outer Limits: Temple Policy in the Centuries Prior to Destruction." In *Redefining First-Century Jewish and Christian Identities*, edited by Fabian E. Udoh, 88–103. South Bend, IN: University of Notre Dame Press, 2008.

Bond, Helen. *Caiaphas: Friend of Rome and Judge of Jesus?* Louisville: Westminster John Knox, 2004.

———. *Pontius Pilate in History and Interpretation*. Cambridge: Cambridge University Press, 1999.

Boyarin, Daniel. *The Jewish Gospels: The Story of the Jewish Christ*. New York: New Press, 2012.

———. *A Radical Jew: Paul and the Politics of Identity*. Berkeley: University of California Press, 1997.

Brustein, William. *The Logic of Evil: The Social Origins of the Nazi Party, 1925–1933*. New Haven: Yale University Press, 1998.

Bücher, A. *Das Synedrion in Jerusalem und das Grosse Beth-Din in der Quaderkammer des Jerusalemischen Tempels*. Vienna: Hölder, 1902.

Cape, Ruth I., ed. *Youth at War:* Feldpost *Letters of A German Boy to His Parents, 1943–1945*. New York: Lang, 2010.

Carroll, John T., and Joel B. Green. *The Death of Jesus in Early Christianity*. Grand Rapids: Baker Academic, 2007.

Chilton, Bruce. *Rabbi Jesus: An Intimate Biography*. New York: Image, 2000.

Clare, George. *Berlin Days: 1946–1947*. London: Macmillan, 1989.

———. *Last Waltz in Vienna*. London: Macmillan, 1981.

Cohen, S. J. D. *From the Maccabees to the Mishnah.* 2nd ed. Louisville: Westminster John Knox, 2006.

Flew, Anthony. *There is a God: How the World's Most Notorious Atheist Changed His Mind.* San Francisco: HarperOne, 2009.

Ford, Henry. *The International Jew: The World's Foremost Problem.* 4 vols. Detroit: The Dearborn Press, 1920–22.

Frank, Anne. *Anne Frank: The Diary of a Young Girl.* Translated by B. M. Mooyaart-Doubleday. New York: Bantam, 1993.

Gay, Peter. *My German Question: Growing Up in Nazi Berlin.* New Haven: Yale University Press, 1999.

Gompertz, Rolf. *Abraham the Dreamer: An Erotic and Sacred Love Story.* New York: iUniverse, 2003.

———. *A Celebration of Life.* North Hollywood: Word Doctor, 1983.

———. "The Day of the Messiah." *The Jewish Spectator* (September 1973) 11–13.

———. *Jesus, mein jüdischer Bruder.* Neukirchen-Vluyn: Aussaat Verlag, 2010.

———. *A Jewish Novel about Jesus.* New York: iUniverse, 2003. (Originally published as *My Jewish Brother Jesus.* North Hollywood: Word Doctor, 1977.)

———. *Menachem's Mantras & Other Verses, Stories and Thoughts.* 2002. Reprint. North Hollywood: Word Doctor, 2007.

———. *The Messiah of Midtown Park.* New York: iUniverse, 2004. (Originally published as *The Messiah of Midtown Park: Stage Play (Comedy Drama).* North Hollywood: Word Doctor, 1983.)

———. "The Messiah—Where Do We Go From Here?" *The Jewish Spectator* (Summer 1993) 24–29.

———. *Promotion and Publicity Handbook for Broadcasters.* Blue Ridge Summit, PA: Tab, 1977.

———. *Publicity Advice & How to Handbook.* North Hollywood: Word Doctor, 1992.

———. *Publicity Writing for Television and Film: A How-to Handbook.* North Hollywood: Word Doctor, 1992.

———. "The Regulars." *The Jewish Spectator* (Fall 1975) 63–65.

———. *Sparks of Spirit (A Handbook for Personal Happiness): How to Find Love and Meaning in Your Life 24 Hours a Day.* 1983. Reprint. New York: iUniverse, 2004.

———. *To Life, To Love: In Poetry and Prose. A Spiritual Memoir.* New York: iUniverse, 2004.

Goodman, Martin. *The Ruling Class of Judaea: The Origins of the Jewish Revolt against Rome, A.D. 66–70.* Cambridge: Cambridge University Press, 1993.

Grabbe, Lester L. *Judaic Religion in the Second Temple Period: Belief and Practice from the Exile to Yavneh.* London: Routledge, 2000.

The Hamburg Institute for Social Research. *The German Army and Genocide: Crimes against War Prisoners, Jews, and Other Civilians, 1939–1944.* New York: New Press, 1999.

Hays, Richard B. *The Faith of Jesus Christ: The Narrative Substructure of Galatians 3:1–4:11.* 2nd ed. Grand Rapids: Eerdmans, 2002.

Heym, Stefan. *Ahasver.* Gütersloh: Bertelsmann Verlag, 1981.

Hoehner, Harold. *Chronological Aspects of the Life of Christ.* Grand Rapids: Zondervan, 1978.

Johnson, Eric A., and Karl-Heinz Reuband, eds. *What We Knew: Terror, Mass Murder, and Everyday Life in Nazi Germany.* New York: Basic, 2003.

Kassoff, David. *The Book of Witnesses*. San Francisco: Fount, 1971.

Kaufmann, David, and Max Freudenthal. *Die Familie Gomperz . . .* 1907. Reprint. Charleston: Nabu, 2011.

Kazantzakis, Nikos. *The Last Temptation*. Reprint. London: Faber and Faber, 2003.

Kershaw, Ian. *Hitler, the Germans, and the Final Solution*. New Haven: Yale University Press, 2006.

Kertesz, Imre. *Kaddish for a Child Not Born*. 3rd ed. Evanston, IL: Northwestern University Press 1997.

Levin, Jeff, and Stephen G. Post, eds. *Divine Love: Perspectives from the World's Religious Traditions*. West Conshohocken, PA: Templeton, 2010.

Lohse, E. "*sunédrion*." In *Theological Dictionary of the New Testament, Vol. 7*, edited by Gerhard Kittel, 862. Grand Rapids: Eerdmans, 1971.

Longenecker, Bruce W. "The Challenge of a Hopeless God: Negotiating José Saramago's Novel *The Gospel according to Jesus Christ*." In *Art, Imagination, and Christian Hope: Patterns of Promise*, edited by Trevor Hart et al., 129–48. Aldershot, UK: Ashgate, 2012.

Maccoby, Hyam. *Judas Iscariot and the Myth of Jewish Evil*. London: Halban, 1992.

Mantel, H. *Studies in the History of the Sanhedrin*. Cambridge: Harvard University Press, 1961.

McLaren, James S. *Power and Politics in Palestine: The Jews and the Governing of Their Land, 100 BC–AD 70*. Sheffield, UK: Sheffield Academic Press, 1991.

Monhollon, Michael. *Divine Invasion*. Abilene, TX: Reflection, 1998.

Mossinsohn, Igal. *Judas*. New York: St. Martin's Press, 1963.

Neusner, Jacob. *A Rabbi Talks with Jesus*. Montreal: McGill-Queen's University Press, 2000.

Ollenberger, Ben C. "Suffering and Hope: The Story behind the Book." In *Suffering and Hope: A Biblical Vision and the Human Predicament*, by J. C. Beker, 1–16. Grand Rapids: Eerdmans, 1994.

Reinhartz, Adele. *Caiaphas the High Priest*. Minneapolis: Fortress, 2013.

Rensberger, David. *Johannine Faith and Liberating Community*. Louisville: Westminster John Knox, 1988.

Rivkin, E. "Beth Din, Boule, Sanhedrin: A Tragedy of Errors," *Hebrew Union College Annual* 17 (1975) 181–99.

Rosenberg, Solomon. *Face to Face with Sholem Asch*. Miami: Aber, 1958.

Rubenstein, Richard L. *My Brother Paul*. San Francisco: Harper & Row, 1972.

Sanders, E. P. *Judaism: Practice and Belief 63 BCE–66 CE*. London: SCM, 1992.

Schäbitz, Michael. "The Flight and Expulsion of German Jews." In *Jews in Nazi Berlin: From Kristallnacht to Liberation*, edited by Beate Meyer et al., 36–63. Chicago: University of Chicago Press, 2009.

Siegel, Ben. *The Controversial Sholem Asch: An Introduction to His Fiction*. Madison, WI: Popular, 1976.

Smith, Michael. *Foley: The Spy who Saved 10,000 Jews*. London: Hodder and Stoughton, 1999.

Stanton, Graham N. *Matthew for a New People*. Edinburgh: T. & T. Clark, 1992.

Starck, Renate. "Krefelder Juden berichten von ihrem Leben." *Die Heimat* 59 (1988) 26–39.

Stendahl, Krister. *Meanings: The Bible as Document and as Guide*. Philadelphia: Fortress, 2008.

Taylor, Joan E. *The Immerser: John the Baptist within Second Temple Judaism.* Grand Rapids: Eerdmans, 1997.

Taylor, Kressmann. *Address Unknown.* London: Souvenir, 2002.

Toland, John. *Adolf Hitler.* London: Book Club Associates, 1977.

Traverso, Enzo. *The Origins of Nazi Violence.* Translated by Janet Lloyd. New York: New Press, 2003.

Turner, Henry Ashby Jr. *German Big Business and the Rise of Hitler.* Oxford: Oxford University Press, 1987.

Vermes, Geza. *Jesus the Jew.* London: Collins, 1973.

Volf, Miroslav. *The End of Memory: Remembering Rightly in a Violent World.* Grand Rapids: Eerdmans, 2006.

Wiesel, Elie. *Night.* Rev. ed. New York: Hill and Wang, 2006.

Wink, Walter. *Engaging the Powers: Discernment and Resistance in a World of Domination.* Minneapolis: Fortress, 1992.

Zelizer, Barbie. *Remembering to Forget: Holocaust Memory through the Camera's Eye.* Chicago: University of Chicago Press, 1998.

Zeitlin, Solomon. *Who Crucified Jesus.* New York: Bloch, 1964.

Zullo, Allan. *Survivors: True Stories of Children in the Holocaust.* New York: Scholastic, 2005.

WATER WIND & FIRE

THE NEXT STEPS

W9-CYB-131

WATER
WIND
&FIRE

THE NEXT STEPS

Developing Your New
Relationship With God

MAC HAMMOND

Unless otherwise indicated, all Scripture quotations are taken from the King James Version of the Bible.

Scripture quotations marked NKJV are taken from The New King James Version. Copyright © 1979, 1980, 1982, Thomas Nelson, Inc.

Scripture quotations marked NIV are taken from The Holy Bible: New International Version®. NIV®. Copyright © 1973, 1978, 1984, by International Bible Society. Used by permission of Zondervan Publishing House. All rights reserved.

Scripture quotations marked AMP are taken from The Amplified Bible, New Testament. Copyright © 1958, 1987 by the Lockman Foundation, La Habra, California. Used by permission.

Scripture quotations marked NAS are taken from the New American Standard Bible. Copyright © the Lockman Foundation 1960, 1962, 1963, 1968, 1971, 1972, 1973, 1975, 1977. Used by permission.

Scripture quotations marked MESSAGE are taken from The Message: New Testament, copyright © 1993 by Eugene H. Peterson, published by NavPress, P.O. Box 35001, Colorado Springs, Colorado 80935. Used by permission.

09 08 07 06 05 10 9 8 7 6 5 4 3 2 1

Water, Wind, & Fire—The Next Steps
Developing Your New Relationship With God

ISBN 978-1-57399-3463

Copyright © 2005, 2008 by Mac Hammond

Published by Mac Hammond Ministries
PO Box 29469
Minneapolis, MN 55429

Contents

Chapter 1
Hearing and Doing God's Word 3

Chapter 2
The Local Church and Your Role in It . . 17

Chapter 3
Passing the First Faithfulness Test . . . 29

Chapter 4
Prayer and Intimacy With God 53

Chapter 5
The Power of Our Words 69

Chapter 6
Walking in Love. 81

Chapter 7
Looking Outward—How to Share Jesus . 93

Chapter 8
Three Baptisms 103

Introduction

Welcome to the family of God!

I want to personally rejoice with you that you have been born again and filled with the Holy Spirit. Not only will you live for eternity with God in heaven, but you have begun the Christian life here on earth, one of the greatest adventures a human being can experience. However, the richness of that adventure depends upon how much you grow in your faith from a newborn babe to a mature Christian. Paul writes in Philippians 3:14:

I press toward the mark for the prize of the high calling of God in Christ Jesus.

The life of a Christian is a press that ultimately culminates with the prize of our high calling in Christ Jesus. What is that press? How do you press forward? What things are you reaching for, especially as a new Christian? That's what I want to show you in this book. The Bible outlines a path for you to walk as you grow in the Lord, and this book will show you what steps are on that path.

Your new life of faith will require commitment, change, and courage; but it will also provide rewards in this life and in the life to come that will go beyond your wildest dreams.

Chapter 1

Hearing and Doing God's Word

All scripture is given by inspiration of God, and is profitable for doctrine, for reproof, for correction, for instruction in righteousness: that the man of God may be perfect, thoroughly furnished unto all good works.
2 Timothy 3:16,17

In your Christian life are many necessary elements, but nothing is more important than God's Word. It is the foundation upon which your life must be built; it is the light that shows you how to navigate life successfully. (Ps. 119:130)

The Bible reveals the general will of God for all believers of all ages. Its timeless truths and practical principles provide the doctrine, correction, reproof, and instruction you need to become everything God has designed you to be.

In the simplest of terms, it is the owner's manual for life given by the Creator of life! To begin growing in God, you must embrace the Bible's importance, hear it on a regular basis, and yield to its direction by becoming a "doer" of the Word!

Hearing but Not Doing

In James 1, God reveals to us a major hindrance to our spiritual growth and a doorway to self-deception. Verse 22 teaches us, "Be ye doers of the word, and not hearers only, deceiving your own selves."

As important as it is to read and study the Bible, you must keep as your aim and focus living out what it teaches. Every time that you read or hear the Word of God and fail or refuse to act on it, you leave the door wide open for deception. In effect, you say by your actions that you don't believe God's Word is true for you and that you have a better plan.

Remember: James 2:17 declares that faith without action is dead. Yes, faith comes by hearing and hearing by the Word of God, and James is talking to you who have heard and believed. But without corresponding action, that faith is powerless to help you. In fact, the word translated *hearers* in verse 22 is the same Greek word translated *hearing* in Romans 10:17,1. So James is not talking about hearing with your natural ears but rather hearing with your heart, which is how faith comes. But if you don't do that Word, you can still be deceived.

Closely related to this form of deception is the way Satan stops people's spiritual ears with religious tradition. Jesus told the religious leaders of His day—the scribes and Pharisees—that their traditions had made the Word of God of no effect. (Matt. 15:6; Mark 7:13.) Since the Word of God is intended to have the effect of bringing faith, Jesus is saying that the tradition of man will stop faith from coming because traditional people don't have ears to hear what the Spirit of God is saying. Folks steeped in religious tradition have no capacity to receive revelation knowledge from the Word, so faith can't come to them.

Jesus defined tradition as the commandments of men. You'll find that the commandments of men have no root in the Word of God and many times even contradict God's Word. An example would be the teaching that if you were sprinkled as an infant, then your eternity in heaven is secure. Those who have accepted this tradition have a difficult time accepting the truth that they must be born again. They simply don't have ears to hear that truth.

Why Would Anyone Hear and Believe, and Not Do?

There are three main reasons why believers hear but don't do His Word even though they truly believe that it would be best for them to be obedient to it.

The Lust of the Flesh

The first reason is simply the lust of the flesh. Lust is any powerful desire of the flesh; it is usually thought of with a sexual connotation, but it really includes anything that your flesh strongly craves or wants to do.

Addictive behavior is a form of lust that illustrates this truth quite well. I'm sure that everyone who has ever used drugs or smoked cigarettes for any length of time knows deep down in their hearts that they are slowly killing themselves. They may even believe that their bodies are the temple of the Holy Ghost and are to be presented as a living sacrifice to God, but the desire is so powerful that they can't overcome it.

Others may hold onto a grudge and refuse to forgive someone who hurt them. It feels good to their flesh to exact vengeance and to try to repay the wrong that has been done, even though they know that they are to walk in love and forgive as Christ forgave them.

Selfishness is another area where people's flesh can give them trouble. Their spirits have received the revelation that they should tithe and be givers and sow to the Spirit to reap life everlasting, but the flesh has other things that it wants to do with that money to satisfy itself.

Fear of Man

The second reason people don't do the Word is fear— and perhaps I should say, more specifically, the fear of man. God has called all of us to preach the Gospel, lay hands on the sick, and cast out devils; but most Christians don't tell folks what Jesus has done for them because they are afraid of being mocked, rejected, or persecuted.

Many don't walk in love because they are fearful of being hurt in some way. And how many don't receive the baptism in the Holy Spirit and speak with other tongues because of what their families and other church members might think.

Procrastination

The third, and possibly most prevalent, reason for not doing the Word is procrastination.

If you have ever said, "Lord, I'm going to do what Your Word says about this—tomorrow," then you have fallen for this deception. It is always easier to say, "I'll quit smoking tomorrow," or "I'll start tithing next month," or "I'll go witnessing next week." And the thing is, you'll always have a seemingly good reason to put off being obedient.

The Amplified Bible's rendering of James 1:22 clarifies how this happens. It says, "Be doers of the Word [obey the message], and not merely listeners to it, betraying yourselves [into deception by reasoning contrary to the Truth]."

If you don't do the Word that you know you ought to, then in order to still that guilty conscience, in order to live with yourself, you have to engage in something called self-justification. You start reasoning contrary to the truth to come up with an excuse for your failure to act. You say, "I can't do that now because..." and then give some reason that keeps you from feeling too bad about it.

The moment you do that, you open a door to deception, and Satan immediately begins to promote death and cursing in your life. Death and cursing seldom become evident overnight; and the longer you reason against the truth, the more comfortable you become living opposed to it. Therefore, by the time you realize the touch of death in your life, you may not make the connection that it is there because you are not doing the Word.

Then you'll begin reasoning, trying to figure out why that death is there. "Why is this happening to me? Maybe this faith stuff doesn't really work all the time. Is God trying to teach me something? Did I do something to make Him angry with me?" And the deception will deepen, and the death will become more and more manifest.

> *...betraying yourselves into deception by reasoning contrary to the truth.*
> *James 1:22 Amp.*

How to Do the Word

Without a doubt, psychologically or chemically addictive behavior, selfishness, fear, and reasoning can be powerful forces in a person's life. Even secular studies demonstrate that most people cannot consistently change these kinds of behaviors. And from them, we can see that just exercising willpower and self-control is not going to effect permanent change in most lives. Government drug rehabilitation programs with their 10 percent success rate clearly show that.

So how do you begin to close the common doors to not doing the Word? As always, the answer to this is found in the Word of God. In Ephesians 2:19, we are told there is an exceeding greatness of His power toward those who believe. The same power that raised Christ Jesus from the dead is certainly more than enough to overcome any fear or contrary behavior in our lives.

I should say here that since none of us has achieved perfection, until Jesus returns, we are all going to have to deal with these issues from time to time. What you must learn to do is to not just exercise your willpower but rather to tap into the power that is available to you because you believe. Don't ever let Satan deceive you into thinking that your faith isn't important. Believing comes first. But then what? How do you tap into that power?

Let's go back to James 1:22 and read on to verse 25:

> *But be ye doers of the word, and not hearers only, deceiving your own selves. For if any be a hearer of the word, and not a doer, he is like unto a man beholding his natural face in a glass: For he beholdeth himself, and goeth his way, and straightway forgetteth what manner of man he was. But whoso looketh into the perfect law of liberty, and continueth therein, he being not a forgetful hearer, but a doer of the word, this man shall be blessed in his deed.*

In verses 24 and 25, the Greek word translated *forgetteth* and *forgetful* means "to put out of mind."[3] If you want to be a doer of the Word, you have to do something about what's in your mind.

The Word says, "...being not a forgetful hearer but a doer..." (v. 25). A hearer of what? A hearer of the perfect law of liberty, or God's Word, of course. So you could say, "Being not a forgetful hearer of God's Word, but a doer." Insert the definition of forgetful and you read, "Not putting out of mind God's Word, but being a doer." Another way to say it, then, is this: "Keep God's Word in your mind, and be a doer of the Word."

Let's look at the next key to doing the Word, which is found in the next verse: "If any man among you seem to be religious, and bridleth not his tongue, but deceiveth his own heart, this man's religion is vain" (v. 26).

The previous verses said that deception comes when you hear the Word but don't do it, and that you can only do the Word if you keep it in your mind. In the very next verse, God says that deception occurs when you don't control your tongue.

Don't we all eventually speak what we think about? Remember: "Out of the abundance of the heart, the mouth speaks" (Matt. 12:34 NKJV).

The two principal factors that define doers of the Word are what they think upon and what they speak. If you think on God's Word and then speak God's Word, you will tap into the exceeding greatness of His power to those who believe—and that power can and will change your behavior. You will become a doer of the Word, not by your own strength and willpower but by the power of God that is in His Word.

In Joshua 1:8, God plainly tells Joshua how to do the Word. Keep in mind that if this worked for Joshua, it will work for you too. God is no respecter of persons. He recorded this so that you could benefit from His instruction as well.

This book of the law shall not depart out of thy mouth; but thou shalt meditate therein day and night, that thou mayest observe to do according to all that is written therein: for then thou shalt make thy way prosperous, and then thou shalt have good success.

Notice that you observe to do the Law, or the Word, only after you've meditated on the Word and spoken the Word. Consistent behavior is always preceded by thoughts and words. Also notice that thinking the Word, speaking the Word, and then doing the Word lead to prosperity and success. On the other hand, not doing the Word leads to deception; and deception leads to cursing and death.

Think It, Speak It, Do It

The connection between thinking and speaking and doing is so vitally important. We need to focus on the process so we can understand how it works.

You have the capacity to imagine yourself experiencing life in a particular way. How you see or imagine your life is how you will experience it. Your thoughts and imaginations will prompt and motivate your behavior to bring that image to pass in your life. Satan wants you to have vain (empty and foolish) imaginations. He wants you to fantasize about sinful things. He wants you to see yourself as defeated, sick, and broke. He wants you to only think about yourself and your needs. He knows that as you dwell on those kinds of thoughts, your life will go in that direction. If you are there now, Satan can keep you there with vain imaginations running loose in your head. As it says in Proverbs 23:7, "As he thinketh in his heart, so is he."

Don't let Satan's thoughts stay in your mind. Cast down vain thoughts, and bring them captive to the obedience of Christ. (2 Cor. 10:5) Begin imagining yourself doing mighty works for God. See yourself as being more than a conqueror and able to do all things through Christ who strengthens you. (Rom. 8:37; Eph. 4:13)

Pray in the Holy Spirit and yield your life to His ministry, and God will begin to show you things that your eye hasn't seen, your ear hasn't heard, neither has entered into your heart. He'll begin to show you what He has prepared for you who love Him. (1 Cor. 2:9) Not only can you imagine God's Word being true in your life, but you can also receive by the Holy Spirit a grand image or vision of what God has specifically planned for you.

As you meditate on God's plan and then talk about that plan, you'll tap into the exceeding greatness of His power. The things in your life that would stand in the way of God's purpose for you will begin to fall away. You'll be delivered and set free from all of Satan's hindrances. Most importantly, you'll become an immediate doer of the things you've heard and believed. And when you do, a major door to deception in your life will be closed and you will become all that God intends you to be.

A Part of Doing the Word

Although much of this chapter has focused on how you can personally receive and act upon the Word of God, it is important to recognize that a major component in this process is the local church.

There are many important topics on the subject of church attendance, and space does not permit me to discuss all of them here. However, Ephesians 4:11-16 reveals the central one: God has ordained ministers and anointed them by the Holy Spirit to equip you with the Word so you can grow up in all things. In other words, it is vital that you recognize and embrace God's planned process for your hearing and doing the Word. God's plan for your growth is eternally linked to your placing yourself under the influence and teaching of His gifted ministers— apostles, prophets, evangelists, pastors, and teachers.

In practical terms, this happens when you commit to be part of a local church where the call of God on the pastor is designed to feed you the Word so you can "come to the unity of the faith and of the knowledge of the Son of God, to a perfect (mature) man, to the measure of the stature of the fullness of Christ" (Eph. 4:13).

Embracing God's strategy for your ongoing spiritual growth—becoming part of the local church—is your first step toward becoming a hearer and doer of the Word of God. We'll explore this important subject more fully in the next chapter.

Chapter 2

The Local Church and Your Role in It

Is church attendance really necessary? Is it actually that important?

Ask people these questions and the diversity of answers you will hear, even from long-time Christians, will astound you. Many people lack understanding concerning the benefit, purpose, and importance of the local church. As a result, church attendance has become a dead, religious ritual for many, and a casual and sometimes unnecessary distraction for others.

An in-depth study of the Word will reveal that God's directive for church attendance is actually quite specific in purpose. The Word reveals that "assembling" is a supernatural design orchestrated by God to interconnect believers with one another for the purpose of impact and increase.

In fact, Scripture reveals that properly plugging into the company of believers with whom God has connected you will position you to access the power of God in a way nothing else can, causing increase and growth in your life.

A God-Ordained Place

Let's start with the most oft-quoted verse on the subject of church attendance and involvement. In Hebrews 10:25, we are told to not forsake "the assembling of ourselves together." Although many seek to minimize the direct connection between this verse and church attendance, the author of Hebrews isn't talking about gathering for dinner over at a Christian friend's house or about a spontaneous prayer meeting with friends. Both of these things are great and should be done, but this verse is addressing something different.

The meaning of the word "assembly" can be likened to an erector set, where pieces are designed to fit together in a particular group.[1] In effect, this verse might as well have said, "Don't forsake going to your local church," because that is what it means.

Moreover, according to the Word of God, attendance to just any church will not do. The Bible gives a clear indication that God wants to place each of us in a specific church where His power will flow to and through each one of us.

We see this truth demonstrated in Acts 4. After Peter and John were apprehended by the temple priests for preaching about Jesus, they were brought before the high priest, who interrogated them, threatened them, and then let them go.

Then Peter and John, after "being let go... went to their own company" (Acts 4:23).

Notice that it says they went to their "own company." That means there were other companies of believers available, but they identified a particular company as their own.

Now I want you to see what happened next. After Peter and John shared all that the chief priests had said and done to them, all the members in their company lifted up their voices together in one accord and prayed. The result? The power of God came in such strength that it shook the building!

What was the result of this release of power? The Bible says that the believers in their company were emboldened to go out and share the Gospel fearlessly.

> *...they were all filled with the Holy Spirit and spoke the word of God boldly.... With great power the apostles continued to testify to the resurrection of the Lord Jesus, and much grace was upon them all.*
> Acts 4:31,33 NIV

They had a powerful impact on their community. Furthermore, we see that this supernatural power affected their individual and personal lives as well. The Bible says that not one of them lacked in material need.

There were no needy persons among them. For from time to time those who owned lands or houses sold them, brought the money from the sales and put it at the apostles' feet, and it was distributed to anyone as he had need. Acts 4:34,35 NIV

When they plugged into their company of believers, the power of God flowed through them to drive out insufficiency!

The power available to believers assembling with their "own company" is confirmed in 1 Corinthians 12:12-18, where the apostle Paul compares the body of Christ to the natural human body. This comparison is practical yet profound in its application, revealing how the Church is to operate and function in the earth.

First Corinthians 12:14 says, "For the body is not one member, but many." Every time I read this, the picture of a jigsaw puzzle comes to my mind. A jigsaw puzzle may have hundreds of pieces; yet when put in their right places, all the pieces fit together perfectly to form a whole picture that is a blessing to others. That is how you and I are to fit into the church body that God has called each of us to be a part of.

More specifically, I want to draw your attention to 1 Corinthians 12:18 NKJV, which says, "But now God has set the members, each one of them, in the body just as He pleased." Notice it says God sets the members in the body as it pleases Him.

Without a doubt, there is a specific church in which God is pleased to set you. It won't necessarily be the church that your parents and grandparents have attended for the last fifty years. It might not be the church that's closest to where you live. It might not even be the church that has the biggest pipe organ that you like so much. It is a place— a specific place—where it pleases God to place you.

Finding Your Place

You may be thinking, *But how do I find that place I'm supposed to be in?* I can assure you, God is not trying to hide this place from you. He desires that you know which church He wants you to join. Let me share with you three foundational steps to finding your "own company."

First of all, the Bible says:

If any of you lacks wisdom, let him ask of God, who gives to all liberally and without reproach... But let him ask in faith....
James 1:5,6 NKJV

It's a simple but important step. Ask the Lord in faith, "Where do You want me to be?" God won't make this a difficult step, but be sure you haven't fashioned a list of acceptable answers beforehand. The book of James also reveals that selfish motives and desires will hinder us from receiving what we ask for. (James 4:3) So when you ask, be completely open to God's direction.

Take advantage of every opportunity that crosses your path, and view it as a possible answer to your prayer. When people mention their church or invite you there, don't write it off as a coincidence.

The next step is to follow your heart and pay attention to the inward witness of the Holy Spirit. The presence of God within a believer will always confirm a right decision. Visit a few churches, and when you walk into the right place, it will seem right. It will feel like putting on a pair of comfortable bedroom slippers or coming home to your favorite dinner.

The reverse is also true. If you visit a church that's not the right place for you, you'll feel uncomfortable. It will be like dragging a fingernail across a blackboard; your spirit will know it's not the right church for you. That doesn't mean it's an ungodly church; it simply means that it's not the place where it has pleased God to place you.

The third principle for finding your place is revealed in John 10:4, in which Jesus says that the sheep will follow their true shepherd because they know (distinguish, recognize) His voice. Jesus is the Chief Shepherd of the body of Christ, and pastors are called under-shepherds. Because God's children know the voice of the Chief Shepherd, I believe they will also know the voice of their appropriate under-shepherd.

In other words, when you are in the proper church, the pastor will be someone whom you consistently receive ministry from, someone who feeds you spiritually—and maybe sometimes even steps on your toes. In other words, there will be times when the pastor's preaching will seem to be directed specifically at you. In fact, sometimes irritated husbands will come up to me after a service I've preached and ask, "Has my wife been talking to you about me?"

The reality is that when you are in your company of believers, the preaching and teaching of the Word will be right on target and what you need—not just what you want—to hear! Your shepherd's "voice" will provide a balanced spiritual diet that will cause you to grow. This is simply another confirmation that you are in the church where it has pleased God to place you.

An Important Attitude Adjustment

There is one more important issue to address concerning finding the place where it has pleased God to place you. When you are in your company of believers— your church— you will submit to and flow with them, for as Amos 3:3 says, "Can two walk together, except they be agreed?"

Incredibly, I've talked to many people who actually attend churches where they are in direct contradiction with their vision, doctrine, and conduct. They believe God has called them there to be an agent of change and bring revelation to that pastor and congregation—to alter their vision, adjust their doctrine, and change the way they operate.

Though their intent might be for good, they are dreadfully deceived. They end up placing themselves in a position to cause strife, promote rebellion, or experience rejection because of their differences. These are definite signs of being in the wrong church or simply that you have the wrong attitude toward church and your role in it!

As you search for the company of believers God has chosen for you, always remember that He will not place you in a church to straighten them out or instigate change. In fact, the opposite is true: He will place you in a church that does these things for you!

Getting Plugged In

Finding your church home where it has pleased God to place you is vitally important, but there is an additional step required to properly develop your new relationship with God. You must become a contributing member of the body of Christ. That means doing something more than becoming a member of a church and warming a pew every Sunday. Look at Ephesians 4:16:

> *From whom the whole body fitly joined together and compacted by that which every joint supplieth, according to the effectual working in the measure of every part, maketh increase of the body unto the edifying of itself in love.*

Did you catch it? The key is in the phrase "every joint supplieth." This is what will increase, edify, and build up the body of believers in love. Every joint (or member) needs to give of its supply. Simply put, just coming to church every Sunday will not enable you to walk out your divine destiny. Your next step must be to get involved and share your "supply" as you have something that your church needs.

Not only will the church benefit when you give your supply to the body by plugging in and getting involved, when you give your supply to the church body, the church grows and increases, which means your life does too.

It's a fact. The normal growth process of the human body is that every part of a body grows in unison. You won't see a baby's arm or leg remain infant size while the rest of the body increases in size. All the contributing members of a body develop at the same time.

What happens when a member fails to contribute? Compare it again to the functioning of the human body. What would happen if you taped your arm firmly to your side, making it unable to move? In a couple weeks, it would begin to wither in strength and would eventually become atrophied.

Likewise, when members of the church body fail to plug in and make a contribution to the increase of the body, they are disconnected from the power source designed to bring them growth and increase.

This is why your focus needs to be plugging in and faithfully offering your supply within your company of believers. Being faithful is "where the rubber meets the road." Sadly, every Sunday in churches throughout the world, far too few faithful people are in attendance.

Faithfulness involves commitment, consistency, and loyalty. Sadly, these values are declining and at times, even mocked in our current culture. This should not be the case with Christians, especially when the Scripture clearly reveals the rewards of faithfulness.

A faithful man will abound with blessings.... Proverbs 28:20 NKJV

Hebrews 11:6 says that God is a rewarder, and this verse clearly reveals that abundant blessings will be the reward at the finish line for faithful people.

So, is church attendance really necessary? Is it really that important?

To successfully develop your new relationship with God, you must solidify in your heart the Bible's answer to these questions. The answer according to the Word of God is a resounding and resolute yes!

But remember: simply sitting in a church isn't being plugged into a church. As you begin your journey to becoming a productive part of the family of God, it is vital that you recognize that faithfulness is a requirement. (1 Cor. 4:2) It is important that you not only find your God-ordained local church, but that you faithfully fill your place in it. How do you do that? We'll explore the ways in the next chapter.

Chapter 3

Passing the Faithfulness Test

As we have seen, it is important that you not only find the church where it has pleased God to place you, but that you also faithfully fill your place in it. Taking these steps is crucial to your spiritual development. In this chapter, I want to address the next step in your journey by answering a question I have often been asked: "I found my church home; now what do I do?"

Considering the diversity of arenas in which we could offer our supply and be faithful, the challenge is knowing where to begin. The good news is that the answer is clearly revealed in the Bible.

> *He that is faithful in that which is least is faithful also in much: and he that is unjust in the least is unjust also in much. If therefore ye have not been faithful in the unrighteous mammon, who will commit to your trust the true riches?* Luke 16:10,11

Here we see that the least God expects us to be faithful in is our handling of "unrighteous mammon." (The phrase "unrighteous mammon" is a reference to worldly riches, or money. However, this is not saying that money is either good or evil. Mammon, or money, only becomes "unrighteous" when it is used wrongly.)

Mammon is simply another word for material resources or money. Thus, the clear universal starting line for plugging into a church and becoming a faithful member is managing our material resources in line with God's Word. If we are not faithful with our financial supply, how can God trust us with anything else?

You see, the most basic call of God on our lives is to be His stewards. Stewardship is the one calling that we all have in common; it transcends all dispensations and follows us into eternity. We are created to manage creation on God's behalf—to manage (or administrate) the household (or estate) of our Lord. The essence of the principle of stewardship is this: we don't own anything. We are God's stewards, and we need to see our lives as resources—of time, talent, money, and so forth—to accomplish God's purpose in the earth.

As a steward, you need to be faithful to follow God's commands, particularly in the area of finances. Faithfulness on any level is impossible until you become faithful in the use of your money. You see, prosperity doesn't involve just your bank account. Prosperity also includes prosperity in your soul, an abundance of health, your every need provided for—body, soul, and spirit. That is why it is vital to understand that giving of our natural resources (money) is the least that we are called to be faithful in. It is intricately entwined with everything else in our lives.

Understand, however, that learning to be faithful with your money doesn't automatically make you faithful in all the other areas of your life. Other steps must be taken to yield to faithfulness in those areas. What the Scripture does mean, however, is that you simply cannot become faithful in any other area without first taking care of the money matter.

How important is this? Look at the latter portion of Luke 16:11: "...who will entrust to you the true riches?"

What are the true riches? They are the gifts and callings of God, His power and anointing, and His divine endowments. These are the true riches that God desires for each of us to manage as His stewards on the earth—for the purpose of initiating change on His behalf.

This change is designed to happen through the local church. Yet even if we find the place where it has pleased God to place us, if we don't understand and function in this most basic of all callings, then nothing else will work properly.

God's Pathway to Financial Faithfulness

As you begin your journey toward financial faithfulness, the first thing that must be clear in your mind is that God does want you to prosper and is not against you having things. A wealth of Scripture clearly reveals this fact, while also showing us that He is against things having you! Things (money) have you when they occupy the place God is supposed to hold in your life and when you forget God by placing your trust in riches. (1 Tim. 6:17; Deut. 8:10,11.)

The issue is our perspective toward money and how we use it, not whether God wants us to prosper. There is only one reliable way to be assured of God's desire: by going to His Word. There is no shortage of Scripture that speaks directly to the issue of God's provision. Although space does not permit us to look at all of the relevant Scriptures here, a sampling will give us a clear picture of God's intentions.

In Deuteronomy 8:18, God makes a remarkable statement:

> *But thou shalt remember the Lord thy God: for it is he that giveth thee power to get wealth, that he may establish his covenant which he sware unto thy fathers, as it is this day.*

Ask yourself a question. Why would God tell His covenant people He was giving them the power to get wealth if He didn't want them to have any?

You may be thinking, *But Mac, that verse isn't for us! It was written to the Old Testament Jews!*

Many believers rob themselves of hundreds of wonderful Bible promises through such assumptions. They think that because the promises were originally made to Israel (the children of Abraham) in the Old Testament, they don't apply to them.

However, the New Testament says that we have a better covenant established on better promises.

> *But now He [Jesus] has obtained a more excellent ministry, inasmuch as He is also Mediator of a better covenant, which was established on better promises.* Hebrews 8:6 NKJV

Also, if you are a child of God, then the blessings of Abraham are yours to claim:

That the blessing of Abraham might come on the Gentiles through Jesus Christ; that we might receive the promise of the Spirit through faith.

And if ye be Christ's, then are ye Abraham's seed, and heirs according to the promise.
Galatians 3:14,29

As a born-again believer, you are Abraham's heir according to the promise and are, therefore, entitled to the promises God made to Abraham and Israel. Part of your birthright as a seed of Abraham is the God-given power to acquire wealth. He placed that power within you. You won't offend Him by using it.

Does God really want you to prosper? Look to Psalm 35:27 and see:

Let them shout for joy, and be glad, that favour my righteous cause: yea, let them say continually, Let the Lord be magnified, which hath pleasure in the prosperity of his servant.

According to this verse, watching His servants prosper doesn't give God heartburn; it gives Him pleasure! Think of it: God is pleased when you increase!

This theme is woven throughout the entire Old Testament and continues right on into the New. Look at 2 Corinthians 9:11, for example. Paul says Christians who give to the work of the Gospel are "being enriched in every thing to all bountifulness, which causeth through us thanksgiving to God."

The New International Version translation of this verse is enlightening. It says:

You will be made rich in every way so that you can be generous on every occasion, and through us your generosity will result in thanksgiving to God.

In this verse and throughout the entire chapter of 2 Corinthians 9, Paul says to expect great financial increase if you are a giver to the work of God. The clear aim of this passage is to raise your level of expectancy concerning your financial harvest. Look at verses 6-8, for example:

But this I say, He which soweth sparingly shall reap also sparingly; and he which soweth bountifully shall reap also bountifully. Every man according as he purposeth in his heart, so let him give; not grudgingly, or of necessity: for God loveth a cheerful giver. And God is able to make all grace abound toward you; that ye, always having

all sufficiency in all things, may abound to
every good work.

Here is one of the clearest expressions
of the will of God for your finances in all
of Scripture! When you give cheerfully and
abundantly, God wants you to expect Him to
bless your finances. Why? So you can squander
money on the desires of your flesh? No! So you
may continue to "abound to every good work."

It would take volumes to cover all that
the Bible has to say about God's desire to see
His faithful ones prospered and successful.
Just look at the lives of some of the great men
of God mentioned in Scripture. God blessed
Abraham, David, and Solomon with great
wealth. We are also His children and heirs
according to the promise. The blessing of God
is meant to be a part of our lives.

Our Motive and Method in Working

Another foundational perspective we must
embrace is that God expects us to earn our
money and not rely on the lottery if we want to
experience His blessing. Ephesians 4:28 says:

Let him that stole steal no more: but rather
let him labour, working with his hands the

*thing which is good, that he may have to
give to him that needeth.*

Some people read this verse casually and assume it merely says that if you've been a thief, then you have to get a job and start living right. But Paul is actually giving us his definition of a thief.

First, he says that if you don't want to be a thief, if you don't want to steal anymore, then you have to get a job and begin to labor at that which is good. Labor involves diligent, consistent effort. This is God's way for you to generate an income: He wants you to be hard-working and persistent in your vocation.

Unfortunately, a lot of folks punch the clock in the morning, do as little as they can during the day, and leave early in the afternoon. That's not God's way. He wants you to give it your most consistent, diligent effort. God says that if you don't do that, then you're a thief. You won't have Him involved in your financial life if you're not making a diligent, consistent effort at that which is good.

In Luke 10:7, Jesus said that the laborer who works diligently is worthy of his hire. Whatever you do, if you do it as unto the Lord, God will see to it that you receive a fair wage.

Ephesians 4:28 also shows us what our motive should be for laboring: "That [you] may have to give to him that needeth." If this isn't your perspective, then the Bible says that you're a thief. I know that's a strong statement, but the reasoning behind it is this: you're God's steward. When you start laboring for motives that are self-centered, the income that you generate will be consumed on your desires instead of on God's. As God's steward, if you're consuming resources only on you, then He says you're a thief.

God wants our paradigm regarding prosperity to focus outwardly and not inwardly—to meet the needs of others and not to be consumers only for the sake of our own flesh. That outward focus, my friends, is the ultimate purpose of financial prosperity at the hand of God.

Understanding the Tithe

As I said before, God expects us to be faithful to Him with the money He has given us, His stewards. Being faithful with our money begins with the tithe. There are those in the body of Christ who argue that the tithe is not in the New Testament, that it was under the Law, and that Christians are, therefore, not required to tithe. These assumptions are wrong. The fact is that the tithe predates the Law and is in the New Testament.

Before you get tripped up with these erroneous teachings, let's see what the Bible says. Look at Hebrews 6:20 Amp:

Where Jesus has entered in for us [in advance], a Forerunner having become a High Priest forever after the order (with the rank) of Melchizedek.

Jesus' present-day ministry is as our High Priest. He is seated at the right hand of God. He is our Mediator, our Advocate, and our Intercessor. This Scripture says that Jesus is a High Priest after the order of Melchizedek. He is not a High Priest after the order of Aaron, whose priesthood was established under the Mosaic Law.

To better understand Jesus' high priestly ministry, we need to know more about Melchizedek, who is first mentioned in Genesis 14:18-20:

And Melchizedek king of Salem brought forth bread and wine: and he was the priest of the most high God. And he blessed him [Abraham], and said, Blessed be Abram of the most high God, possessor of heaven and earth: and blessed be the most high God, which hath delivered thine enemies into thy hand. And he gave him tithes of all.

Abraham had just been victorious in battle and was returning with the spoils when he met Melchizedek. Upon meeting Melchizedek, Abraham acknowledged him as a priest of the most high God and, therefore, paid him tithes of the spoil of battle. Abraham tithed before God gave Moses the Law, so we can see clearly that tithing is not under the Law.

In his meeting with Abraham, Melchizedek did two things. He received Abraham's tithes, and then he conferred blessing upon him. Like Melchizedek, Jesus too receives tithes. Look at Hebrews 7:8 NKJV:

Here mortal men receive tithes, but there he receives them, of whom it is witnessed that he lives.

Just as Abraham acknowledged Melchizedek by paying him the tithe, we acknowledge Jesus as our High Priest by paying Him the tithe. And just as Melchizedek blessed Abraham in return, Jesus confers His blessing on our lives.

It is extremely arrogant and inconsistent with Scripture to expect the blessing of God when we have not acknowledged Jesus as our High Priest with our tithes.

Where Does the Tithe Go?

Does God need your money? No. But it is through the tithe that we acknowledge His sovereignty. God looks at the tithe as our recognition that He is the owner and we are the stewards. It is how we acknowledge His lordship and declare that we have submitted our interests in this material world to Him. Leviticus 27:30 shows us that God views the tithe as His.

And all the tithe of the land, whether of the seed of the land, or of the fruit of the tree, is the Lord's: it is holy unto the Lord.

The tithe is not something we give God. It's something that we return to Him. Where and how to pay the tithe is a question for many people. Malachi 3:10 gives us the answer:

Bring ye all the tithes into the storehouse, that there may be meat in mine house, and prove me now herewith, saith the Lord of hosts, if I will not open you the windows of heaven, and pour you out a blessing, that there shall not be room enough to receive it.

This verse clearly states that we're to bring all the tithe to the storehouse. (Notice that it does not say, "Divide your tithe up and send it to a number of different storehouses.") What, then, is the storehouse? In the dispensation of the church age, the word *storehouse* is analogous to the local church. In other words, you are to bring your tithe to the local church of which you are a member.

Too often, I hear of people sending off their tithe checks to their favorite traveling ministers. Although they are on the right track in giving to ministries that are doing God's work, they are doing it out of order. First, all the tithe (10 percent of your income) goes to your home church. After that, you are free to give offerings (monetary gifts above and beyond the tithe) to other ministries.

Malachi 3:10 explains why all the tithe goes to the storehouse:

Bring ye all the tithes into the storehouse [church], that there may be meat in mine house....

The term "meat" here is a reference to natural provision. The tithe provides unencumbered, general fund income to pay for the cost of ministry. Also, the word "meat" is used in the New Testament to describe the Word of God. (Heb. 5; 1 Cor. 3.) When you bring your tithe to your storehouse, you will provide what is needed for the operation of ministry and you will position yourself to receive the meat of God's Word. (This is another confirmation of the importance of being part of a local church.)

This spiritual exchange is also illustrated in 1 Corinthians 9:11, in which the apostle Paul says:

> *If we have sown unto you spiritual things, is it a great thing if we shall reap your carnal things?*

This verse indicates that there is an exchange of natural things for supernatural things—an exchange of money for spiritual provision. Furthermore, this exchange is made glaringly clear in the last part of Malachi 3:10: "...prove me now herewith, saith the Lord of hosts, if I will not open you the windows of heaven, and pour you out a blessing, that there shall not be room enough to receive it."

To the tither, God says that He will open the windows of heaven and pour out a blessing so big that there won't be room enough to receive it all. That's quite a supernatural return for your giving, wouldn't you say?

But before you start jumping up and down, you need to understand that the phrase "there shall not be room enough to receive it" is not to be taken literally. God was not saying that you'd have so much money that you wouldn't be able to open enough bank accounts to accommodate it all. He was saying that you wouldn't have enough room in your heart to receive all that He'd brought you, and the result would be that your heart's desires would change.

The tithe turns a hard heart into a sowing heart. Why is that? Jesus said in Matthew 6:21:

For where your treasure is, there will your heart be also.

When you begin investing your money the way God says a faithful steward should, your heart will begin to change.

Now, when people hear about God pouring out a blessing, sometimes they begin to conjure up in their minds pictures of winning the lottery, inheriting a million dollars, or catching a bag of coins dropping out of heaven. Don't hold your breath waiting for any of that to happen!

The blessing of God will manifest in your life through various means, such as God giving you witty ideas to save or earn extra money. Many people testify that before tithing they lived paycheck to paycheck, but after they began tithing, their current income somehow became more than enough to meet their needs.

Another interesting phenomenon that tithers experience is that their number of financial emergencies drastically decreases. They find that the lawnmower doesn't break down, the car keeps running smoothly, and the refrigerator keeps "fridging." Like the children of Israel wandering through the desert, they find that their sandals never wear out (figuratively speaking). For the tither, God opens doors of opportunity that no man can shut.

Meeting the Needs of Your Family

So far, we've learned that as God's stewards, we are at least to be faithful in the use of our money. We are to generate income by laboring at that which is good. From the fruits of our labor, we are to pay God the tithe, which is 10 percent of our income. We are to pay all the tithe to the storehouse, which is the church we attend.

Now, after we've generated an income and given God 10 percent, 1 Timothy 5:8 shows us what to do next:

> But if any provide not for his own, and specially for those of his own house, he hath denied the faith, and is worse than an infidel.

This verse says the next thing we do with our money is to take care of the needs of our families. Before we go on a vacation, before we buy that boat, and before we give offerings above and beyond the tithe to the Gospel, we are to meet the needs of our families. If we don't, it's tantamount to being infidels, unbelievers.

Meeting the needs of our families is a serious matter to God. It's vital that they have the necessities in life. Food, clothing, and shelter are the barest essentials.

How do we define a need? We need to keep two things in mind. First of all, need is a very personal thing. Only you and God know what needs your family has. Don't let anybody else define for you what need is for your family, and don't ever get in the business of trying to define somebody else's need.

Furthermore, your level of need will change with the level of responsibility God entrusts to you. For example, a person who is single will have fewer needs in life than someone who is married and has children. The level of need rises drastically when someone becomes married and then rises again after he or she has children.

Secondly, God knows when you've stepped across the line and tried to define something as a need when it really is a desire. Don't try to con God. He knows the difference between genuine need and false need. When you're honest before God about it, He will see to it that you will always have enough left over to meet the needs of others.

Do you know what we call money that is left over after all of your genuine needs are met? We call it seed. Seed is what we use to meet the needs of those around us. It is also the instrument God will use to bring increase into your life. So we will wind down our discussion about money by talking about the seed.

The Seed—Your Instrument for Increase

When we talk about using our leftover money to meet the needs of others, we need to have an understanding of how the needs of others are met. Do we use our excess money to purchase a bag of groceries for someone who can't afford any food? Do we fill up his car with gas? Do we slip him a twenty-dollar bill when we shake his hand?

Though these are all charitable things to do, they will not meet the greatest need in a person's life. No amount of money can purchase anyone's salvation. No amount of money can purchase a healing. The only thing that ultimately meets human need on every level consistently and permanently is the Word of God. So the seed that you have left over is best used to get the Word of God into the hearts of others.

As a matter of fact, in Matthew 13, Jesus defines seed as the Word of God. The soil that the seed is planted in is the human heart. When the seed of God's Word concerning salvation, healing, or deliverance is sown into the hearts of the lost, the people who have sown the seed are entitled to a harvest from that seed.

You see, when you give your money to a ministry to help spread the Gospel, you are planting the seed of God's Word into the hearts that receive from that ministry. Galatians 6:7 says:

> *Be not deceived; God is not mocked: for whatsoever a man soweth, that shall he also reap.*

Your experience of prosperity is based on how effectively you use what is left over to spread the Word to other people. Your harvest in life is not dependent on tithing. It's not dependent on how much you grow and mature in the knowledge of the Word. Your harvest in life is dependent upon how you use your life's resources to give the Word of God to other people.

The Multiplication Effect of Ministry

I want to show you a Scripture passage that illustrates this very point. It's the account of the feeding of the five thousand. John 6:5-7 NKJV says:

> *Then Jesus lifted up His eyes, and seeing a great multitude coming toward Him, He said to Philip, "Where shall we buy bread, that these may eat?" But this He said to test him, for He Himself knew what He would do. Philip answered Him, "Two hundred denarii worth of bread is not suffi-cient for them, that every one of them may have a little."*

Phillip was puzzled by what Jesus said; he clearly didn't get the picture. He was trying to tell Jesus that they didn't have enough money to buy enough bread for everyone.

Then Andrew piped up and said, "There is a lad here who has five barley loaves and two small fish..." But then his mind got the best of him too. He said, "...but what are they among so many?" (v. 9 NKJV).

Jesus then said, "Make the people sit down" (v. 10 NKJV). In Mark's account, Jesus had them all sit down in companies and ranks to prepare them to receive a supernatural miracle.

The Bible says there were five thousand men there. Most Bible commentaries suggest that with women and children present, the number of people would have probably totaled fifteen to twenty thousand people.

After everyone was seated, Jesus took the bread and when He had given thanks, broke it and began to distribute it to the disciples. Then they, in turn, distributed it to the multitude. He did the same thing with the fish.

When the people had gotten their fill, Jesus had the disciples gather up the leftovers. After they gathered everything up, they had a total of twelve baskets of leftovers. Approximately twenty thousand people were fed with five barley loaves and two small fish, and they had twelve baskets full of leftovers!

Commentaries say that the baskets were most likely woven market baskets, and that one of those baskets would have accommodated at least thirty to fifty of the little boy's lunches. They ended up with twelve baskets full! That's six hundred lunches left over after one was sown!

So what is the lesson learned from this account of the feeding of the five thousand? It's this. The little boy could have given his lunch to someone who seemed to be hungrier than he was. According to the Word, he would have received a return on his giving. But because he gave it to ministry (represented by Jesus), twenty thousand people were fed with the little boy's lunch instead of just one.

We see in this example that giving to ministry ordained by God multiplies the effectiveness of the seed sown. And I would suggest that it multiplies the magnitude of the harvest returned.

So again, we see the big picture of God's purpose for our natural resources.

Remaining Faithful in Your Finances

As I said at the beginning of this chapter, many principles in the Word of God contribute to our being empowered to prosper. I encourage you to study all of them because they work together and none of them can be disregarded.

I have shared with you the importance of financial faithfulness and how you can begin walking out God's plan for using your material resources to promote His purposes in the earth.

Allow the Bible to adjust your thinking in this arena. At this stage of your spiritual journey, you may not understand intellectually the connection between your use of money and your ability to serve successfully in other areas within the body of Christ. Yet over the years, I've often seen the clear connection between a person's faithfulness with their natural resources and God's provision of spiritual resources in that person's life.

People who never get plugged in at church, never grow spiritually, and eventually disappear altogether are those people who fail this first test of faithfulness. But those who honor God with their possessions and the first fruits of their increase (Prov. 3:9) are the ones who are the most blessed and are set apart by God for various responsibilities and calls on their lives. God is not a respecter of persons. He'll do the same for you!

Chapter 4

Prayer and Intimacy With God

[For my determined purpose is] that I may know Him [that I may progressively become more deeply and intimately acquainted with him, perceiving and recognizing and understanding the wonders of His Person more strongly and more clearly].... Philippians 3:10 Amp.

Paul didn't say that his determined purpose was to be healed, to win souls, to feed the hungry, or to clothe the naked. He said that his primary pursuit in life was intimacy with God. If this was Paul's first priority, then it should be our first priority. Everything we desire is wrapped in intimacy with the Lord. Jesus came to restore us to intimacy with God. What is intimacy?

Pertaining to the inmost character of a thing ... most private or personal ... closely acquainted or associated; very familiar ...

resulting from careful study or investigation ... thorough ... knowledge of.[1]

We cannot be intimate with someone we casually acknowledge or only call upon when it's convenient or when life is tough. Intimacy results from careful study and ongoing communication. Believers who want to be intimate with God study His Word, which reveals His thoughts, feelings, will, personality, and ways of doing things, and they communicate with Him in prayer.

Prayer is more than getting on your knees at bedtime. It is communing with God. You talk to Him, and He talks to you. Intimacy comes from an exchange of personal thoughts and feelings over a period of time.

And the glory which thou gavest me I have given them; that they may be one, even as we are one: I in them, and thou in me, that they may be made perfect in one; and that the world may know that thou hast sent me, and hast loved them, as thou hast loved me.
John 17:22,23

The pursuit of intimacy leads to oneness, the unity Jesus prayed for us to have with Him and with each other. We enter into oneness and unity as we pray and fellowship with Him and with each other. And that's powerful.

Matthew 18:19-20 and other verses declare that nothing is impossible to us when we are one. John 17:23 says that when we are one, the world will see that God sent Jesus and that He loves them. That's why the Devil fights to keep us from praying individually and corporately. He knows that all the power of heaven is unleashed in earth when we are one and agree in prayer.

Personal Identity

Something interesting happens to our personal identity when we become one with God. Paul said it this way in Philippians 3:9 Amp. "And that I may [actually] be found and known as in Him...." In John 14:9 Jesus referred to the same condition when He said, "He that hath seen me hath seen the Father." When you are intimate with Jesus in prayer, people will see Jesus through your life. The greatest witness of Jesus is His followers' being like Him.

> *For whosoever will save his life shall lose it: and whosoever will lose his life for my sake shall find it.* Matthew 16:25

People of prayer lose their personal identity in Christ, but it is no loss! Being one with the Prince of Peace, they have His love, His peace, and His joy. Being one with the Healer, they have health and healing. Being one with the Provider, they have all the provision they need. Being one with the Lord of the Harvest, they win souls for the kingdom.

> *But seek ye first the kingdom of God, and his righteousness; and all these things shall be added unto you.* Matthew 6:33

The irony of the Christian life is that when we lose ourselves in God, we find ourselves. We seek His kingdom, and He reveals who we are in it. This is one of the great benefits of prayer and intimacy with God. Knowing who you are in Him gives you security, confidence, and rock-solid faith.

Change Your Desires

Prayer does not necessarily equate to intimacy, but you can't have intimacy without prayer. The highest quality prayer occurs when you are hungry for God. How do you get hungry for Him? You think about Him! You develop a taste for a certain food by eating it regularly, and you develop a desire for God by thinking about Him and His Word regularly. What you give your attention to is what you will desire.

If you do not choose what you think about, your flesh will supply plenty of ungodly thoughts. Thinking about how much fun all that drinking and partying was before you got saved will cause you to desire that life and eventually go back to it. But if you think about God, you will desire Him.

> *Set your affection on things above, not on things on the earth.* Colossians 3:2

The Greek word translated "affection" means "to exercise the mind."[2] Exercise your mind in spiritual things instead of natural things. Think about God instead of why someone doesn't like you or what the next terrorist act will be. Thinking about God causes a hunger for God. What you exercise your mind to think about becomes your desire, and what you desire is where you excel.

When I was in the Air Force, a friend asked me to play handball. I had never played and was soundly beaten, an experience I didn't like! So I started thinking about handball, and then I was at the court practicing handball, and it wasn't long before I became a handball advocate. Because I exercised my mind toward handball it became a desire of my heart, and I became good at it.

What is simple is not always easy. However, God is not telling you to do something you can't do. It takes discipline to change your desires and pursuits from the things of the world to the things of God. But the more you read the Word, the more you want to read the Word. The more you pray, the more you want to pray. And the reward is intimacy with Him.

Quality Prayer

We assume that believers who pray a lot have an intimate relationship with the Lord, but prayer can become a religious, legalistic, meaningless exercise that has no intimacy. Intimacy requires quality time. If all you do is ask God for things, you will not become intimate with Him. You must share your life with Him and then hear what He has to say to you.

God is a person. If I want to pursue intimacy with a person, I study about the person and then I talk with the person. Intimacy between a husband and a wife is impossible if the husband is determined to be the strong, silent type or if the wife is determined to be so submissive that she never expresses her opinions or feelings. Likewise, intimacy is impossible if neither one will listen to the other.

The only way the deepest parts of people's nature can be revealed to one another is through communicating their innermost thoughts and feelings. Honest and open communication is the means to achieve intimacy with another person. This is not a man-made system; it is the way God set things up.

Let no corrupt communication proceed out of your mouth. Ephesians 4:29

The Greek word for "communication" means "something said."3 It denotes the simple exchange of information or ideas.

Notwithstanding ye have well done, that ye did communicate with my affliction. Philippians 4:14

Here, the Greek word for "communicate" means "to share in company with ... co-participate ... have fellowship ... be partaker of."4 This is more than an exchange of information and ideas. It is an intimate understanding.

Paul commended the Philippians for identifying with his affliction. They had shared their lives to the point that, though separated physically, they were one spiritually. They were one with God and one with each other.

Intimacy requires a mutual exchange of hearts and minds, experiences and dreams. If all you do is talk to God and never listen for a response, you won't get to know Him. But if all you do is sit and wait for Him to speak and you never share what's in your heart, you will not know how He feels and what He thinks about you and your life. Quality prayer involves trust, and no one is more trustworthy than God. He already knows your secrets! In your prayer time, tell Him what is on your heart, and then listen.

Knowing God's Voice

The Bible mentions different ways the Lord communicates with us. He speaks in an audible voice, as He did with Saul in Acts 9; or in a still, small voice, as He did with Elijah in 1 Kings 19:12.

He gives us the inward witness in our spirits, when we experience peace or the lack of peace. This is the Holy Spirit's way of helping us make decisions in line with God's will.

God can also speak to us through visions and dreams; the preaching and teaching of the Word; the gifts of the Spirit; and as we read, study, and meditate on His Word.

And when he putteth forth his own sheep, he goeth before them, and the sheep follow him: for they know his voice. And a stranger will they not follow, but will flee from him: for they know not the voice of strangers.
John 10:4,5

As a believer, you have Jesus as your shepherd and you know His voice. You follow only Him because every other voice is strange to you. When you have a thought and it strikes you as strange, it is probably the enemy trying to influence you. The Holy Spirit is in your heart, and He speaks to you there; the enemy speaks from the outside, introducing thoughts to your natural mind. If your mind is renewed with God's Word, you will know that the enemy is speaking because the thought will not line up with the Word of God. It will seem strange.

But as it is written, Eye hath not seen, nor ear heard, neither have entered into the heart of man, the things which God hath prepared for them that love him. But God hath revealed them unto us by his Spirit: for the Spirit searcheth all things, yea, the deep things of God.
1 Corinthians 2:9,10

The Holy Spirit reveals the deep things of God, and He lives in your spirit. Your spirit communicates with the Holy Spirit when you pray—both in English and in tongues. When you pray in tongues, don't check out mentally!

Speaking in tongues can become a dead, religious exercise if you are not diligent to stay focused on God and His Word.

It is possible to pray in tongues while your mind is at the golf course or the mall, so it is important to remain attentive to the Holy Spirit and listen for His response. He may speak through God's Word, give you the interpretation of tongues, or just give you the inward witness that you have prayed what needed to be prayed and everything is going to be fine.

Effective Prayer

But when ye pray, use not vain repetitions, as the heathen do: for they think that they shall be heard for their much speaking.
Matthew 6:7

I am always amazed at how easy it is to fall into "vain repetitions" in prayer, repeating something without my heart being in it. This is ineffective prayer because it is a work of the flesh. When I pray like this, no spiritual exchange is occurring between my spirit and the Holy Spirit.

Nothing is more boring than vain repetition, and you'll notice before long that if you don't catch yourself doing it, you will have no desire to pray and will quit altogether. When you are fully engaged with the Holy Spirit, however, prayer brings great results.

James outlines other reasons our prayers are ineffective.

> *...ye have not, because ye ask not. Ye ask, and receive not, because ye ask amiss, that ye may consume it upon your lusts.*
> James 4:2,3

We may not ask for anything, we may ask for something that is not in line with God's Word or will, or we may ask with the wrong heart attitude.

If you are frustrated, have you taken the issue to the Lord? Are you making a selfish request, not in keeping with His plan for your life? The Holy Spirit will alert you if you are asking amiss. Then you can pray correctly so that your prayers will be answered.

> *Confess your faults one to another, and pray one for another, that ye may be healed. The effectual fervent prayer of a righteous man availeth much.* James 5:16

Once you know what to pray, then you need to know how to pray. This verse says that effective prayer is fervent, but first you need to make sure your heart is right. If you need to confess a fault or pray with someone else to get something straight, then do it. Why? Because then your conscience is clear and you can pray fervently—with hot, boiling passion to see what you are praying come to pass. The Amplified Bible says, "The earnest (heartfelt, continued) prayer of a righteous man makes tremendous power available [dynamic in its working]."

> *For verily I say unto you, That whosoever shall say unto this mountain, Be thou removed, and be thou cast into the sea; and shall not doubt in his heart, but shall believe that those things which he saith shall come to pass; he shall have whatsoever he saith.*

> *Therefore I say unto you, What things soever ye desire, when ye pray, believe that ye receive them, and ye shall have them.*
> Mark 11:23,24

Effective prayer is a result of faith. To receive the answer to your prayer, you have to believe that you receive. This teaching has bothered a lot of the religious community, but this is what the Bible says. You must believe in your heart and have faith to receive what you are praying for.

Extremists have taken this verse to mean that you can have whatever you desire as long as you believe it in your heart, but we have seen from James 4:2-3 that you also must be asking with the right heart motive and according to God's Word. Believers who use Mark 11:23-24 to justify their own lust are not rightly dividing the Word of truth.

When we pray God's Word and will with the right heart motive, we can pray in faith, believing that we receive. I believe the main obstacle to believing we will receive is sin. We saw this in James 4:2-3. John also talks about it.

Beloved, if our heart condemn us not, then have we confidence toward God. And whatsoever we ask, we receive of him....
1 John 3:21

If there is sin standing between us and God, then we have no confidence to ask Him for anything. It's very hard to believe we receive financial blessing if we just embezzled money from our company. I'm not talking about missing it now and then, or being in the process of overcoming a fault when we are keeping our hearts right. I'm speaking of habitually and knowingly sinning, while doing nothing to change our hearts or behavior.

God does not expect you or me to be perfect. Our righteousness is through the blood of Jesus—not anything we do. But rebellion breaks fellowship with God and prevents Him from hearing our prayers. If He cannot hear them, He cannot answer them. When

Jesus prayed for Lazarus to be raised from the dead, He said, "Father, I thank thee that thou hast heard me" (John 11:41). Because He was one with the Father, Jesus knew His prayers would be heard and answered.

Maintaining intimacy with God in prayer helps us to resist temptation and overcome sin. We will not want to rebel against God if we are intimate with Him. And one of the rewards is that our prayers will be effective.

Corporate Prayer

> ...if two of you shall agree on earth as touching any thing that they shall ask, it shall be done for them of my Father which is in heaven. For where two or three are gathered together in my name, there am I in the midst of them. Matthew 18:19,20

These are powerful verses. Jesus is right there, and whatever you ask in His name will be done. So don't ever be afraid to ask for someone to pray for you, and don't be afraid to pray with other believers. Praying together is one of the joys of the Christian life. But the key word is agreement. You need to know that the two of you are in full agreement about the issues being addressed and the Word that applies. Then you can lock your shields of faith together and pray with total confidence.

When a large number of believers pray together, it can shake a city for God. This is what happened when Peter and John were released from prison and returned to their company in Acts 4:31:

And when they had prayed, the place was shaken where they were assembled together; and they were all filled with the Holy Ghost, and they spake the word of God with boldness.

Intimacy with God through prayer will change your life. At the end of this book, we will pray a prayer of commitment. Let that prayer be the beginning of your intimate relationship with Him!

Chapter 5

The Power of Our Words

So shall my word be that goeth forth out of my mouth: it shall not return unto me void, but it shall accomplish that which I please, and it shall prosper in the thing whereto I sent it. Isaiah 55:11

What kind of power do our words hold? In Genesis 1, we see that the same God who spoke the worlds into existence made us in His image; therefore, our words possess that same creative power. When we believe and confess God's Word, we create a godly destiny for ourselves. When we believe and confess the enemy's word, we create an ungodly destiny for ourselves.

The power of our words begins with what we truly believe in our hearts. The Word equates the spirit to the heart, but it is not referring to our feelings; it is referring to our core belief system, what we base our lives upon. Every decision we make emanates from what we truly believe in our hearts, or spirits. What we believe is the power behind our words.

What Do You Believe?

What you truly believe deep in your heart is the basis for every decision you make, from what you're going to eat at lunch to whom you marry. What you believe also determines the power of your words.

> *For verily I say unto you, That whosoever shall say unto this mountain, Be thou removed, and be thou cast into the sea; and shall not doubt in his heart, but shall believe that those things which he saith shall come to pass; he shall have whatsoever he saith.*
>
> *Therefore I say unto you, What things soever ye desire, when ye pray, <u>believe that ye receive them</u>, and ye shall have them.*
> Mark 11:23,24

Believing God's Word is the dynamic power of our speaking. We can speak God's Word day and night, but if we do not believe it, our words carry no power to bear fruit. That's why people who habitually say, "That kills me" or "I'll die if that happens," don't drop dead. They don't really believe that what they are saying is true. The reason I bring this up is that many believers have taken the power of confessing God's Word to an extreme. They are judgmental speech monitors, correcting and chastising anyone who says anything they disagree with or are afraid will happen. They are not acting in faith or wisdom; they are acting in fear and ignorance. They don't understand the full meaning of Mark 11:23-24: that you must believe in your heart what you confess (speak) with your mouth.

This doesn't mean you don't need to monitor your speech. Thoughtless, mindless talk is not pleasing to God or beneficial in any way. Believers are expected to mean what they say and say what they believe in their hearts.

Ephesians 1:19 says the exceeding greatness of God's power is released when we believe. By believing God, we release His power. If we find that we don't really believe Him, then confessing His Word over ourselves can help us to believe in our hearts what we know to be true in our heads.

Ask yourself each day if you really believe what you are saying. You may discover that you really don't believe God loves you, and that's why you can't receive His blessings. That's nothing to be ashamed of; we all feel like that at times. That's why the Holy Spirit wrote so many Scriptures that tell us how much God loves us. Meditate on those verses. Pray in tongues, and the Holy Spirit will make

God's love for you a living reality in your heart. It won't be long before you will know you are the apple of God's eye and can confess it with full confidence. Then, when you say, "By His stripes I am healed," your belief in His love for you will enable you to receive your healing.

Don't Get Weary

In Galatians 6:7-9, the Lord says we are not to be weary in well doing because God always performs His Word, and what we have sown we will reap at just the right time. One of the biggest challenges to believers is given in this verse: Don't get weary! Don't stop believing and agreeing with what you have sown, because one day you will reap.

As a pastor, I hear people complain that they have been believing God for years and He hasn't done anything. I asked God to show me what was holding back their blessings, and He gave me this verse.

> *Your words have been stout against me, saith the Lord. Yet ye say, What have we spoken so much against thee?*
>
> *Ye have said, It is vain to serve God: and what profit is it that we have kept his ordinance, and that we have walked mournfully before the Lord of hosts?* Malachi 3:13,14

Our words are powerful and can be the reason we're not reaping what we have sown. You may be obeying the Word, but then your words may betray a heart of unbelief, anger, or sometimes even bitterness. In essence, you come out of agreement with the Word of God that you have sown. You dig up your seed and throw it around. Malachi 3:13-14 says you are opposing God when you do this.

God cannot strengthen and encourage you when you oppose Him with your words, and without His strength you cannot persevere and overcome. Weariness and the words of your mouth go hand in hand. If you speak words of doubt and unbelief or anger and frustration, you're going to be weary and discouraged—and it may not be long before you quit.

It is hard not to become discouraged when you are waiting for the promise of God to manifest, but don't be like Job. He moaned and complained until God finally said to him, "Shall he that contendeth with the Almighty instruct him?" (Job 40:2). When we murmur and complain, we are essentially saying that God is not keeping His Word or performing it the way we think He ought to perform it.

When we feel discouraged and weary, we should not contend with the Lord; we should run to Him for help! He's our answer, not our problem. Discouragement will only get worse and eventually lead to depression and other serious problems if we do not go to God—which we do by praying, getting in His Word, listening to the Holy Spirit, and then confessing the truth He illuminates in our hearts.

If things get so bad that you can't hear God, then I encourage you to see your pastor or a church counselor. Surround yourself with believers who can understand your battle and speak God's Word into you and over you, believers who will help you to believe and confess God's truth instead of Satan's lies. Confession of God's Word frees us from discouragement, gives us new hope, and keeps us in agreement with God's will.

This is something you have to be on top of every single day because it's so easy to fall into old patterns of speech, particularly if you rub elbows with the world and work a secular job. If you don't persevere in watching your words, the next thing you know you're speaking what the world says instead of what the Word of God says—and believing it!

James 3:2-13 is a passage of Scripture every believer should read before getting out of bed in the morning. It tells us how important, and difficult, it is to maintain control of our tongue. In fact, watching our words is one of the most difficult challenges in the Christian life. We quickly see the importance of it, master it in some areas, then fail in other areas. However, if are not weary in well doing, Galatians 6:9 says that we will win. We can, and will, conquer our tongue!

Word Seeds or Weed Seeds

When I refer to the power of confession, I'm not talking about the "name it and claim it, confess it and possess it, blab it and grab it" extremism some teach. I'm not saying that whatever you want you can have if you just keep saying it. I'm talking about you making your words line up with the Word of God, saying the things the Word says about yourself and your life.

You are planting seed every time you speak, and the seed is either the Word or a weed. You are either blessing or cursing. Therefore, after you read, study, and meditate God's Word, be diligent to see that your words line up with what has been revealed to you.

As a pastor, I know that some members of my congregation have said, "Yes, praise God, I'm healed by the stripes of Jesus" in church, then have gotten in the car and moaned about all their aches and pains. With their words, they have stopped God's Word from coming to pass in their lives and set in motion a continuing scenario of sickness. Instead of keeping the Holy Spirit busy by confessing God's Word, their words have opened the door for the Devil to do his work. They have planted weed seed. If they had continued to confess God's Word, healing would have continued to flow toward them until they received the full manifestation of health.

Think before you speak. Are you about to plant a weed seed or a Word seed into your life and the lives of those you touch?

Let no corrupt communication proceed out of your mouth.... Ephesians 4:29

When God sent Israel to conquer the city of Jericho, He didn't tell Joshua to make the people be quiet as they marched six days around its walls. Joshua did that.

Now Joshua had commanded the people, saying, "You shall not shout or make any noise with your voice, nor shall a word proceed out of your mouth, until the day I say to you, 'Shout!' Then you shall shout." Joshua 6:10 NKJV

You might think six days of silence sounds extreme, but war is extreme. Lives were at stake. God's battle plan could not be compromised. As a commander, Joshua knew the weaknesses of the flesh, and an army marching around the walls of Jericho in the hot sun day after day might begin to mutter, "What kind of hair-brained scheme is this? Does Joshua have sunstroke or something? This is stupid! Why don't we just scale the walls and get the job done?"

Joshua knew that murmuring and complaining could spoil the plan of God, so he required silence. As soldiers of the cross, we need to be like Joshua, especially when we are in the heat of a battle. If we can't speak words of faith and encouragement, we should remember the battle of Jericho and have the wisdom to be quiet.

Don't let corrupt communication come out of your mouth. The phrase "Sticks and stones will break my bones but words will never hurt me" is a lie! That is not what God's Word says. Again, we must think before we speak. We want to be certain that our confession is planting the Word, not a weed, into our lives.

Speak the Answer

Death and life are in the power of the tongue: and they that love it shall eat the fruit thereof. Proverbs 18:21

The words of your mouth that come out of your heart determine your state of mind, your physical well being, and your destiny. Your words can be the difference between life and death. Sometimes when people come to my office for counsel, I want to shake them and say, "Be quiet! The best thing I can do for you right now is to sew your lips together." Their confession is only making matters worse. They need to speak the answer and stop giving power to the problem.

When you make it a habit to confess the Word of God, the Word of God possesses your heart and flows out of your mouth, even when things go wrong. When you hit your finger with the hammer, you declare that by the stripes of Jesus you are healed. When your children rebel, you confidently proclaim that they are taught of the Lord, they love Him, and they will never depart from Him. This is giving God authority over the situation and releasing the Holy Spirit into it because He watches over His Word to perform it.

My wife, Lynne, has a special call to prayer, and for a long time, I believed her call made it easier for her to pray. This was my confession: "Lynne, it's easier for you to pray. You're called to do it. I have to work to get the time to pray. It's something that I have to labor in. A lot of times, I just pray in faith. It's bone dry." Needless to say, I experienced everything I was confessing!

One morning in prayer the Holy Spirit said, "Change your words." For the first time, I believed my prayer time could be different. Then I started speaking it. "I can't wait to pray. It's my first priority. I'm going to be filled with the glory of God. I'm going to be refreshed and revitalized." Guess what? My confession became reality, and that's the way it will work for you too.

> *If any man among you seem to be religious, and bridleth not his tongue, but deceiveth his own heart, this man's religion is vain.*
> James 1:26

Is your faith in God real? Are you born again and filled with the Holy Spirit? Then you should talk like it! Everything you believe will become empty and you can even get to the place where you deceive yourself with lies if you do not tame your tongue to confess God's truth. You must refuse to give power to the enemy, and persevere in speaking what God says. Confess the answer.

I pray that you now have the clear understanding that the words you speak today create the environment in which you will live tomorrow. It's that plain and simple. Tomorrow you step into the words you speak today. If you say you're afraid that the ceiling is going to collapse the next day, get ready to move out of the way. If you confess God's Word, then you're creating an environment of blessing and prosperity to enjoy tomorrow.

The book of Proverbs has many verses regarding the power of confession. Here are just a few for you to meditate on.

The mouth of a righteous man is a well of life: but violence covereth the mouth of the wicked. Proverbs 10:11

He that keepeth his mouth keepeth his life: but he that openeth wide his lips shall have destruction. Proverbs 13:3

A wholesome tongue is a tree of life: but perverseness therein is a breach in the spirit. Proverbs 15:4

There is that speaketh like the piercings of a sword: but the tongue of the wise is health. Proverbs 12:18

The wicked is snared by the transgression of his lips: but the just shall come out of trouble. Proverbs 12:13

As you continue to meditate on these Scriptures, they will help you to speak the answer and defeat the problem.

Chapter 6

Walking in Love

If I speak with the tongues of men and of angels, but do not have love, I have become a noisy gong or a clanging cymbal.

But now faith, hope, love, abide these three; but the greatest of these is love.
1 Corinthians 13:1,13 NASB

You have just read the first and last verses from one of the most famous passages of Scripture, 1 Corinthians 13, known as "The Love Chapter." What is interesting is that the Holy Spirit placed this chapter in the middle of His teaching about the gifts of the Spirit and how the church is to operate in them. Right in the middle of a discussion of the supernatural power of God manifesting through believers, He stops to talk about love.

If you hang around believers very long, you are going to hear about the power and glory of God. His manifest presence in our lives is what takes Christianity out of the realm of religion and into a dynamic relationship. This is what we all want because when God comes on the scene, everything gets dealt with. But in comparison to her scriptural capacity, the church as a whole is living well below her means in power and authority. Why is that? I believe 1 Corinthians 13 gives the answer: We're not walking in love.

What Is This Love?

The Greek word translated "love" most of the time in the New Testament is agape. It's generally referred to as the God-kind of love.

In respect of *agapao* as used of God, it expresses the deep and constant love and interest of a perfect Being toward entirely unworthy objects, producing and fostering a reverential love in them toward the Giver, and a practical love toward those who are partakers of the same, and a desire to help others to seek the Giver.[1]

John 3:16 says, "God so loved [*agape*]... that He gave." *Agape* gives unconditionally, without expecting anything in return and without selectivity. God loves you no matter who you are or what you've done. His love is based upon His goodwill and not emotion. It is decision driven, not feelings driven. *Agape* gives and gives. If you are walking in *agape*, you are not thinking of yourself; your life is a gift to God and to others.

Another word translated "love" in the Greek is *phileo*, which means "tender affection."[2] Feelings are important because they are the primary motivator for consistent behavior. You can make a decision to act lovingly regardless of how you feel from time to time (*agape*), but most of the time you will act lovingly as a result of your emotions (*phileo*). If you want to change your behavior (to walk in the love of God), then you need to cultivate the feelings that produce that behavior (tender affection for God and His people).

For example, if you make the decision to give to a minister (*agape*), you need to get your feelings to line up with that decision. You need to cultivate a tender affection (*phileo*) for that minister, and you will be more consistent in your giving. It is much easier to give to someone you have strong feelings for, is it not? We base our relationships and decisions on the *agape* love of God, then develop affection—or *phileo*—for those with whom God connects us in the body.

Remember: God has chosen specific people for you to be in relationship with. It's easier to walk in love and stay committed when you know God has connected you to a person. So when you meet someone new, listen to the Holy Spirit. Let Him tell you if you are to be in relationship with that person and what the nature of that relationship should be. This will save you a lot of needless pain and suffering!

Love Moves Everything in the Kingdom of God

Beloved, let us love one another: for love is of God; and every one that loveth is born of God, and knoweth God.

He that loveth not knoweth not God; for God is love. 1 John 4:7,8

If you want to experience and know God, then you must learn about love and walk in love because He is love. Love describes God's person and character, His essence and nature. He chooses to love, and He loves unconditionally.

For in Jesus Christ neither circumcision availeth any thing, nor uncircumcision; but faith which worketh by love. Galatians 5:6

When the early church disputed over whether or not new male converts should be circumcised, Paul settled the issue by pointing out that everything in the New Covenant is based on faith in God, which works by love. You have faith in God and His Word because you know He loves you. To be filled with faith, you need to be filled with His love. Again, the power of God works by love. Faith works by love. All things in the kingdom work by love because God is love.

> *Jesus said unto him, Thou shalt love the Lord thy God with all thy heart, and with all thy soul, and with all thy mind. This is the first and great commandment. And the second is like unto it, Thou shalt love thy neighbour as thyself. On these two commandments hang all the law and the prophets.* Matthew 22:37-40

When I started getting serious with God and reading the Bible, it was almost overwhelming. Everything I read, especially about love, told me how far I was from living the truth. All I saw was what was wrong with me and all these new rules I had to live by: "Do this," "don't do that." But then I found out that if I just concentrated on loving God and loving my brothers and sisters in the Lord, I would do all right. Walking in love simplified my walk with the Lord.

You actually fulfill the Law by simply walking in love toward God and other human beings. Most of what God does in your life is through and with people—by love. When you get discouraged, He will send somebody to exhort you and build you up. However, if they refuse to walk in love and exhort you, or if you refuse to walk in love and receive them, nobody is blessed and God's will is unfulfilled. Walking in God's love is critical to believers' functioning as a productive, healthy body because love moves everything in God's kingdom.

The Mark of a Believer

Herein is love, not that we loved God, but that he loved us, and sent his Son to be the propitiation for our sins. Beloved, if God so loved us, we ought also to love one another. No man hath seen God at any time. If we love one another, God dwelleth in us, and his love is perfected in us. 1 John 4:10-12

These verses show the origination and progression of God's love. He loves us first; then we can love Him and others. He revealed His love for us by sending Jesus to die for us, and His love for us incites us to love Him and love others the way He loves us.

And hope maketh not ashamed; because the love of God is shed abroad in our hearts by the Holy Ghost which is given unto us. Romans 5:5

If you have any doubt that you now have the capacity to walk in God's love, then you need to meditate on this Scripture. When you were born again and the Holy Spirit came to reside in you, so did God's love. His love for you and working in you gives you the ability to love Him and love other believers.

> *A new commandment I give unto you, That ye love one another; as I have loved you, that ye also love one another. By this shall all men know that ye are my disciples, if ye have love one to another.* John 13:34,35

Jesus gave a new commandment to the church: We are to love each other the way He loves us. That is the mark of the believer. Our love for one another tells the world that we are His disciples.

> *If I have the gift of prophecy and can fathom all mysteries and all knowledge, and if I have a faith that can move mountains, but have not love, I am nothing.*
>
> *If I give all I possess to the poor and surrender my body to the flames, but have not love, I gain nothing.*
> 1 Corinthians 13:2,3 NIV

We are nothing without love. We can flow in the gifts of the Spirit, feed the poor, and even die as martyrs, but if we don't grow up in God's love, all our good works amount to nothing. This doesn't mean we should not do these things. What it means is that they are worthless to God if they are not done in love.

Christians get so busy doing what God has called them to do that they often forget to grow up and walk in love. Instead, they walk all over each other, causing hurt and division, using the excuse that they must fulfill the vision God has given them. However, the Word says that none of it will mean anything without love.

The Bible never says that all men will know you are a Christian if you go to church three times a week, if you pray and read your Bible every day, or if you spend all your time and money feeding the poor. The mark that you are a true Christian is that you show love for other Christians, that you love and take care of your own.

How do I know that a brother is truly a member of the family of God? I know that brother is real because he spends time with his immature brother, counseling him and encouraging him in the Lord. He's over at his house helping him clean up his yard and teaching him the Word about how to be a good husband and father. If the guy offends him, he forgives him, prays for him, and provokes him to love and good works. (Heb. 10:24.)

If you are a Christian because you want some order and structure to your life and a good value system to live by, then you have a problem. Why? Because being a Christian means the Holy Spirit fills your heart with God's love, and all you want to do is love Him and love His children. If you don't walk in love, then you don't know God and you aren't a Christian—because the mark of a believer is love.

Perfected in Love

There is no fear in love; but perfect love casteth out fear: because fear hath torment. He that feareth is not made perfect in love.
1 John 4:18

As we are perfected in the love of God, we are going to be less tormented by fear. Every believer is touched by fearful thoughts. Many people—especially men—don't like to admit they've tasted fear, but it's a fact. Some people are fearful of failing in business; others are afraid of being in poor health. They spend all their time at work or at the gym, driven by fear, because they neglect and disregard the love of God in their lives. If they knew how much He loved them, they would not be so frightened!

Worry and complaining are expressions of fear, and fear brings torment. Fear's torment can incapacitate you in your relationships, your work, and every area of life. In truth, fear is the opposite of faith in God and is rooted in self-interest. You will not be afraid if you aren't thinking about yourself, especially if you are so in love with God that He consumes you. The love of God is the miracle cure for any phobia!

Love forces your attention outward because love is always looking for someone to bless. And "practice makes perfect" certainly applies here. When you consistently practice the love of God, you are perfected in love. You grow up and become like Jesus. What are the specific things you are to practice?

> *Love is patient, love is kind and is not jealous; love does not brag and is not arrogant, does not act unbecomingly; it does not seek its own, is not provoked, does not take into account a wrong suffered, does not rejoice in unrighteousness, but rejoices with the truth; bears all things, believes all things, hopes all things, endures all things.*
> 1 Corinthians 13:4-7 NASB

We could spend hours studying patience alone. Read and meditate on the topic of patience in these verses, and also on the fruit of the Spirit in Galatians 5:22-23, in various translations. Get a revelation of what love is and what love is not.

Here is what the Bible says love is not:

...Love doesn't want what it doesn't have.
Love doesn't strut, doesn't have a swelled
head, doesn't force itself on others, isn't
always "me first," doesn't fly off the handle,
doesn't keep score of the sins of others,
doesn't revel when others grovel....
1 Corinthians 13:4-7 MESSAGE

Turn to these Scriptures on love whenever you struggle in a relationship. As you develop these attitudes and behaviors, here are some of the rewards you will begin to receive.

You will know God and develop an intimate relationship with Him.

You will love your brothers and sisters in Christ and will have good relationships with friends and family in the Lord.

You will be filled with faith, hope, and joy.

You will trust God and believe His Word, having great faith to move mountains.

You will cast out all fear.

You will fulfill all the Law and the prophets, which will result in your being mightily blessed of God in every area of your life.

You will be holy and without blame in Him.

One more thing about the love of God: the Bible says that love never fails, but how it succeeds is often known only by Him. You cannot force others to receive the Lord or be made whole by loving them unconditionally. Some people you will endure and persevere to love, and you may never see a change. But you are not to try to control and manipulate them with love. That is perverting the love of God into witchcraft. Just love them, pray for them, and know that the Holy Spirit is moving heaven and earth to save them, heal them, and set them free.

The love of God gives us faith for the impossible. Whether or not we see the fruit of it in this life, we know His love never fails. One day we will see the eternal fruit of His love expressed through us. In the meantime, we can rejoice that we are being perfected in His love today.

Chapter 7

Looking Forward— How to Share Jesus

Sharing Jesus with people often strikes terror in the hearts of believers, but it is a basic and fundamental part of what we do as Christians. That is why we need to discuss it openly and look to God's Word for instruction and confidence so that we can do what God has called us to do.

> *From that time Jesus began to preach, and to say, Repent: for the kingdom of heaven is at hand. And Jesus, walking by the sea of Galilee, saw two brethren, Simon called Peter, and Andrew his brother, casting a net into the sea: for they were fishers. And he saith unto them, Follow me, and I will make you fishers of men.*
> Matthew 4:17-19

Anyone who is born again is a disciple of Jesus and called to be a fisher of men. He was not speaking only to full-time ministers. He was talking to anybody who followed Him.

He didn't say, "Follow Me, and I'll make you a bank president." He said, "Follow Me, and I'll make you a fisher of men."

You will be successful in your calling if you fulfill your primary purpose, which is to be a fisher of men. As you do this, you will find yourself blessed and fulfilled. As you view life through the proper lens of being a fisher of men, the Holy Spirit can reveal the specifics of your calling. Being a fisher of men gives eternal meaning and brings the power of God to everything you do in life.

The Heart of Jesus

Unbelievers cannot understand God's Word until they see it demonstrated. This is important to Jesus. In Matthew 25:34-40, He said that if we feed the hungry, provide a home for the homeless, clothe the naked, and visit prisoners and the sick, we have done this to Him.

Jesus is in the midst of every relationship and encounter. None is casual or accidental. He brings people into your life, and some you may not like! If they are not saved, then you do a little fishing. Visit someone in prison or baby-sit for a single parent who can't afford daycare. God will give you opportunities to meet people's needs so that you can share Jesus with them.

A pastor in northern Minnesota had a small building with a little parking lot. He bought a plow for his truck to keep the parking lot free of snow. One morning the Lord told him to clear the driveways of the houses near his church. He left a church card on each door that said, "Jesus loves you. Come visit us sometime." Within a year he was clearing a lot more driveways and had several hundred people coming to his church. This is not just a formula for church growth; this is a believer seeing Jesus in everyone he meets.

You're Not Alone!

And he said unto them, Go ye into all the world, and preach the gospel to every creature. Mark 16:15

Go ye therefore, and teach all nations. Matthew 28:19

How can we go into the entire world to preach the Gospel and teach all nations? We only can if every believer does his part in his part of the world. Individually, we can serve others, lead them to Jesus, and teach them about the kingdom of God. But we can also invite them to church and give the five-fold ministers a chance to preach, teach, and minister to them.

In Luke 14:23, Jesus taught about the master who told his servants to "Go out into the highways and hedges, and compel them to come...." The church is where spiritual needs are met. The Word goes forth, people are saved, and the Holy Spirit breaks every yoke of bondage. Children receive the Word in children's church, while their parents receive the Word in the sanctuary. A rebellious teen can go to the youth group, while someone with a drug or alcohol problem can attend a meeting just for him or her.

Some discipleship programs make you feel like you've got to do everything yourself, but no one person can disciple another person alone. You are doing great if you minister to those God puts in your path, influence them to look to Jesus, and invite them to your church.

Your Style

When you are a fisher of men, God will use you in certain ways that He may not use others. Look at how different the apostles were. In Acts 2, Peter is an example of confrontational evangelism. There's no diplomacy involved. You simply say, "You're a sinner in need of a Savior, and that's Jesus." Some flow effectively in this style, and the Holy Spirit convicts many through them.

Some of us use intellectual evengelism like Paul did in Acts 17. There are unbelievers who have to see the logic of the Gospel. They get hooked on Jesus in their hearts through their minds.

In Mark 5, the maniac of the Gadaranes shared his testimony with family and friends. Relational evangelism is natural for some who are uneasy sharing with strangers but have great success with those to whom they are close.

In Acts 9:36, Dorcas was a seamstress who helped widows and orphans. Service evangelism is for those whose idea of a great day is mowing someone's lawn or cooking a meal for someone who is sick.

The woman at the well in John 4 yelled in the street, "Come, see a man, which told me all things that ever I did: is not this the Christ?" (v. 29). Invitational evangelism is inviting people to church, a revival meeting, a crusade, a prayer meeting, a Bible study, or anywhere the Gospel is preached and the Word is taught.

You may have another style, or you may find you operate in a combination of styles. Just be who God called you to be. Sharing Jesus flows out of any heart that desires to see eternal life imparted to somebody else. You don't need to go to Bible school. God will use you to share Jesus in day-to-day activities. Just allow the Holy Spirit to lead you.

The Holy Spirit Calls the Shots

The Holy Spirit convicts the unbeliever of sin and is the agent of the new birth. Therefore, when you are "fishing," you must listen to Him. He will not only lead you to deal wisely and effectively with unbelievers, but He will comfort you if you must endure rejection or persecution.

Jesus told us that if people persecuted Him, they would persecute those who followed Him, and that's what the Devil will hit you with when you begin to share Jesus with others. Nobody likes to be rejected or labeled a religious weirdo. But what you need to remember is that they are not rejecting you; they are rejecting Jesus. So don't take it personally!

Some believers incite persecution and rejection because of actions they take without being led by the Holy Spirit. For example, some people act as if they know everything because they're saved, slapping people in the face with their spirituality. This won't happen if you stay humble and listen to the Holy Spirit.

According to Acts 1:8, the Holy Spirit was given so we could be witnesses for Jesus. Jesus doesn't baptize us in the Holy Spirit so we can feel superior to others but to help us to be fishers of men. If you want to experience the power and the gifts of the Holy Spirit, then align yourself with the purpose for His power: fishing for men.

Your Motivation

The Bible tells us how to cultivate a desire to share Jesus: by giving our attention to the reality of hell. If eternal torment is real to you, then you will share your faith! You will be so grateful to Jesus that you don't have to go there, and you will not want anyone else to go there—especially your loved ones.

I asked God to make hell real to me, and He gave me a dream. A multitude of people pressed toward a cliff, and those in front were falling into a dark abyss. Screams and cries came from below. Then I noticed a nice looking man moving toward the cliff. He was a macho guy, but he was uneasy. He held his little girl's hand. She looked up at him and asked, "Is everything going to be all right?" He said, "Yes," and they continued moving toward the abyss.

If you lack motivation to share Jesus, I strongly encourage you to read and study what the Bible says about hell. Ask God to make it real to you. Why? If you're more concerned that your ungodly friends will call you a Jesus freak than you are that they are going to hell, then you will not be a fisher of men.

You need to think in eternal terms. Everything you do in this life has an eternal impact. You have an eternal impact on every person the Holy Spirit brings to you. You will either influence them toward eternity in heaven or eternity in hell.

Another great motivation to share Jesus is the fruit you see in this life: new believers with the peace of God in their hearts, restored marriages, children receiving the love and direction they need, and financial stability. In 2 Corinthians 5:14-18, Paul wrote that the love of God constrained him to share Jesus and that every believer has the ministry of reconciliation. We are compelled by the love of God to be ministers of reconciliation, reconciling others to God.

Your Message

Your message to the lost person is simple: "You need Jesus." If they are skeptical that the Bible is the Word of God or carries the truth they need to be set free, challenge them to try it. It can't do any more damage than the drugs, alcohol, pornography, crime, violence, working night and day, or other things they are doing to fill the emptiness inside them.

Share how Jesus changed your life—past, present, and for eternity. When you humbly admit your struggles and then tell how the Lord helped you and continues to help you, they can relate to you. Your humility and transparency give you credibility.

Every believer has a great and continuous testimony. No testimony is better than any other. The Holy Spirit will use you and your life to say to someone, "You know, I went through that. I have struggled with that." Then they will want to hear what you have to say. The most effective message is one heart sharing the love and saving power of Jesus with another heart.

Chapter 8

Three Baptisms

Baptism is a foundational concept for the Christian, but it is often misunderstood. We need to know what the Bible says about it so we can fully obey the Lord. The Greek word that is translated "baptized" or "baptism" is *baptizo*. It means, "to dip, immerse, submerge for a religious purpose, to overwhelm, saturate."[1] There are three baptisms in a believer's life.

The Baptism of Regeneration

Know ye not, that so many of us as were baptized into Jesus Christ were baptized into his death?

Therefore we are buried with him by baptism into death: that like as Christ was raised up from the dead by the glory of the Father, even so we also should walk in newness of life.
Romans 6:3-4

When you were born again, you were baptized into Jesus Christ by the Holy Spirit and became a member of the body of Christ. Your spirit was regenerated by the Holy Spirit, and that is why it is called the baptism of regeneration. It is amazing how many believers don't know that when they were saved, they were baptized or immersed into Christ.

The baptism of regeneration says that our old man of sin died with Jesus Christ on the cross and was buried with Him. This is called "identification." We identify with Jesus in His death. When we are baptized into Christ by the Holy Spirit, our old man dies. But that's not all.

For if we have been planted together in the likeness of his death, we shall be also in the likeness of his resurrection. Romans 6:5

Our baptism into Christ also means we were raised into newness of life, and the Bible says, "if any man be in Christ, he is a new creature" (2 Corinthians 5:17). We were born again "in the likeness of his resurrection." The Holy Spirit regenerates our spirit.

For by one Spirit are we all baptized into one body, whether we be Jews or Gentiles, whether we be bond or free; and have been all made to drink into one Spirit.
1 Corinthians 12:13

Underscore "one Spirit." The Holy Spirit immerses us into "one body," which is the body of Christ. We become a part of the universal and eternal Church. The baptism of regeneration is a miracle, and the agent of that spiritual transformation is the Holy Spirit. It is His work that causes us to be born again and spiritually made new or regenerated.

First Corinthians 12:13 says that it doesn't matter whether you are a Jew or a Gentile, slave or free, rich or poor. Every true child of God is baptized into Christ by the Holy Spirit. Therefore, the very first baptism for believers is the baptism of regeneration, or salvation, which is spiritual.

Water Baptism

After we experience the baptism of regeneration, we are baptized in water as an outward show of what has happened to us inwardly. Being immersed in water is the natural act that symbolizes the spiritual act of being immersed into the body of Christ. Throughout the New Testament, we are commanded to be baptized immediately after being born again. Most believers have a desire to be baptized, such as when Philip led the Ethiopian eunuch to Jesus.

*Then Philip opened his mouth, and began at
the same scripture, and preached unto him
Jesus.*

*And as they went on their way, they came
unto a certain water: and the eunuch said,
See, here is water; what doth hinder me to
be baptized?*

*And Philip said, If thou believest with all
thine heart, thou mayest. And he answered
and said, I believe that Jesus Christ is the
Son of God.*

*And he commanded the chariot to stand
still: and they went down both into the
water, both Philip and the eunuch; and he
baptized him.*

*And when they were come up out of the
water, the Spirit of the Lord caught away
Philip, that the eunuch saw him no more:
and he went on his way rejoicing.*
Acts 8:35-39

The qualification for water baptism is
stated clearly in verse 37: you must believe
with all your heart that Jesus Christ is the Son
of God. In other words, you must have already
experienced the New Birth. That is the prereq-
uisite for water baptism.

That if thou shalt confess with thy mouth the Lord Jesus, and shalt believe in thine heart that God hath raised him from the dead, thou shalt be saved.

For with the heart man believeth unto righteousness; and with the mouth confession is made unto salvation. Romans 10:9-10

When people believe in their hearts unto righteousness and confession is made unto salvation, the Holy Spirit works the miracle of the new birth. He spiritually baptizes them into the body of Christ. Once they are saved, they can be water baptized. If you were saved spiritually after you were water baptized, then you should be water baptized again. Now it will really mean something to you!

We also see in Acts 8:38 how to baptize. Philip and the eunuch went "down both into the water," and verse 39 says, "And when they were come up out of the water." No room for sprinkling in this passage of Scripture. They went down into the water, and they came up out of the water. That means Philip completely immersed the eunuch in water.

There are many denominations that just sprinkle a person when they are water baptized, so forgive me for correcting you if this has been your experience. However, the word "baptize" clearly means that you must be totally engulfed by water. Why is this so important? Because being totally immersed in water signifies that you have been totally immersed in Christ—not just sprinkled here and there with Him. Your baptism should demonstrate in the natural exactly what has occurred in your spirit.

The Baptism of the Holy Spirit

After the baptism of regeneration, we can be water baptized; and we can also be baptized with the Holy Spirit. This is the third baptism for the believer. Like water baptism, you must be born again before you can be baptized in the Holy Spirit. The Bible tells us that Jesus baptizes us with the Holy Spirit.

I indeed baptize you with water unto repentance. He that cometh after me is mightier than I, whose shoes I am not worthy to bear: he shall baptize you with the Holy Ghost, and with fire. Matthew 3:11

He that sent me to baptize with water, the same said unto me, Upon whom thou shalt see the Spirit descending, and remaining on him, the same is he which baptizeth with the Holy Ghost.

And I saw, and bare record that this is the Son of God. John 1:33-34

In these verses, John the Baptist is refer-ring to Jesus. He states that Jesus is the Son of God, who will baptize with the Holy Ghost. In Acts, we see the first instance of Jesus baptizing believers in the Holy Ghost.

And suddenly there came a sound from heaven as of a rushing mighty wind, and it filled all the house where they were sitting.

And there appeared unto them cloven tongues like as of fire, and it sat upon each of them.

And they were all filled with the Holy Ghost, and began to speak with other tongues, as the Spirit gave them utterance. Acts 2:2-4

Jesus said in Acts 1:5, "Ye shall be baptized with the Holy Ghost not many days hence." In Matthew 3:11 and 1:33, John the Baptist said Jesus would "baptize you with the Holy Ghost," and that Jesus was "he that baptizeth with the Holy Ghost." Then in Acts 2:4, the Bible says "they were all filled with the Holy Ghost." Since Jesus is obviously doing what He and John prophesied He would do, we can logically conclude that the baptism of the Holy Ghost is the same as being filled with the Holy Ghost. When Jesus baptizes believers with the Holy Spirit, they are filled with the Holy Spirit.

I want to add this about being baptized with fire. The only time fire appears with the baptism of the Holy Spirit is in Acts 1:3. My guess is that it is because it is the first time Jesus baptizes believers with the Holy Spirit, and the "cloven tongues of fire" were a miraculous sign that the day had come and they had received what Jesus and John had prophesied. Nowhere else in God's Word do we see fire manifest when the baptism with the Holy Spirit is given.

> *The next day John seeth Jesus coming unto him, and saith, Behold the Lamb of God, which taketh away the sin of the world.*
> John 1:29

> *And I knew him not: but he that sent me to baptize with water, the same said unto me, Upon whom thou shalt see the Spirit descending, and remaining on him, the same is he which baptizeth with the Holy Ghost.* John 1:33

By the Spirit of God, John is illuminating the coming ministry of Jesus. He takes away our sin, and He baptizes with the Holy Ghost. The same Lamb who removes the sin of the world also baptizes with the Holy Ghost. Both are part of His ministry. Although the Church has tried to separate them for generations, we can't take one and not the other without perverting Scripture. Furthermore, Hebrews 13:8 states, "Jesus Christ the same yesterday, and today, and forever."

One of the primary ways that religious tradition tries to sweep the baptism of the Holy Ghost under the rug is by saying that it was a one-time phenomenon to demonstrate the birth of the New Testament Church, that the baptism of the Holy Ghost is not applicable to today's believers. However, if He is still the Lamb of God who cleanses us from sin, then He must still be the One who baptizes in the Holy Ghost. "Yesterday, and today, and forever."

You can be baptized with water and with the Holy Ghost if you have been born again and experienced the baptism of regeneration. Your pastor will gladly baptize you in water, and Jesus will gladly baptize you with the Holy Ghost, just like He has countless other believers through the centuries. (If you want to know more details about this experience, I discuss this thoroughly in the first book of the *Water, Wind, & Fire* series: *Understanding the New Birth and the Baptism of the Holy Spirit.*)

Prayer of Commitment

Father, in Jesus' name, I come to submit myself fully to You. Jesus has paid the price for my sin, and I have risen with Him into a new life. I embrace the importance of Your Word, and I ask You to help me be a doer of what I hear. I thank You for leading me to the church You want me to attend, where I can grow up in You as I yield to Your plan for my growth. I commit to be a faithful steward who promotes Your purposes with my material resources.

Father, more than anything else I want to know You, and I will pursue an intimate relationship with You in prayer. I recognize the power of my words and will put a guard on my tongue. I will walk in Your love, seeking forgiveness when I sin or offend another, and forgiving those who sin against me. I will not let anything come between me, You, Your people, and Your church.

I will take my place in sharing with others what You have done for me. I ask You to help me make being a fisher of men a part of my lifestyle.

Please continue to perfect me in Your love, Father. I thank You for this incredible new life as Your child. Amen.

Endnotes

Chapter 2

The Local Church and Your Role in It

1 Webster's New World College Dictionary, Fourth Edition, Michael Agnes, Editor-in-Chief (New York: Macmillan, Inc., 1999), p. 85.

Chapter 3

The Church and Your Role in It

1 Spiros Zhodiates, The Complete Word Study Dictionary: New Testament, (Chattanooga, TN: AMG Publishers), p. 640.

2 James Strong, Exhaustive Concordance of the Bible, "Greek Dictionary of the New Testament" (Nashville, TN: Thomas Nelson Publishers, 1984), #3618.

Chapter 4

Prayer and Intimacy With God

1 Webster's New World College Dictionary, Third Edition, Victoria Neufeldt, Editor-in-Chief (New York: Macmillan, Inc., 1996), p.707.

2 James Strong, Exhaustive Concordance of the Bible, "Greek Dictionary of the New Testament" (Nashville, TN: Thomas Nelson Publishers, 1984), #5426.

3 Ibid., #3056. 4 Ibid., #4790.

Chapter 5

The Importance of God's Word

1 James Strong, ##6612, 6601. 2 Webster's New World College Dictionary, p. 1251. 3 James Strong, #995. 4 Ibid., #1897.

Chapter 7
Walking in Love

1 W. E. Vine, *Expository Dictionary of New Testament Words* (Iowa Falls, IA: Riverside Book and Bible House), pp. 702-703. 2 Ibid., p. 703.

ABOUT THE AUTHOR

 Mac Hammond is senior pastor of Living Word Christian Center, a large and growing body of Christian believers in Brooklyn Park (a suburb of Minneapolis), Minnesota. He is the host of the *Winner's Way* broadcast and author of several internationally distributed books. Mac is broadly acclaimed for his ability to apply the principles of the Bible to practical situations and the challenges of daily living.

Mac Hammond graduated from Virginia Military Institute in 1965 with a Bachelor's degree in English. Upon graduation, he entered the Air Force with a regular officer's commission and reported for pilot training at Moody Air Force Base in Georgia. He received his wings in November 1966, and subsequently served two tours of duty in Southeast Asia, accumulating 198 combat missions. He was honorably discharged in 1970 with the rank of Captain.

Between 1970 and 1980, Mac was involved in varying capacities in the general aviation industry including ownership of a successful air cargo business serving the Midwestern United States. A business acquisition brought the Hammonds to Minneapolis where they ultimately founded Living Word Christian Center in 1980 with 12 people in attendance.

After more than 27 years, that group of twelve people has grown into an active church body of more than 9,000 members. Today some of the outreaches that spring from Living Word include Maranatha Christian Academy, a fully-accredited, pre-K through 12th grade Christian school; Maranatha College, an evening college with an uncompromising Christian environment; Living Free Recovery Services, a state licensed outpatient treatment facility for chemical dependency; The Wells at 7th Street, a multi-faceted outreach to inner-city residents; CFAITH, an online cooperative missionary outreach of hundreds of national and international organizations providing faith-based content; and a national and international media outreach that includes hundreds of audio/video teaching series, the *Winner's Way* broadcast, the *PrayerNotes* e-newsletter, and the *Winner's Way* e-magazine.

To contact Mac Hammond, please write to:
Mac Hammond Ministries
PO Box 29469 Minneapolis, MN 55429-2946
Or visit us onlone at: www.mac-hammond.org

OTHER BOOKS

BY MAC HAMMOND

Following the Fire
Discerning How God Leads You
by the Desires of Your Heart

Angels at Your Service
Releasing the Power of Heaven's Host

Doorways to Deception
How Deception Comes, How It Destroys,
and How You Can Avoid It

Heirs Together
Solving the Mystery of a Satisfying
Marriage

The Last Millennium
A Revealing Look at the Remarkable
Days Ahead and How You Can Live
Them to the Fullest

Living Safely in a Dangerous World
Keys to Abiding in the Secret Place

Plugged In and Prospering
Embracing the Spiritual Significance and
Biblical Basis for the Local Church

Positioned for Promotion
How to Increase Your Influence and
Capacity to Lead

Real Faith Never Fails
Detecting (and Correcting) Four Common Faith Mistakes

Simplifying Your Life
Divine Insights to Uncomplicated Living

Soul Control
Whoever Controls Your Soul, Controls Your Destiny

Water, Wind, & Fire
Understanding the New Birth and the Baptism of the Holy Spirit

Water, Wind, & Fire—The Next Steps
Developing Your New Relationship With God

The Way of the Winner
Running the Race to Victory

Who God Is Not
Exploding the Myths About His Nature and His Ways

Winning In Your Finances
How to Walk God's Pathway to Prosperity

Winning Your World
Becoming a Person of Influence

Yielded and Bold
How to Understand and Flow With the Move of God's Spirit

By Mac and Lynne Hammond

Keys to Compatibility
Opening the Door to a Marvelous
Marriage

By Lynne Hammond

Dare to Be Free!

Heaven's Power for the Harvest
Be Part of God's End-Time Spiritual
Outpouring

Living in the Presence of God
Receive Joy, Peace, and Direction
in the Secret Place of Prayer

Love and Devotion
Prayer Journal

The Master Is Calling
Discovering the Wonders of
Spirit-Led Prayer

The Master Is Calling Workbook
Discovering the Wonders of
Spirit-Led Prayer

Renewed in His Presence
Satisfying Your Hunger for God

Secrets to Powerful Prayer
Discovering the Languages of the Heart

Staying Faith
How to Stand Until the Answer Arrives

The Table of Blessing
Recipes From the Family and Friends of
Living Word Christian Center

When Healing Doesn't Come Easily

When It's Time for a Miracle
The Hour of Impossible Breakthroughs
Is Now!

Whispers From the Secret Place
A 31-day Journey

*For a complete catalog of our books, CDs, and
DVDs, please contact us at:*

Mac Hammond Ministries
PO Box 29469
Minneapolis, Minnesota 55429-2946

You can also visit us on the web at
www.mac-hammond.org.